Negotiating Globally

Negotiating Globally

How to Negotiate Deals,
Resolve Disputes, and
Make Decisions Across
Cultural Boundaries

Jeanne M. Brett

JOSSEY-BASS
A Wiley Company
San Francisco

Published by

JOSSEY-BASS
A Wiley Company
350 Sansome St.
San Francisco, CA 94104-1342

www.josseybass.com

Jossey-Bass books and products are available through most bookstores. To contact Jossey-Bass
directly, call (888) 378-2537, fax to (800) 605-2665, or visit our website at
www.josseybass.com.

Substantial discounts on bulk quantities of Jossey-Bass books are available to corporations,
professional associations, and other organizations. For details and discount information, contact
the special sales department at Jossey-Bass.

We at Jossey-Bass strive to use the most environmentally sensitive paper stocks available to us.
Our publications are printed on acid-free recycled stock whenever possible, and our paper always
meets or exceeds minimum GPO and EPA requirements.

Library of Congress Cataloging-in-Publication Data

Brett, Jeanne M.
    Negotiating globally : how to negotiate deals, resolve
disputes, and make decisions across cultural boundaries / Jeanne
M. Brett.
    p. cm.—(The Jossey-Bass business & management series)
    Includes bibliographical references and index.
    ISBN 0-7879-5586-8 (alk. paper)
    1. Negotiation in business—Cross-cultural studies   2.
Negotiation—Cross-cultural studies.   3. Decision
making—Cross-cultural studies.   4. Conflict
management—Cross-cultural studies.   I. Title.   II. Series.
HD58.6 .B74 2001
658.4'052—dc21   00-011770

FIRST EDITION
HB Printing   10 9 8 7 6 5 4 3 2 1

**The Jossey-Bass
Business & Management Series**

Contents

List of Exhibits

To all the negotiators
who shared their experiences
so that others could learn

Preface

Mickey and Minnie Mouse are building a new residence in Hong Kong to complement their theme park homes in California, Florida, Japan, and France.[1] The familiar Disney cartoon characters are the same around the world, but the deals that took them abroad, first to Japan, then to France, and now to Hong Kong, are very different and illustrate a highly respected U.S. company's growing sophistication in negotiating across cultural boundaries.

A private Japanese company owns Toyko Disneyland. In 1979, Disney invested $2.5 million in Toyko Disneyland in return for a forty-five-year contract for 5 percent of the food sales and 10 percent of the gate and the corporate sponsorships. By 1985, when Disney began negotiating with the French government, the Tokyo theme park was generating $40 million a year for Disney and hundreds of millions a year for its Japanese owners.

Disney was determined to negotiate a better deal for itself in France, and at first glance it seems it did. Through a wholly owned subsidiary, Disney invested less than $200 million for a 49 percent stake in a venture that was worth $3 billion. The rest came from four banks that provided loans and letters of credit worth about $1.4 billion. The French government did its part too, arranging for Disney to buy five thousand acres of land at 1971 prices and spending more that $400 million on highways and a suburban rail link. Although now profitable, in 1992 EuroDisney was in serious financial trouble, overwhelmed by debt, low attendance, and cold, rainy weather. Disney, it seems, had badly misjudged the appeal of American pop culture in France.

The Hong Kong deal is different still. Disney will invest $316 million for a 43 percent stake. Its partner is not a private investor, not a consortium of banks, but the Hong Kong government! Hong Kong is making a direct investment of $419 million for a 57 percent stake and arranging for loans bringing its stake to $1.5 billion out of a $1.8 billion investment. Somewhat surprising is Disney's choice of Hong Kong over another China location. Chinese citizens will need special permits to go to Hong Kong to visit Disneyland. Estimates are that Disney and the Hong Kong government will need five million Chinese and other visitors annually to break even, compared to the ten million break-even figure for Disneyland Paris (the former EuroDisney).

Experience has taught Disney to pay attention to cultural differences and to negotiating fundamentals. Negotiating across cultural boundaries is not easy. Ethnocentrism (the belief that your culture's way is the best way) often makes negotiators ignore highly relevant information that is coming across the table. Disney should have known that the French were concerned about cultural domination. One of the stipulations in the agreement was that one attraction "depict French and European civilization." The language of the park was to be French. But Disney did not realize just how concerned the French were about Disney's wholesale export of Mouse culture to France until the park opened and French tourists stayed away in droves. Disney also did not anticipate the decided lack of enthusiasm with which they were received by local citizens and government in Marne-la-Vallée, where at one point during construction French farmers carried out a threat to block access to the park entrance, causing delays and embarrassment. Disney's experiences in France illustrate how flawed cross-cultural deal making leads to tense cross-cultural dispute resolution.

Purpose and Audience of This Book

This book is for you if you must negotiate deals, resolve disputes, or make decisions in multicultural environments. If you have had formal training in negotiation but no training in culture, you will find that old familiar negotiation concepts, such as "power" and "interests," take on different meanings in different cultures. This book extends what you already know about negotiating in the global environment. If you have had no formal training in negotiation, the book will introduce you to all the fundamental concepts and explain how they apply in different cultural settings.

The book emphasizes negotiations in a multicultural business environment. The advice it contains, however, is relevant not just to managers and management students who expect to be negotiating across cultural boundaries but also to lawyers and law students and to government officials and students of public policy who are concerned with economic development in a global environment. Global negotiations occur in multiple legal environments. International agencies and national and local government officials are frequently at the table in negotiations that bridge cultural boundaries. Lawyers, government officials, and managers need expertise in negotiating globally.

The book focuses on national culture because nation-state boundaries are both geographical and ideological. The ideology or theory underlying a nation's social, economic, legal, and political institutions affects the way its people interact. When negotiators are from the same culture, they approach the table with a shared cultural understanding, and institutional ideology is the backdrop against which deals and decisions are made and disputes are resolved. When negotiators are from different cultures, however, each may rely on quite different assumptions about social interaction, economic interests, legal requirements, and political realities.

In today's global environment, negotiators who understand cultural differences and negotiation fundamentals have a decided advantage at the bargaining table. This book is all about what you can do to negotiate across boundaries of national culture successfully. It explains how culture affects negotiators' assumptions about when and how to negotiate. It discusses how culture affects the negotiators' interests and priorities and their strategies, the way they go about negotiating. It explains how confrontation, motivation, influence, and information strategies shift due to culture. It provides strategic advice for negotiators whose deals, disputes, and decisions must bridge cultural boundaries.

Background of This Book

Until recently, most of the knowledge about how to negotiate deals, resolve disputes, and make decisions in teams came from U.S. researchers studying U.S. negotiators negotiating with other U.S. negotiators. The evidence is overwhelming that U.S. negotiators leave money on the table when they negotiate deals, escalate disputes to the point where costs outweigh gains, and make suboptimal decisions in teams,[2] and the more emotional they become, the worse the outcomes they achieve. The gap is often significant between the outcomes negotiators reach and the ones they could have reached had they fully integrated their interests using all the information available to them.

Armed with knowledge of this gap and techniques for reducing it, my colleagues at the J. L. Kellogg Graduate School of Management at Northwestern University and I have worked with thousands of students, managers, and executives who sought to improve their negotiation skills. In the early 1990s, the profiles and interests of our students began to broaden. Managers from all over the world started coming to our executive programs. We were invited to teach negotiation in Europe, Latin America, and Asia. Kellogg's enrollment became more and more international. We could not avoid dealing with the question of whether what we were teaching applied across cultures. Was the same gap present in other cultures, or was it a uniquely American problem? Would the same skills close the gap in other cultures? What about negotiating across cultures? What adjustments needed to be made to take what we knew about negotiations effectively across cultures?

These questions motivated the research that underlies this book. The task was to determine how culture affects negotiation processes and outcomes in the settings of deal making, dispute resolution, and multicultural team decision making. Since 1992, I have traveled widely and worked with scholars around the world, studying how managers negotiate in different cultures and what they do when the setting is multicultural. I have talked with managers from many different cultures about their negotiation strategies, collected their stories, and shared some of my own. But I have also systematically collected data on their negotiation strategies, processes, and outcomes, using the same methods that my colleagues and I have used with U.S. managers.[3] These data provide a strong foundation for the insights in the book. Although the book does not dwell on the data, it does use the data to illustrate cultural differences in negotiation and to develop strategies to deal with those differences.

The book is not about how to negotiate in Israel, Russia, Japan, Brazil, Thailand, Spain, India, France, Germany, Sweden, or China—all countries where managers and management students have helped me understand culture and negotiation and where I have done research. Instead, the book focuses on what we in the field know theoretically and empirically about negotiation and how negotiation strategy needs to be modified and expanded to take cultural differences into account. Rather than giving advice about how to act when in Rome negotiating with a Roman, I provide practical advice about how to manage cultural differences when they appear at the bargaining table. The book challenges negotiators to expand their repertoire of negotiation strategies so that they are prepared to negotiate deals, resolve disputes, and make decisions regardless of the culture in which they find themselves.

Major Themes

Chapter One lays the groundwork for understanding how culture affects deal-making, dispute resolution, and multicultural team decision-making negotiations. It explains different types of negotiations and negotiated agreements. It explains how culture affects assumptions about what to negotiate and when. It provides a framework for understanding how culture affects negotiators' interests, priorities, and strategies. It explains how negotiators' confrontational, motivational, influence, and information strategies vary across cultures. It provides links between negotiators' strategies and culture, identifying where and why negotiators use one strategy rather than another.

Chapter Two offers concrete advice about negotiating deals across cultures. It provides criteria for distinguishing good deals from poor ones. It explains distributive and integrative negotiations. Understanding these two types of negotiation will significantly improve your deal making. If you already know about integrative negotiations, do you know how to get the information you need to construct an integrative deal when the other negotiator is from a culture, such as China, where negotiators may be reluctant to answer questions directly?

Chapter Two takes distributive and integrative negotiation strategies across cultural boundaries. It gives advice on setting goals and using power and influence across cultures to maximize your own interests. It also explains how to acquire information across cultures to create value in integrative negotiations. The main ideas in the chapter are illustrated with data from Israeli, Chinese, German, Japanese, and U.S. negotiators. Chapter Two reveals that negotiators all over the world leave about the same amount of money on the table when negotiating deals. Outcomes are quite similar across cultures; however, the strategies negotiators use to make deals are culturally linked and distinct. The advice in Chapter Two is grounded in systematic research, and it should help managers know what to expect and how to react when negotiating in a multicultural environment.

Chapter Three moves from making deals to resolving disputes. Few books on negotiation address dealing (buying and selling) separately from resolving disputes (claims and counterclaims). But in some cultures, managers who would negotiate directly and aggressively to make a deal would not confront directly when they have a dispute; this means that the strategies needed to resolve disputes across cultures are not quite the same as those that are needed to make deals. Chapter Three provides negotiators with practical advice about how to resolve conflict via direct confrontation and how to use peers, bosses, and information indirectly to confront and resolve conflict. The chapter also discusses what options negotiators have when dispute resolution negotiations break down. In the global environment, there is no culturally common or culturally neutral legal system to turn to when disputants cannot reach an agreement. The chapter discusses third-party conflict resolution and provides managers with information about where to find appropriate third parties and how to select them.

Chapter Four focuses on multicultural teams. It explains why these teams have difficulty achieving their goals and provides concrete advice for team leaders and members on how to make high-quality integrative decisions and manage conflict. It argues that multicultural teams cannot be left to their own devices to make decisions and manage conflict "as best they can." It describes how to gather information from different team members and then integrate this information into a series of high-quality decisions. It suggests ways to prevent gratuitous conflict and to manage dysfunctional team conflict when it occurs.

Social dilemmas are special cases of team decision making. Teams with members representing many different nations are currently struggling with dilemmas concerning global resources, including forests, fisheries, air, and water. Social dilemmas are multiparty extensions of the famous prisoner's dilemma: if everyone on the team acts to maximize personal gain, everyone is worse off than if everyone acts to maximize collective gain, yet acting to maximize personal gain is always better for the individual team member. Within a culture, social dilemmas can be handled by regulation, but the only global authority is the one that is self-regulatory. Chapter Five describes different types of social dilemmas and how to use psychology to manage them.

Chapter Six returns to Disney's global expansion to analyze the role of government at and around the negotiating table. Why did Disney choose Hong Kong instead of another China location where there would be no travel restrictions on Chinese citizens? Why did Disney partner with the Hong Kong government instead of a private investor, as in Japan? If government is not actually at the table in negotiations that cross cultural boundaries, it is usually in the immediate vicinity. Cross-cultural negotiators often find themselves in unfamiliar legal and ethical environments with a governmental or quasi-governmental agency on the other side of the table.

Chapter Six uses real-world examples to set the stage for strategic advice about how political and legal contexts affect interests, hedging political and economic stability, and dealing with corruption. This chapter suggests Internet resources for researching the global competitiveness of nations and their reputations for combating bribery in international business transactions.

Chapter Seven addresses the question of whether Western negotiation strategies will soon dominate global negotiations, just as the English language dominates global communications. It then turns to practical advice for encountering cultural differences in interests and priorities, as well as strategic differences in confrontation, motivation, influence attempts, and information sharing.

A Word on Words

A lot of terms in this book have specific meanings in the context of intercultural negotiation. Do not let the terminology you encounter throw you. Each term is defined when it is introduced, and for handy reference, all the defined terms appear in a glossary at the back of the book. A good grasp of negotiation terminology will help you incorporate new negotiation strategies into your own negotiations.

The Value of Becoming an Excellent Global Negotiator

As you improve your cross-cultural negotiating skills, you will find yourself making deals you might otherwise not have made, creating value that might otherwise have been left on the table, and avoiding and resolving disputes by considering new possibilities and alternatives. The value of becoming a better cross-cultural negotiator can also be measured by the relationships you preserve, the costs you minimize, and the flexibility you retain by managing conflict rather than becoming a captive of it. The benefits of your cross-cultural negotiation skills will also be reflected in the quality of your team's decisions when all group members' distinct knowledge gets incorporated and in the ease with which those decisions are implemented. The advantages of your negotiation skills will be in the way you manage dilemmas of self-interest and collective interests. Finally, the benefits of becoming a better cross-cultural negotiator will be in having strategies for dealing with government bureaucrats who value the status quo and corrupt officials who are acting normatively in their own culture when asking for a personal payment.

Negotiating across cultures is never easy, but it can be made easier by paying close attention to strategy and knowing how to adjust your strategy when you cross cultures. That is what this book will help you do.

Evanston, Illinois   Jeanne M. Brett
February 2001

Acknowledgments

I have had the privilege of working in an environment where many scholars are investigating negotiations. Max Bazerman, Margaret Neale, and Leigh Thompson have taught me much about deal making. Laurie Weingart and Mara Olekalns challenged my understanding of the negotiation process. My coauthors in writing *Getting Disputes Resolved*, Stephen Goldberg and William Ury, led me to think about the similarities and differences in negotiating deals and resolving disputes. Zoe Barsness, Maddy Janssens, Anne Lytle, Catherine Tinsley, and I spent two years studying the cross-cultural research in psychology and developing facility with cross-cultural research paradigms. Without these colleagues, I would never have taken the plunge into this challenging area of research and practice. Anne Lytle's dissertation was our first comparative cross-cultural negotiation study. The study of U.S.-Japanese intercultural negotiations I conducted with Tetsushi Okumura was our first attempt to understand cross-cultural negotiations. Wendi Adair has expanded that research by investigating the negotiation process. She collected the Russian data, Alain Lempereur the French data, Anne Lytle the Hong Kong and later the Thai data, and Tetsushi Okumura the Japanese data that allowed us to develop an important comparative-culture perspective on deal-making negotiations. Catherine Tinsley's dissertation and the subsequent research done jointly with her provided many of the ideas for the chapter on dispute resolution.

Research done with Maddy Janssens and Ludo Keunen enriched my understanding of multicultural teams. Studies done with Laurie Weingart and Debra Shapiro, along with research they have done without my involvement, have enriched my thinking about multi-cultural, multiparty, multi-issue negotiations in a global context. Kim Wade-Benzoni and Tetsushi Okumura worked with me to understand social dilemmas. James Gillespie, Wendi Adair, Shirli Kopelman, Dania Dialdin, and Ashleigh Rosette have stimulated my thinking about what happens when cultures clash and were involved in collecting the U.S.-Israeli, U.S.-German, and U.S.–Hong Kong Chinese intercultural data. Wendi Adair became the expert on reciprocity in negotiations, Shirli Kopelman on social motives and social dilemmas, Dania Dialdin on distributive negotiations, and Ashleigh Rosette on virtual negotiations. Kwok Leung and Mara Olekalns have been thoughtful and extremely helpful commentators throughout the research process.

I owe an enormous intellectual debt to all of these people. I hope that they have learned as much and enjoyed as much working with me as I have with them. I am confident that they will not agree with all my conclusions and encourage the interested reader to seek out the original research papers and my colleagues' independent work.

Max Bazerman and Ann Tenbrunsel wrote the original exercise on which Cartoon was based. I am grateful to them for letting us adapt it for research and use it in this book. The dispute between U.S. and Chinese joint venture managers described in Chapter Three was inspired by an example given by Karen Jehn at the 1998 International Association of Conflict Management meeting at the University of Maryland. The rattling bicycle story was told by Jeff Palmer at the 1999 International Executive Masters Program at the J. L. Kellogg Graduate School of Management. Madame Petit has retired from raising pumpkins, but her story is true.

Much of the research underlying this book was supported by the Dispute Resolution Research Center at the J. L. Kellogg Graduate

School of Management, Northwestern University. I appreciate the willingness of the members of the center's research committee—Keith Murnighan, Margaret Neale, Max Bazerman, and Michael Roloff—to comment on and ultimately to invest in cross-cultural research.

Rachel Hamill and Margaret Dash supported the research in countless ways. Man Ho Han and Sara Bachman managed the data sets. Michael Teplitsky and Sara Bachman worked on the references. Linda Stine produced the tables and figures; Jason Bladen formatted the book; Molly Kern read the proofs. Anne Lytle, Maddy Janssens, Jacques Tibau, Wendi Adair, Zoe Barsness, Judy Krutky, Julianna Gustafson, and several anonymous reviewers gave me wonderful feedback, support, and encouragement in making the final revisions.

The staff of the Dispute Resolution Research Center—Rachel Hamill, Margaret Dash, Linda Stine, and Jason Bladen—as well as the staff of the Management and Organizations Department at Kellogg—Linda Piotrowski, Susan La Coppola, and Charlene Jenkins—have been extraordinarily gracious in supporting my getting the book written. I am sure they are looking for another project for me so that I will not be tempted to meddle in their competent and independent running of the center and the department.

There is no way to properly thank my host professors and all the participants in the executive, M.B.A., and law programs I have had the pleasure to work with since 1981. Professor Bala Balachandrin invited me to teach in India; Dean Israel Zang, to teach in Israel; Professor Eric Langeard (deceased), to teach in France; Professor Akihiro Okumura, to teach in Japan; Professor Bing Xiang, to teach in China; Professor Toemsakdi Krishnamra, to teach in Thailand; and Professor Lourdes Munduata to help her teach in Spain. Dean Donald Jacobs encouraged me to teach negotiations in the first place, encouraged me to take the course cross-culturally, and introduced me to many international teaching opportunities.

I am deeply grateful to all the participants in these programs and in Kellogg's M.B.A. and Executive Masters programs for sharing their negotiation insights and experiences. I hope what you learned from me has helped you understand as much about negotiations as what I have learned from you. I see you again from time to time at Kellogg alumni events around the world, in airports, on the lakefront, and in cards and notes where you bring to my attention the odd negotiation term that catches your eye in an ad or a street sign. These brief interchanges do not do justice to my debt to you. You have made all that Kellogg has supported in the area of negotiations possible. Bob Dewar, my department chairman in 1981, encouraged me to take the risk and teach a negotiation course. My husband, Steve Goldberg, gave me the idea to do it in the first place and then negotiated with faculty at Harvard Law School to let me use their cases, even to write the lawyers out! Seventeen students took the course that first year. It was student response in 1982 that brought the course to the attention of Dean Jacobs and caused our infamous negotiation over class size and the beginning of Kellogg's incubator for teaching new negotiations faculty. It was the student response that moved the course from an elective to a core course in the Executive Masters Program, and that encouraged those running Kellogg's far-flung joint ventures to bring their participants to Evanston for the opportunity to learn negotiations in an intercultural setting. It was the student support that justified hiring Max Bazerman and then Maggie Neale and Leigh Thompson. Their research, along with that of psychologists Reid Hastie and Tom Tyler, game theorists Roger Myerson and Robert Weber, and law professor Stephen Goldberg, allowed us to seek the support of the William and Flora Hewlett Foundation and develop the Dispute Resolution Research Center. Funding from the Hewlett Foundation and the Alan and Mildred Peterson Foundation has been instrumental in making Kellogg not just a major site for teaching negotiation but also a major negotiations research center. Thank you to everyone who has made Kellogg's negotiations initiative possible.

My daughters, Gillian and Amanda Goldberg; my husband, Steve Goldberg; and my gardens all have learned to get along with less attention as the book project took shape. I look forward to spending more time with each, and I hope they hold no grudges for the lack thereof over the past year when this project held center stage.

—J.M.B.

The Author

JEANNE M. BRETT is DeWitt W. Buchanan Jr. Distinguished Professor of Dispute Resolution and Organizations at the J. L. Kellogg Graduate School of Management, Northwestern University, where she is also the director and a founding member of the Dispute Resolution Research Center. Brett initiated Kellogg's popular Negotiation Strategies for Managers course and then extended the course to negotiating in a global environment. She conducts research and negotiation training programs at Kellogg and in executive programs around the world. She is the author of several books, including *Getting Disputes Resolved: Designing Systems to Cut the Costs of Conflict* (Jossey-Bass, 1988), written with William L. Ury and Stephen B. Goldberg, and numerous scholarly articles.

Negotiating Globally

1

Negotiation and Culture

A Framework

At the height of foreign investment in Russia, BP PLC spent $484 million to buy 10 percent of Sidanko, one of the five largest Russian oil companies. Eighteen months later, BP was enmeshed in a bankruptcy proceeding and takeover fight that resulted in the loss of BP's investment. What went wrong with this deal? In the race to have a foothold in an emerging market, BP apparently overlooked negotiating fundamentals and cultural issues. A young pro-Western banker with excellent political connections ran Sidanko. He had taken the company private for $470 million, only slightly less than what BP paid for 10 percent ownership, 20 percent voting rights, and a few senior management positions. BP clearly wanted access to Sidanko's oil fields but unfortunately did not negotiate enough leverage to take over the direction of the company and make it profitable. According to one commentator who follows foreign investment in Russia, the BP executives' instructions were not carried out either because Russian management culturally would not do so or because Russian management was getting orders from somewhere else.[1] BP ended up facing off with a recalcitrant creditor who owned part of Sidanko's $450 million in outstanding debt and wanted the oil fields itself.

Culture is often the culprit when deals that cross national borders, like the one between BP and Sidanko, lead to disputes and unanticipated costs. This chapter lays the groundwork for under-standing how culture affects negotiation. It begins by describing negotiation fundamentals, those elements of negotiation that are the same across cultures. It then describes culture and explains how culture affects negotiations.

Negotiation Fundamentals

When you ask people all over the world what comes to mind when you say *negotiation*, most describe some sort of a market in which two people exchange a series of offers. Implicit in their answer is the assumption that a deal is in the making, that the two are speaking directly (though the medium may be electronic), and that they are bargaining to divide a fixed pie of resources. Yet negotiations are not limited to direct deal making over fixed resources. In all cultures, people negotiate to resolve disputes and to make decisions in teams. When negotiators reach agreement, resources are always distrib-uted, but the amount of resources available for distribution is not necessarily fixed. Fundamental to negotiation are the circumstances in which people negotiate and the types of agreements they reach.

Types of Negotiations

All types of negotiations occur because people perceive that their goals are incompatible. When people see themselves as interdepen-dent (or potentially so) but in *conflict*, they naturally negotiate to try to deal with the conflict. Negotiators from BP trying to buy Sidanko wanted to pay as little as possible. Negotiators from Sidanko trying to raise capital by selling a stake to a foreign oil company wanted to gain as much as possible. Their *deal-making negotiations* sought terms that were better than either party could negotiate elsewhere despite their conflicting goals. Conflict is frequently the subtext when groups or teams are trying to make decisions. BP placed managers in top exec-utive positions at Sidanko, but these managers did not have sufficient leverage to influence *decision-making negotiations* at the top. When BP realized that its goals were not being met, it made a series of *claims* for more management control. When its claims were rejected, *dispute resolution negotiations* ensued. Deal-making, decision-making, and dispute resolution negotiations occur in all cultures. However, because culture affects how negotiators reach deals, resolve disputes, and make decisions, it also affects their agreements.

Distributive and Integrative Agreements

Negotiation is about claiming *value*: how much of a set of resources you are going to get and how much the other party gets. Successful *value-claiming negotiation* leads to a *distributive* outcome that divides a fixed set of resources such that your interests or the needs underlying your positions are met. But negotiation can also be about creating value: how you and the other party can increase the resources available to divide. Successful *value-creating negotiation* leads to an agreement that is both integrative and distributive, one that divides an enhanced set of resources.

The concept of *integrative agreements*, much less how to reach them, is not intuitive. To create value takes transforming what appears to be a fixed set of resources into a set of resources that are differentially valued by the negotiators and then distributing resources to the negotiators who value them the most.

There may be opportunities to create value in even the simplest of negotiations. While living in a small village in France, my husband and I offered to organize a traditional Halloween party for the thirty children in the local grade school. Our children had told their French friends about making jack-o'-lanterns (pumpkins are hollowed out, a face is carved, and a lighted candle is placed inside). My job was to purchase enough pumpkins for thirty children to carve. I had difficulty locating any pumpkins but finally found a roadside stand outside a small house with some for sale. I counted; there were exactly thirty. I knocked on the door, and a woman came out. I told her I wanted to buy the pumpkins and asked the price. She named a reasonable figure, and I said, "Fine, I'll take all of them." "Oh, no," she replied, "I cannot sell you all of them." I immediately had visions of making jack-o'-lanterns with pumpkin halves, holding a lottery to determine which children got to carve and which got to take home a jack-o'-lantern, carving melons instead . . . But then I thought, wait a minute, you're supposed to know something about negotiation. So I asked, "Why won't you sell me all the pumpkins?" She answered, "If I sell all of them to you, I won't have any seeds to plant next year." I asked her if having the seeds by November 1 would allow sufficient time for planting. She said it would and sold me all the pumpkins on the condition that I return the seeds on November 1, which I did.

Madame Petit and I negotiated an integrative agreement. We created value by my asking and her answering truthfully a series of questions that led us to separate the pumpkins and the seeds. There are two sources of integrative potential in negotiations: differences in negotiators' *preferences* and compatibility of preferences. Madame Petit had a stronger preference for the seeds and I for the rind of the pumpkins. Madame Petit did not need the seeds immediately and I did not want to give them to her right away. Our interests on the timing issue were compatible. Our integrative negotiation took advantage of our different uses for the pumpkins and our compatible time frame.

Had I accepted Madame Petit's refusal to sell me all the pumpkins, our agreement would have been distributive. I would have bought as many pumpkins as she would sell, and she would have kept as many as she needed for seeds. Neither of our interests would have been as fully satisfied as they were with the integrative agreement. With the integrative agreement, Madame Petit gained more money by selling me all the pumpkins, and she gained all the seeds. I gained all the pumpkins I needed so that every child could make a jack-o'-lantern.

Had I stood on principle, refusing to buy any pumpkins if I could not buy all of them, we would have reached an *impasse*. I thought my best alternative, if I could not buy pumpkins, was to have the children carve melons, a messier prospect at best. Madame

Petit's alternative was to interrupt her housework repeatedly to get rid of her stock of pumpkins.

Note that our integrative agreement over the pumpkins was also distributive. Madame Petit got all of the seeds *and* her full asking price; I got all of the pumpkins. In fact, all integrative agreements also distribute value.

This is one important reason to integrate: negotiators who integrate have more value available to distribute and are therefore more likely to claim what they want. A second important reason to integrate is that negotiators who integrate are sometimes able to structure an agreement when otherwise there would be none. Impasses normally occur when a seller asks more than a buyer can pay. However, if the seller learns why the buyer cannot pay the asking price or the buyer learns why the asking price is so high, the negotiators may be able to structure the deal—for example, with creative financing or with nonfinancial compensation that corresponds to both parties' interests.

The term *integrative* is frequently used with a great deal of imprecision to mean an agreement that is mutually satisfactory. Mutual satisfaction, however, is an evaluation of an agreement, not a type of agreement. Negotiators who have failed to look for or find an integrative agreement may be quite satisfied with a distributive agreement. For example, if I were only able to buy twenty-six pumpkins and evaluated that outcome against the alternative of carving melons, I might have been satisfied. Madame Petit, who had no intention of selling all her pumpkins anyway, would also have been satisfied. Distribution and integration have to do with the *amount* of resources, not with the evaluation of them.

When I tell the pumpkin story in class, someone invariably suggests that I did not get such a great deal because I did not negotiate a discount for buying all the pumpkins. It is possible that had I pushed for a better price, I might have gotten one. Yet I did not for several reasons. First, I knew that haggling over price is not common in the open-air food markets in that part of France. Second, I was concerned that if I did haggle, Madame Petit might refuse to sell me any pumpkins, and my melon alternative was not particularly attractive. Third, I thought it possible that the school might want to continue the Halloween tradition and I might have future interactions with Madame Petit. My poor alternative and my concern for the relationship affected my distributive outcome. In the negotiation literature, especially the cross-cultural literature, the relationship is sometimes represented as an outcome. Yet as the example illustrates, relationship is an issue in negotiation and can be one element of a distributive or an integrative agreement.

Negotiation Fundamentals Affected by Culture: Interests, Priorities, and Strategies

All negotiators have interests and priorities, and all negotiators have strategies. *Interests* are the needs or reasons underlying the negotiator's positions. *Priorities* reflect the relative importance of various interests or positions. My interest in the negotiation with Madame Petit was having a pumpkin for each child. As we negotiated, we realized that we had different priorities: hers was for seeds and mine for the rind. A negotiation *strategy* is an integrated set of behaviors chosen because they are thought to be the means of accomplishing the goal of negotiating. My strategy negotiating with Madame Petit included confronting her directly and asking for information. I could have sent a third party, but I did not. I also refrained from using *influence* because my alternative was so poor.

Negotiators' interests, priorities, and use of strategies are affected by culture. So it is useful to have an understanding of culture before considering how and why culture affects interests, priorities, and strategies.

Culture and Negotiation

Culture is the unique character of a social group, and in this book the focus is on national culture.[2] Cultures consist of psychological elements, the values and norms shared by members of a group, as well as social structural elements: the economic, social, political, and religious institutions that are the context for social interaction.[3] Cultural *values* direct attention to what issues are more and less important and influence negotiators' interests and priorities. Cultural *norms* define what behaviors are appropriate and inappropriate in negotiation and influence negotiators' strategies. Cultural *institutions* preserve and promote values and norms. Cultural values, norms, and *ideologies* serve as shared standards for interpreting situations (this is a negotiation, therefore I ought to . . .) and the behavior of others (she threatened me, therefore I should . . .).[4]

When two parties negotiate, both bring culture to the table with their interests and priorities and their negotiation strategies. Exhibit 1.1 illustrates how culture affects negotiation. It shows culture affecting the interests and priorities that underlie negotiators' positions on the issues. That is, culture may affect why the negotiators have taken the position they have or why one issue is of higher priority than another is. The fit between negotiators' priorities and interests is what generates the potential for an integrative agreement.

EXHIBIT 1.1. How Culture Affects Negotiation.

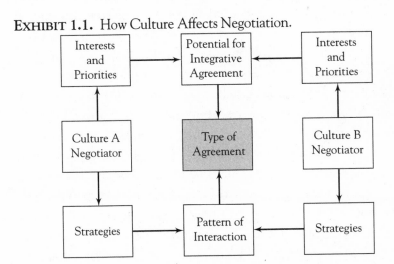

Source: J. M. Brett, "Culture and Negotiation," *International Journal of Psychology,* 2000, 35, 102. Reprinted with the kind permission of the International Union of Psychological Science (IUPSYS).

Culture may also affect the strategies that the negotiators bring to the table—for example, the way they go about negotiating, whether they confront directly or indirectly, their motivations, and they way they use information and influence. Exhibit 1.1 shows that negotiators' strategies cause patterns of interaction in negotiation. Those interaction patterns can be functional and facilitate integrative agreements, or they may be dysfunctional and lead to suboptimal agreements in which integrative potential is left on the table.

Effects of Culture on Interests and Priorities

Cultural values may reveal the interests underlying negotiators' positions. Negotiators from cultures that value tradition over change, for example, may be less enthusiastic about economic development that threatens valued ways of life than negotiators from cultures that value change and development. This was the situation in which Disney found itself after purchasing a large tract of land south of Paris to construct EuroDisney. Although EuroDisney promised jobs and economic development to an area that had high unemployment and few nonfarm jobs for youth, the local populace valued its traditional agricultural lifestyle. EuroDisney management, with its American values for economic development, had difficulty reconciling the local population's preferences for tradition over development.

The example also points out that the same values that generate cultural differences in preferences may also act as cultural blinders. Negotiators from one culture, expecting preferences to be compatible, cannot understand the rationality of negotiators from another culture whose views on the same issue are at odds with their own.[5] It is generally unwise in negotiation to label the other party as irrational. Such labeling encourages persuasion to get the other party to adopt your view of the situation and distributive outcomes, rather than the search for differences and the trade-offs that are the foundation of integrative agreements. There is opportunity for integration in differences. Instead of trying to persuade local French farmers that they should want to give up their traditional way of life, Disney had the opportunity to seek ways to preserve the traditions in the agrarian community in return for the community's support of the new park.

How Culture Affects Negotiation Strategies

When people negotiate, their behaviors are strategic and their strategies may be culturally based. This means that negotiators in one culture are more likely to enact a strategy with one set of behaviors and negotiators from another culture are more likely to enact that same strategy with another set of behaviors. Not only are there differences in strategic behavior between cultures, but there are also differences within cultures and overlap between cultures, with the result that some members of a culture may negotiate less like their own cultural *prototype* and more like the prototype of another culture.

Exhibit 1.2 shows the distribution of a negotiation strategy in two different cultures. The horizontal axis shows the level of strategic behaviors, ranging from low to high. The vertical axis shows frequency in terms of proportions of cultural members who exhibit different strategic behaviors. The normal curves drawn for cultures A and B indicate that the two cultures' prototypes are quite different but there is variability within each culture. Some members' behaviors are more and some less similar to the cultural prototype. There is also some overlap between the two cultures such that Smith from culture A behaves more like the prototype for culture B than the prototype for his own culture and vice versa for Chen from culture B.

Negotiation strategies are linked with culture because cultures evolve norms to facilitate social interaction. Norms are functional because they reduce the number of choices a person has to make about how to behave and because they provide expectations about how others in the culture will behave. Functional norms become institutionalized, meaning that most people use them and new members of the culture learn them because they make social interaction

EXHIBIT 1.2. Cultural Prototypes, Variability, and Overlap.

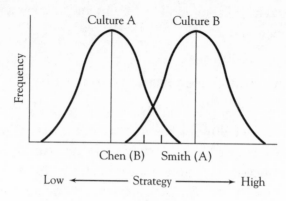

efficient. Our research indicates that there is a range of behaviors available for negotiators to use when enacting confrontation, information, influence, and motivation strategies and that culture has an impact on what behaviors negotiators use. Exhibit 1.3 summarizes these strategies and the alternative behaviors that negotiators can use to enact them.

Confrontation. Negotiations are not always direct verbal interactions between principals. Sometimes the verbal message is indirect. A U.S. company had a contract from a German buyer to sell bicycles produced in China. When the first shipment was ready, there was a problem. The bikes rattled. The U.S. buyer did not want to accept the shipment, knowing that with the rattle, they would not be acceptable to the German customer, whose high-end market niche was dominated by bikes that were whisper-quiet. What to do? In the U.S. culture, the normal approach would be to tell the manufacturer that the rattling bikes were unacceptable and that the problem had to be fixed. In China, such a direct *confrontation* would be extremely rude and cause much loss of *face*. Knowing this, the U.S. manager went to the Chinese plant, inspected the bicycles, rode a few, and asked about the rattle. "Is this rattle normal? Do all

EXHIBIT 1.3. Negotiation Strategies and Behaviors.

Strategy	Behaviors
Confrontation	Direct ←——————→ Indirect
Motivation	Self-Interests Other Interests ←——→ Collective Interests
Influence	BATNAª ←——————→ Status
Information	Direct ←——————→ Indirect

ªBest alternative to a negotiated agreement.

the bikes rattle? Do you think the German buyer will think there is something wrong with the bike if it rattles?" Then he left. The next shipment of bikes had no rattles.

Sometimes nonverbal behavior sends the message. An Asian woman, a new member of a multicultural team I was observing, was participating in discussion at a low level until an issue arose that involved her part of the organization and on which she had clearly been briefed. She spoke clearly and forcefully about the problems the team's plans would cause in her area. The rest of the team listened politely, asked no questions, and went ahead with the plan. Her response was to withdraw and stop participating altogether. Unfortunately, the rest of the team was not attuned to her nonverbal behavior.

At other times, instead of direct confrontation, a third party gets involved. When a U.S. manager in a U.S.-Chinese joint venture did not receive the information he was expecting in a report, he asked the Chinese woman responsible for the report for a meeting to discuss his needs. She politely put him off. A day later, he was called into her manager's office and told that there was no problem with the report, the report had the information it always had, and the report could not be changed.

People from different cultures vary in their preferences for direct verbal confrontation in negotiation. Some who are comfortable negotiating deals face to face are not comfortable engaging in face-to-face confrontation over a dispute or in a team meeting. Global negotiators need to understand how to confront directly and indirectly, a topic that is treated in depth in Chapter Three.

Motivation. *Motivation* is all about negotiators' interests. Negotiators may be concerned about *self-interests*, about the interests of the other party at the table, or about *collective interests* that extend beyond the immediate negotiation table. My negotiation with Madame Petit was motivated by self-interests and *other interests*—mine with the pumpkins, hers with the seeds. Collective interests did not really enter into the negotiation. The children might have been just as happy carving melons! However, in some negotiations, collective interests are very important. For example, when the French automaker Renault bought a large stake in Nissan in 1999, business commentators predicted that the measures required to make Nissan profitable—plant closings, layoffs, winnowing of suppliers—would be extremely difficult to accomplish. Japanese companies traditionally feel responsible for their employees and to the communities in which their plants are located. Laying off employees, closing plants, and generating competition among suppliers is not a normative business practice in Japan, where collective interests dominate.

The relative importance of negotiators' self-interests, other interests, and collective interests vary by culture. Negotiators from some cultures are much more concerned with self-interests; negotiators from other cultures pay as much attention to the interests of others as to their own; and negotiators from still other cultures take the interests of the collective into account when setting priorities and deciding whether to accept a proposal or continue negotiating. Global negotiators need to be sensitive to cultural differences in negotiators' goals and motivation and in negotiators' interests. Culture and goals are discussed in Chapter Two, culture and negotiators' interests in Chapter Three.

Influence. *Power* is the ability to influence the other party to accede to your wishes.[6] There are many different bases of power in social interaction,[7] but two, BATNAs and fairness standards, seem to be particularly important for negotiation and to be relied on differently in different cultures.

BATNA stands for the *best alternative to a negotiated agreement.*[8] The worse a negotiator's BATNA, the more dependent the negotiator is on reaching an agreement and the less powerful in terms of extracting concessions. My BATNA in negotiating with Madame Petit was buying melons—not very good. I could hardly have influenced her to sell me all her pumpkins by threatening to go elsewhere and buy melons!

Fairness standards are decision rules, wrapped in a veneer of justice. The rule might be precedent, it might be contract or law, or it might be social status (for example, age or experience) or social ideology (for example, equity, equality, or need). I could have proposed need as a fair standard to try to convince Madame Petit to sell me all her pumpkins. However, she had needs too, and this illustrates the problem with fair standards as influence strategies: there are almost always competing standards, even within a culture.

Across cultures, differences in ideology are likely to make it difficult to agree on a fairness standard. For example, ideology is at the heart of the long-standing "banana wars" between the United States and the European Union (EU). The fair standard that applies is the open markets standard that both parties have agreed to as members of the World Trade Organization (WTO). Yet France, an EU and WTO member, effectively blocked the importation of bananas from U.S. companies by imposing tariffs, making U.S. bananas more expensive than bananas from former French colonies whose economies in the near term depend on bananas. French ideology has a social welfare slant that extends to its former colonies. U.S. ideology is more capitalistic.[9]

The relative importance of BATNAs versus fairness standards, especially standards based on social status, as a basis of power in negotiations varies by culture and is explained in Chapter Two. The relative frequency of use of influence tactics also varies by culture. Chapter Two discusses culture and the use of influence tactics in deal making. Chapter Three focuses on culture and influence tactics in dispute resolution negotiations.

Information. *Information* is the currency of negotiation. Information about BATNAs, status, and other fair standards affects distributive agreements. Information about interests and priorities affects integrative agreements. When negotiators do not understand the information conveyed by the other party, integrative potential is almost always left on the table, and sometimes negotiations end in impasse.

Consider the inauspicious opening in the following negotiation. A U.S. negotiator on his first trip to Japan was confused by the formal opening meeting, which his Japanese hosts filled with a recitation of the history of their company, a story about the founder, and a litany about their product. After the meeting, the U.S. negotiator turned to his local representative and said, "What was that all about? Do they think I would arrive so unprepared as not to know about their company and their product? I want to buy their product. Why are they treating me as though I've never heard of it or their company? All the information they conveyed this afternoon is readily available in the marketplace, and I already know it." The local representative explained that the Japanese negotiators were attempting to convey information, albeit indirectly, about the status of their company and the product. The U.S. negotiator, fully aware of the Japanese company's status, was eager to get down to direct negotiations.

Culture affects whether information is conveyed directly, with meaning on the surface of the communication, or indirectly, with meaning conveyed within the context of the message. Culture also affects whether information is conveyed at all. Chapter Two discusses direct and indirect influence and information strategies in the context of deal making.

Why Culture Affects Negotiation Strategy

The behaviors that negotiators from a culture characteristically use to enact a negotiation strategy are related to other features of that culture, including its values, norms for social interaction other than negotiation, and ideologies. Three widely studied features of culture seem to be related to the variability in negotiation strategy across cultures: the cultural values of individualism versus collectivism and egalitarianism versus hierarchy, and the low- versus high-context norm for communication.

Individualism Versus Collectivism. The most widely studied cultural value, *individualism* versus *collectivism*, distinguishes between cultures that place individuals' needs above collective needs and cultures that place the needs of the collective above the needs of individuals.[10] In individualist cultures, norms promote the autonomy of the individual. Social and economic institutions reward individual accomplishments. Legal institutions protect individual rights. In collectivist cultures, norms promote the interdependence of individuals by emphasizing social obligation. Social and economic institutions reward classes of people rather than individuals. Legal institutions support collective interests above individual rights.

The way a society treats people affects how they construe themselves and how they interact. People in all cultures distinguish between *in-groups*, of which they are members, and *out-groups*, of which they are not.[11] In individualist cultures, self-identity is likely to consist of attributes that are independent of in-group membership.[12] A negotiator from an individualist culture might say, "I am tall; I am intelligent; I have a sense of humor." In collectivist cultures, self-identity is likely to be interdependent with in-group membership. A negotiator from a collectivist culture might say, "I am a wife, mother, and daughter; I am a Kellogg faculty member."

Two researchers, Geert Hofstede and Shalom Schwartz, have measured social values in many cultures.[13] They used questionnaires and classified cultures by differences in average scores. Exhibit 1.4 summarizes Hofstede's classification of individualist and collectivist cultures, ranked in each category in decreasing order of individualism.

Members of individualist and collectivist cultures differ in many ways. Exhibit 1.5 suggests that both confrontational and motivational behaviors may stem from this cultural value.

Reluctance to confront directly in a negotiation may stem from the emphasis on cooperation in collectivist cultures.[14] Confronting—for example, telling the bicycle maker that the rattles indicated unacceptable quality—signals a lack of respect for an individual with whom you have a relationship.[15] An indirect approach is thought to be relationship-preserving.[16]

EXHIBIT 1.4. Individualist and Collectivist Cultures.

Individualist Cultures	Intermediate Cultures	Collectivist Cultures
United States	Austria	Brazil
Australia	Israel	Turkey
Great Britain	Spain	Greece
Canada	India	Philippines
Netherlands	Japan	Mexico
New Zealand	Argentina	Portugal
Italy	Iran	Hong Kong
Belgium		Chile
Denmark		Singapore
Sweden		Thailand
France		Taiwan
Ireland		Peru
Norway		Pakistan
Switzerland		Colombia
Germany		Venezuela
Finland		

Source: G. Hofstede, *Culture's Consequences: International Differences in Work-Related Values* (Thousand Oaks, Calif.: Sage, 1980), p. 158, copyright © 1980 by Sage. Reprinted by permission of Sage Publications, Inc.

EXHIBIT 1.5. Individualism–Collectivism and Negotiation Strategy.

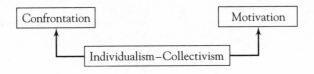

Negotiators' motivational orientations may also stem from their culture's values for individualism versus collectivism. This cultural value reflects a society's goal orientation.[17] Individualist cultures emphasize self-interests. Collectivist cultures emphasize collective interests.

Egalitarianism Versus Hierarchy. The second most widely studied cultural value distinguishes *hierarchical cultures*, which emphasize differentiated social status, from *egalitarian cultures*, which do not. In hierarchical cultures, social status implies social power. Social inferiors are expected to defer to social superiors, who in return for the power and privilege conferred on them by right of their status have an obligation to look out for the well-being of low-status people.[18]

Hofstede and Schwartz have also classified cultures on this dimension, which Hofstede calls "power distance." High-power-distance cultures are hierarchical ones where social status is differentiated into ranks. Exhibit 1.6 summarizes Schwartz's classification of egalitarian and hierarchical cultures, ranked in descending order of egalitarian and hierarchical commitment.

Members of egalitarian and hierarchical cultures may have rather distinct confrontational styles. They may also use influence differently. Exhibit 1.7 suggests that both confrontational and influence behaviors may be related to this cultural value.

People in hierarchical cultures may be reluctant to confront directly in negotiation because confrontation implies a lack of respect for social status and may threaten social structures. The norm in such a culture is not to challenge higher-status members. When

EXHIBIT 1.6. Egalitarian and Hierarchical Cultures.

Egalitarian Cultures	Hierarchical Cultures
Portugal	Thailand
Italy	China
Spain	Turkey
Denmark	Zimbabwe
France	Japan
Netherlands	Taiwan
Germany	Hong Kong
Greece	Singapore
Finland	Brazil
Switzerland	Poland
New Zealand	Malaysia
Turkey	Hungary
United States	United States
Mexico	New Zealand
Australia	Australia
Brazil	Mexico
Israel	Germany
Hong Kong	Netherlands
Poland	Switzerland
Singapore	France
Japan	Portugal
Taiwan	Spain
Malaysia	Finland
China	Greece
Zimbabwe	Denmark
Slovenia	Slovenia
Thailand	Italy

Source: S. Schwartz, "Beyond Individualism/Collectivism: New Cultural Dimensions of Values," in H. C. Triandis, U. Kim, and G. Yoon (eds.), *Individualism and Collectivism* (London: Sage, 1994), pp. 113–114, copyright © 1994 by Sage. Reprinted by permission of Sage Publications, Inc.

EXHIBIT 1.7. Egalitarianism–Hierarchy and Negotiation Strategy.

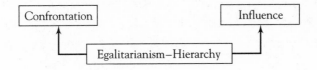

conflict does occur, it is more likely to be handled by a social superior than by direct confrontation.[19] When a higher-status third
party gets involved in a dispute, that party's decision reinforces his
authority without necessarily conferring differential status on the
contestants, as a negotiation that one party lost and the other won
would do. In an egalitarian culture, differentiated status due to success in direct negotiations is not likely to translate into permanent
changes in social status because there are few avenues for setting
precedents in egalitarian cultures.

Negotiators from hierarchical and egalitarian cultures may use
influence rather differently if their views of power in negotiation
reflect the way power is construed in their cultures. In egalitarian cultures, power is transitory and situational; in hierarchical cultures,
power is long-term and general. The concept of BATNA fits well
with the conceptualization of power in egalitarian cultures. BATNAs
are situational and flexible. If a negotiator is unhappy with his
BATNA, he may be able to improve it. Power as status fits well with
the conceptualization of power in hierarchical cultures. Status-based
power should endure over time and across situations.[20]

The reliance on a status-based interpretation of power can be
seen in Japanese commercial relationships in the 1960s and the
1980s. Japan is a hierarchical culture. In the 1960s, when Japanese
automobile companies were trying to break into the U.S. market,
they sold their cars at a very low margin. Presumably, they viewed
themselves as having lower status than the American carmakers,
and that status dictated that they could not charge the same high
prices for their cars as the higher-status Americans. When the
Japanese economy was booming in the 1980s, Japan's self image of

its economic status improved, and Japanese companies paid top dollar, bidding and winning against American companies for commercial real estate and private companies.

These events can be interpreted, as indeed they were in the U.S. press, from an in-group versus out-group perspective. Japan is a collectivist culture. Negotiators from collectivist cultures are said to deal with in-group members cooperatively and out-group members competitively. Japanese commercial behavior in both the 1960s and the 1980s was motivated by competition. This explanation based on competitiveness due to collectivism may be correct, but it is simplistic. Selling at or below margin, as the Japanese automakers did in the 1960s, does not make a lot of competitive sense because it does not build market share when competitors drop their prices too. (Japanese market share for automobiles in the United States was ultimately built on quality, not on price.) Paying significant premiums when you are the powerful buyer in the market and presumably have many options for investment also does not make competitive sense. An explanation based on hierarchy and the status of the Japanese in the marketplace in the 1960s and the 1980s provides additional insight into the behavior of Japanese negotiators.

Low-Context Versus High-Context Communications.

People in low-context cultures prefer to communicate directly. Meaning is on the surface of the message. Information is explicit, without nuance, and relatively context-free. People in high-context cultures prefer to communicate indirectly. Meaning is embedded in the context of the message and must be inferred to be understood.

Exhibit 1.8 identifies national cultures according to whether high- or low-context communication is normative.[21] In general, high-context cultures are those in which people have extensive information networks among family, friends, colleagues, and clients and are involved in close personal relationships.

Negotiators from low- and high-context cultures may have rather distinct confrontational styles. They may also use information differently. Exhibit 1.9 suggests that both confrontational and information-sharing behaviors may be influenced by this cultural value.

The Western manager in the rattling bicycles story was using high-context communication. He expected his Chinese counterpart to infer from his calling attention to the rattle that the bicycles needed to be repaired. He was neither confronting directly nor communicating directly. The Asian manager on the multicultural team was showing her displeasure at being ignored by in turn ignoring the team for the rest of the meeting. Her behavior was a form of indirect confrontation and communication. The Chinese manager in the joint venture confronted and communicated indirectly by having a third party, who just happened to be the boss, communicate the refusal.

EXHIBIT 1.8. Low- and High-Context Cultures.

Low-Context Cultures	High-Context Cultures
Germany	Arab cultures
Scandinavian cultures	France
Switzerland	Japan
United States	Mediterranean cultures
	Russia

Source: E. T. Hall and M. R. Hall, *Understanding Cultural Differences* (Yarmouth, Maine: Intercultural Press, 1990), pp. 7–8, 23.

EXHIBIT 1.9. Low- and High-Context Communication and Negotiation Strategy.

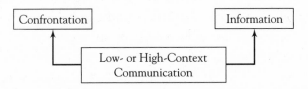

Culture and Negotiation Strategy: A Complex Link

It would be helpful if the relationships between negotiation strategies and other features of a culture were strong and straightforward. The research to date indicates quite clearly that this is not the case. The link between cultural values and cultural ideology and negotiation strategies is complex.

A look back at Exhibit 1.2 reveals two reasons why this link between features of a culture and negotiators' strategy is not straightforward: not all members of a culture behave like the cultural prototype, and cultural profiles overlap.

Another reason for the complex relationship between culture and negotiation strategy is that cultures are not composed of single features. Cultures have profiles of features. Single cultural features may be more or less important, depending on the profile in which they are embedded. Given the state of the research, we can make at most general statements about single cultural features and negotiation strategy.

Yet another reason why negotiation strategy is not perfectly related to other features of a culture is that cultural norms for negotiation may be cued more strongly in some situations than others.[21] For example, members of a multicultural team may act more in accordance with their national cultural norms when they report to local superiors. When they report to a senior manager at corporate headquarters, they may act more in accordance with corporate norms.

Finally, there is the influence of the strategies of the other negotiators at the table. Negotiators are quite likely to reciprocate each other's strategies.[23] When all negotiators are from the same culture, reciprocity reinforces culturally normative negotiation behaviors. When negotiators are from different cultures, reciprocity may help negotiators adjust their strategies to each other.[24]

Given all of these caveats, it is not unreasonable to wonder why we should study culture and negotiation strategy at all. The answer is that there are cultural differences in the behaviors negotiators use to enact a strategy. Anticipating these differences helps negotiators make sense of them and adjust their own behaviors to reinforce or to block the other party's strategy. However, the global negotiator needs to be aware of several important points:

- Research is only beginning to profile the characteristic negotiation strategies of different cultures. There may be important strategic differences between cultures in addition to the motivational, influence, information, and confrontational strategies discussed here. Many cultures have not yet been thoroughly studied.

- Individual cultural members may not act like the cultural prototype, especially in particular situations. The cultural typologies based on individualism–collectivism, egalitarianism–hierarchy, and low- or high-context communication may not characterize the negotiators you are dealing with.

- A negotiator's strategy is not immutable; negotiators adjust their strategies to accommodate one another.

There is a risk in knowing too much about the other party's culture and assuming that he will act according to the cultural prototype. Excellent cross-cultural negotiators proceed slowly, testing their assumptions about what strategy will be effective with the other party. They are willing to adjust their use of negotiation strategy to achieve their goals but not compromise on their goals.

Being an excellent cross-cultural negotiator means understanding the nuances of negotiation strategy as it applies in different contexts. The following chapters develop those nuances.

2

Negotiating Deals

Markets are becoming global at an astonishing rate as suppliers look for new outlets with less competition and buyers look for variety in quality and price. North Americans buy South American fresh fruits and vegetables. South Americans watch television shows and films produced in North America. People in developing countries sew the shoes, footballs, and clothes used by consumers at their leisure in developed countries. High-technology companies compete for contracts to build infrastructure in developing countries. Corporations are merging to enter new markets and to realize global efficiencies that come with size. All these transactions involve negotiations across cultural boundaries.

Global deals are being done. Why then be concerned about the difficulties of negotiating cross-culturally? There are three reasons. First, some deals turn out poorly because in the rush to go global, negotiators fail to pay attention to their alternatives and lack clear standards for evaluating global deals. Second, opportunities are being lost because negotiators assume that bargaining is bargaining regardless of culture. In some ways, bargaining is bargaining regardless of whether you are buying or selling in markets in the Middle East, Latin America, or Southeast Asia. Yet there are subtle and important cultural differences in negotiators' goals and in the ways in which they use power and information that affect distributive outcomes. Third, money is being left on the table either because negotiators do not know how to negotiate integrative agreements or because they are unable to do so when negotiating across cultures. Information is crucial to the search for integrative agreements, and negotiators from different cultures handle information rather differently. Skilled negotiators can avoid making poor global deals by paying attention to standards for evaluating global deals and by learning how culture affects the path to distributive outcomes and integrative agreements.

Good Deals and Poor Deals

Many companies are aggressively pursuing globalization by negotiating deals to acquire a presence in a foreign country by acquisition, venture, alliance, or licensing. In the rush to go global, some rather poor decisions have been made. Not all global deals are good deals. Like any other aspect of business, some deals are better than others.

BP's deal for a 10 percent ownership stake in Sidanko, mentioned in Chapter One, does not look wise simply on the financials: Sidanko had been taken private for $470 million; its outstanding debt was $450 million; BP paid $484 million for 10 percent ownership. The business strategy motivating foreign acquisitions is usually framed as buy versus grow, but BP could not realistically grow a presence in Russia. There were no newly opened oil fields where BP could begin with an initial developmental investment. The Russian government also heavily regulated the oil industry. The cost of growing a presence in the Russian oil industry was essentially incalculable. Without a clearly delineated BATNA (what BP will do if it cannot buy into the Russian oil industry), BP negotiators had no basis for setting a *reservation price* (limit on what can be paid). It is no surprise that BP paid so much for its 10 percent stake in Sidanko.

BATNAs and Reservation Prices

If you are going to negotiate globally, you need a reservation price to serve as a stopping point, and to set a reservation price, you need a BATNA. This requires strategic thinking that extends beyond buy versus grow. It requires a corporate strategy that has multiple options to realize global expansion. With multiple options, you can set your reservation price by comparing, for example, the cost versus return anticipated for investment A, or A's *net value*, to the cost versus return for investment B, or B's net value. Whichever investment provides the least net value (return minus costs) becomes the BATNA for negotiating a deal for the other investment. The reservation price is a number close to the net value (return minus costs) of the less favorable investment.

There is no mathematical formula for determining BATNAs. Costs are not just financial but may extend to loss of reputation, if making the deal involves ethical issues; negative effects on communities, if jobs are at stake, as is so often the case when mergers occur; or damage to the environment. Expected returns are estimates. They may turn out to be wrong, but at least they give you a basis for setting a reservation price that is grounded in the same financial fundamentals that the analysts will use in evaluating the wisdom of your deal.

Even with this analysis, it is still not easy to set a reservation price, because of the transaction costs of negotiating. Let's make A the preferred deal and B the alternative. How close the reservation price for A is to the net value of the alternative investment, B, depends on how easy it will be to negotiate deal B. If deal B is certain, the reservation price for deal A may be higher than deal B's net value. If deal B is uncertain, negotiators may be willing to take a little less at the table for deal A than they think they could get with substantial effort for deal B.

Transaction Costs

Negotiating global deals is likely to generate higher *transaction costs*, or the costs of doing the deal, than negotiating domestic deals. New business relationships almost always call for face-to-face negotiations. When partners are from different parts of the world, negotiations may require substantial investments of time and money.

High transaction costs can be justified only if good deals get done. The better the deal, the more justifiable high transaction costs. But when you are engaged in protracted negotiations, you are not free to negotiate other deals. It is difficult to know at what point you should cut your losses and walk away from a deal. In cultures like the United States, decision makers get committed to even obviously losing courses of action,[1] and as a general rule, the more time and energy the deal takes to negotiate, the less net value there is likely to be in the deal. But this rule of transaction costs may not hold in cultures where great emphasis is placed on relationships or in negotiations that cross cultural boundaries.

Good advice sometimes comes from surprising sources. For many years, the artist Christo has negotiated with private and public officials around the world for permission to mount projects that usually involve large amounts of public space and fabric. Not surprisingly, negotiations have played a central role in his career. For example, he has been negotiating off and on with New York City for more than two decades to install a series of fabric arches in Central Park. In the meantime, Christo has, among other projects, surrounded eleven islands in Biscayne Bay with pink fabric, wrapped the Reichstag with gold fabric (his proposal was turned down twice before the German government came to him), and installed miles of blue parasols in Japan and yellow ones in the United States. Christo understands the transaction costs of negotiating. He also understands the value of his time. But the key to his success as an artist who has actually mounted these large public projects is that he understands the concepts of BATNA and reservation price. He is willing to cut his losses and move away from one project, though not necessarily abandon it forever, because he always has another project to develop.

Christo's strategy pays close attention to BATNA and transaction costs. Global negotiators would be wise to follow Christo's model: always have a BATNA, and trust your intuition when transaction costs are too high.

Setting BATNAs and Reservation Prices

The most important standard for evaluating global deals in the short term is the value of the deal versus the value of the BATNA. This is the primary focus of this chapter: how to negotiate to maximize the gain in your distributive outcome and your integrative agreement over your alternative and do so successfully when negotiating across cultural boundaries. However, no amount of attention to strategy for negotiating integrative and distributive deals across cultures will compensate for a flawed analysis of fundamentals like BATNA and reservation price. Here is some advice:

- Understand how the deal you are negotiating fits into the larger strategic picture. What goal is this deal supposed to meet? How else might that goal be met?

- Know your BATNA. You always have a BATNA; figure out what it is.

- If your BATNA is poor, try to improve it: generate some other alternatives.

- Evaluate transaction costs before finalizing your reservation price.

- Set a reservation price. Do not change your reservation price unless you have new, credible information that changes your BATNA.

Net-Value Deals and Culture

Analyzing a negotiation agreement in terms of its net value is certainly a rational approach, and rationality is closely linked with free-market economic models. Does this mean that this standard for evaluating a negotiated deal is applicable only in cultures with free-market economies? Am I imposing an American cultural standard on the rest of the world? I think not, because as discussed in Chapter One, alternatives or BATNAs are perceptions that take negotiators' interests into account. A BATNA is a judgment: if I do not make a deal with you, what is the next best way to get my interests met? My interests may be personal or they may be communal, depending on my culture and other factors. The standard works across cultures because even though the judgment is rational, the basis for that judgment is psychological and therefore open to cultural or other influences.

Integrative and Distributive Deal Making: An Example

One of the best ways to learn about negotiation is to put yourself in a simulation and negotiate. When we teach managers negotiation skills, we do not start off telling them how to negotiate. We give them a role, buyer or seller; a partner with the opposite role; and some confidential information about the issues to be negotiated, their interests and priorities, and their alternatives. We then ask them to try to negotiate a deal. We encourage them to use what they know about negotiating to see how far their current skills take them. We tell them we will post everyone's results, and we often ask them to make an audiotape, for us to listen to and for them to take home and evaluate after the course.

A simulation is a very good way to evaluate your negotiation skills and identify areas for improvement, because while what is being negotiated is a constant, how it is negotiated is a variable. Few deal makers get the same deals, and few use the same strategies. By looking at all the different deals that were reached and discussing all the different strategies that were used, negotiators can gain a lot of insight into their own negotiating strengths and weaknesses.

For the same reason that simulations provide an excellent source of feedback, they also provide a very good way to learn about how people from different cultures negotiate. When we began to study deal-making negotiations across cultures, we chose a simulation, Cartoon, that involved a film company (seller) and a TV station (buyer).[2] The negotiation is over the rights to broadcast one hundred episodes of a half-hour animated cartoon called *Ultra Rangers*.

We made our product a cartoon because cartoons are produced in many different countries and are quite easy to sell in the global marketplace because dubbing in a new language is inexpensive.

Managers find the Cartoon simulation challenging. Most get deals that are better than their BATNAs, but most leave money on the table. With a clearer understanding of the fundamentals of integrative and distributive negotiation, they might have negotiated a better deal.

Cartoon provides an opportunity for negotiating an agreement that is both integrative and distributive. Integrative opportunity in deal-making negotiations is embedded in the differential interests and priorities of the buyer and seller. Exhibit 2.1 shows this information for the buyer and seller in Cartoon. To find the *integrative potential* in Exhibit 2.1, look at the "Runs-per-Episode Adjustment" and "Financing Savings or Cost" rows. Runs refer to how many times each of the hundred episodes of *Ultra Rangers* can be shown during the term of the contract. Notice that the buyer gains significant revenue from showing *Ultra Rangers* more than six times, because the buyer receives advertising revenue each time an episode is shown. The seller estimates some loss of future revenue if *Ultra Rangers* episodes are shown too frequently. Interest in *Ultra Rangers* may wane, and the seller may not receive as much the next time it is sold in that same market. However, the estimated loss to the seller is much less than the estimated gain to the buyer. Of course, the negotiators do not know each other's interests unless they share this information.

Now look at the "Financing Savings or Cost" row. This information indicates that the cost of capital is different for the buyer and the seller. Here the seller is more sensitive to financing than the buyer is. The buyer would like to put off paying for *Ultra Rangers* as long as possible, but the seller really needs the cash at the time of the sale.

Exhibit 2.2 plots buyers' and sellers' net values for three different agreements. In outcome A, the price per episode is $46,000, the parties agreed on six runs, and 25 percent of the purchase price was

EXHIBIT 2.1. Preferences in Cartoon.

Issue	Buyer	Seller
Revenue	$8.4 million	N.A.
Price per Episode		
Limit	$60,000	$35,000
Aspiration	$30,000	$70,000
Runs-per-Episode Adjustment		
4	$(1,680,000)	$500,000
5	$(840,000)	$250,000
6	$0	$0
7	$840,000	$(250,000)
8	$1,680,000	$(500,000)
Financing Savings or Cost		
Year 1	10%	–20%
Year 2	20%	–35%
Year 3	30%	–50%
Year 4	40%	–60%
Year 5	50%	–70%
Strums		
Reservation Price	$20,000	$10,000
Ratings (Estimated Likelihood)[a]		
6–7	20%	10%
7–8	50%	10%
8–9	10%	10%
9–10	10%	50%
10–11	10%	20%
BATNA	$3.0 million	$2.5 million

Source: A. E. Tenbrunsel and M. H. Bazerman, "Working Women," in J. M. Brett (ed.), *Teaching Materials for Negotiations and Decision Making* [compact disk] (Evanston, Ill.: Dispute Resolution Center, Northwestern University, 2000).

[a]A rating point is the percentage of all TV households watching a particular show (number of households watching divided by total number of TV households).

EXHIBIT 2.2. Runs and Financing Trade-Offs in Cartoon.

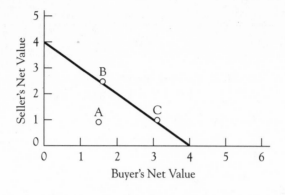

Outcome	Net Value ($ millions)		Price per Episode	Number of Runs	Financing
	Buyer	**Seller**			
A	$1.5	$0.9	$46,000	6	25% Years 0–3
B	$1.6	$2.5	$55,000	8	100% Year 0
C	$3.1	$1.0	$40,000	8	100% Year 0

Source: A. E. Tenbrunsel and M. H. Bazerman, "Working Women," in J. M. Brett (ed.), *Teaching Materials for Negotiations and Decision Making* [compact disk] (Evanston, Ill.: Dispute Resolution Center, Northwestern University, 2000).

paid immediately, with the rest paid annually in three equal parts. The net value for the buyer is $1.5 million and for the seller, $0.9 million. Exhibits 2.3 and 2.4 show the math for figuring the buyer's and seller's net value for outcome A. Look at outcomes B and C in the key at the bottom of Exhibit 2.2. Both outcomes B and C move the runs and financing to the extremes. Both of these outcomes are better for both parties than outcome A. Negotiators have created integrative value by trading off low-priority issues for high-priority issues.

Looking at the key in Exhibit 2.2, you can see that outcomes B and C contain the same amount of integrative value, $4.10 million

EXHIBIT 2.3. Example of Buyer Net Value in Cartoon.

Proposal: $46,000 per episode, 6 runs, financing 25% up front and 25% equal payments in Years 1–3.

Expected Revenue $8.4 million

Price $4.6 million

Runs Adjustment $0

Payment Savings $0.69 million

Year	Percent Paid	Amount Paid	Savings (%)	Savings ($ million)
0	25%	$1.15 million	0	0
1	25%	$1.15 million	10%	$0.115
2	25%	$1.15 million	20%	$0.230
3	25%	$1.15 million	30%	$0.345
Total Savings				$0.69

Other $0

Net Profit of Cartoon: $4.49 million
    [Revenue – (Price + Savings + Other)]
    $8.4 million – ($4.6 million + $0.69 million + $0) = $4.49 million

Net Value of the Agreement: $1.49 million
    (Net Profit – BATNA)
    $4.49 million – $3.0 million = $1.49 million

EXHIBIT 2.4. Example of Seller Net Value in Cartoon.

Proposal: $46,000 per episode, 6 runs, financing 25% up front and 25% equal payments in Years 1–3.

Revenue $4.6 million

Financing Cost $1.2075 million

Year	Percent Paid	Amount Paid	Savings (%)	Savings ($ million)
0	25%	$1.15 million	–0%	–$0
1	25%	$1.15	–20%	–$0.23
2	25%	$1.15	–35%	–$0.4025
3	25%	$1.15	–50%	–$0.575
Total Savings				–$1.2075

Runs Adjustment $0

Other $0

Net Revenue from Cartoon: $3.3925 million
    [Revenue – (Costs + Other)]
    $4.6 million – ($1.2075 million + $0) = $3.3925 million

Net Value of the Agreement: $0.89 million
    (Net Revenue – BATNA)
    $3.3925 million – $2.5 million = $0.8925 million

(buyer's net value plus seller's net value). In fact, any agreement for eight runs and no financing could be plotted on the B–C line in Exhibit 2.2. Exactly where on the line the agreement falls depends on how the integrative value is distributed, and this depends on what price per episode the parties agree to. In outcome B, the price of $55,000 per episode results in a deal that is better for the seller than the buyer. In outcome C, the price of $40,000 per episode results in a deal that is better for the buyer than the seller. Exhibit 2.2 makes clear that deal makers need to be concerned about integrative value, or they will end up with a deal like outcome A that leaves money on the table. Exhibit 2.2 also makes clear that deal makers need to be concerned with distributive outcomes or, as illustrated by the case of the seller in outcomes A and C, all or most of the integrative value will go to the buyer.

There is another source of integrative value in the Cartoon simulation. Buyers and sellers have compatible interests in a second animated cartoon series, *Strums*. The seller would also like to sell *Strums*, and the buyer has an available time slot for another cartoon. Exhibit 2.1 shows that the buyer has a reservation price for *Strums* of $20,000 per episode. The seller's reservation price is $10,000 per episode. Although it is not necessary to include *Strums* in a deal for *Ultra Rangers*, if the negotiators can agree to a price within the range of their reservation prices, *Strums* adds $1 million in integrative value to be distributed.[3] Exhibit 2.5 illustrates the effect of adding *Strums* at a price of $15,000 per episode. At this price, *Strums* increases each negotiator's net value by $0.5 million. There is no particular reason to split the difference on *Strums*. If the price were lower, say, $12,000 per episode, the buyer would gain more, $0.8 million, and the seller less, $0.2 million. If the rest of the deal were as in outcome E, this would move point E down to the right. Again, integrative value is also distributed.

Many of the ideas in this chapter about negotiating integrative and distributive agreements across cultures are grounded in the experience of managers around the world who have negotiated Cartoon. When managers negotiate Cartoon within their own culture,

EXHIBIT 2.5. Adding a Compatible Issue in Cartoon.

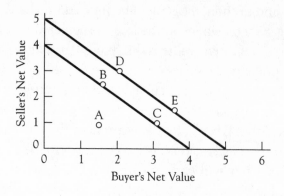

Outcome	Net Value ($ millions)		Price per Episode	Number of Runs	Financing	Other
	Buyer	Seller				
A	$1.5	$0.9	$46,000	6	25% Years 0–3	
B	$1.6	$2.5	$55,000	8	100% Year 0	
C	$3.1	$1.0	$40,000	8	100% Year 0	
D	$2.1	$3.0	$55,000	8	100% Year 0	*Strums* ($15,000)
E	$3.6	$1.5	$40,000	8	100% Year 0	*Strums* ($15,000)

Source: A. E. Tenbrunsel and M. H. Bazerman, "Working Women," in J. M. Brett (ed.), *Teaching Materials for Negotiations and Decision Making* [compact disk] (Evanston, Ill.: Dispute Resolution Center, Northwestern University, 2000).

their behavior illustrates what negotiation strategies are normative in their culture. When managers negotiate Cartoon across cultures, their culturally normative negotiation strategies may be compatible or may need some adjustment. Knowing what is normative in each of their cultures allows us to anticipate what adjustments they will need to make to negotiate successfully across cultures.

Negotiating Integrative and Distributive Deals

Recall from Chapter One that there are two reasons to try to reach integrative agreements in negotiations. First, with integrative agreements, there is more value to distribute. Second, without integration, there may be no room for agreement. Keep in mind that integrative agreements result from identifying trade-offs among issues like runs and financing in Cartoon on which negotiators' preferences are different, and finding *compatible issues*, like *Strums* in Cartoon, on which negotiators' preferences are not opposed.

Cultural Differences in Integrative Agreements and Distributive Outcomes

Over the past several years, U.S., Israeli, German, and Hong Kong Chinese[4] managers who are enrolled in Kellogg's International Executive Master's Program have convened at Northwestern University in the fall for a week of cross-cultural negotiations. Cartoon is their very first exercise. The deals they negotiate along with those of Japanese managers participating in a Kellogg-type executive program in Japan or in special U.S.-Japanese executive programs at Kellogg provide a way to evaluate cultural differences in integrative and distributive agreements.

The participants in these programs are all quite similar in many respects except culture. All are successful managers, average age thirty-eight; all have been selected by their employers and by Kellogg and its academic partners in Israel, Germany, and Hong Kong for this M.B.A. program. Their language of instruction is English.

Japanese companies similarly selected the Japanese managers. The U.S.-Japanese program was taught in English; however, the within-culture program was taught in Japanese. All negotiated Cartoon under very similar circumstances. The same introduction and the same materials were used.[5] The data set represents two or sometimes three different executive sessions, however, there are no significant between-session within-culture differences.

The similarities among the participants in our programs cut against finding cultural differences. This means that the differences that we do find are likely to be conservative estimates of differences between managers from these cultural groups.

Integrative Agreements. In the Cartoon negotiation, the highest possible integrative value is $5.10 million. This integrative deal results from trading off runs and financing and including *Strums* in the deal at a price between $10,000 and $20,000 per episode. The white bars in Exhibit 2.6 show the average integrative agreements negotiated by managers in U.S., Japanese, Hong Kong Chinese, German, and Israeli cultures. The shaded bars show the average integrative agreements negotiated interculturally between U.S. and Japanese, Hong Kong Chinese, German, and Israeli managers. The first thing to notice in Exhibit 2.6 is that there is no U.S. hegemony in negotiating integrative agreements. The Israelis were the most successful integrative negotiators both when negotiating within culture (white bar, average $4.24 million) and across cultures with a U.S. negotiator (shaded bar, average $4.45 million). The second thing to notice is that crossing cultures does not necessarily mean performance decrements in negotiation. On average, Hong Kong Chinese negotiators' integrative agreements were enhanced by more than a half a million dollars when negotiating with a U.S. buyer or seller. Japanese negotiators' integrative agreements were decreased by over three-quarters of a million dollars when negotiating with a U.S. buyer or seller. When you think about these results in net financial terms, culture and type of negotiation, whether same culture or across cultures, certainly make a difference. The

EXHIBIT 2.6. Integrative Agreements in Same-Culture and Across-Culture Negotiations.

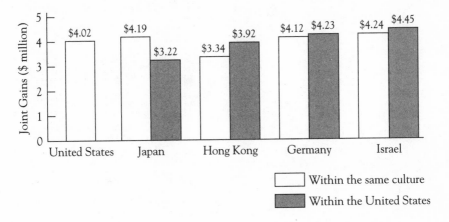

third thing to notice is that even the highest-performing U.S.-Israeli teams on average left more than half a million dollars of potential value on the table.

Cultural differences in integrative agreements were due to differences in how many times *Ultra Rangers* could be shown, or runs, and *Strums*, the second cartoon. Japanese negotiators, especially those negotiating across cultures, were much less likely to increase the number of runs beyond six, which the case indicates is the norm. Hong Kong Chinese negotiators and Japanese negotiators negotiating across cultures were least likely to include *Strums*. This latter decision may reflect a cultural difference in relationship building. Chinese and Japanese negotiators often commented in the debriefing that they saw *Strums* as an excuse to continue negotiating in the future and continue building a relationship.

Distributive Outcomes. Exhibit 2.7 shows the buyers' distributive outcomes, or net values, in the Cartoon negotiation. Buyers negotiating with a seller from their own culture are the white bars. Buyers negotiating across cultures with a U.S. seller are the shaded bars. The exhibit shows buyers' data only because buyers' and sellers'

EXHIBIT 2.7. Buyer's Distributive Outcomes in Same-Culture and Across-Culture Negotiations, Controlled for Seller's Gains.

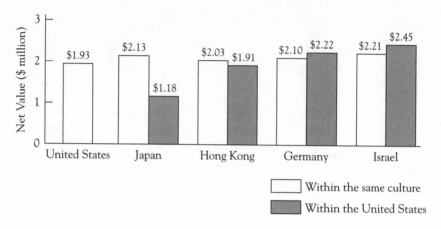

distributive outcomes are related both in terms of the integrative value the buyer and seller create together and because the seller receives the portion of the integrative value that the buyer does not.[6] To control for these interdependencies, we do not present the sellers' distributive outcomes, and we control the buyer's outcome statistically for the seller's. This all sounds very complicated, but it is just so we can look at the data in Exhibit 2.7 as buyers' distributive outcomes without worrying about all the interdependencies in the data.

The Israelis were also the most successful distributive negotiators. The Israeli buyers claimed the most, both when negotiating with same-culture sellers, $2.21 million on average, and when negotiating across culture with U.S. sellers, $2.45 million on average. Notice that Japanese and Hong Kong Chinese buyers claimed less on average when negotiating across culture with a U.S. seller than with a same-culture seller. This is not so surprising in the case of the Japanese because their across-culture integrative agreements were so low. However, the Hong Kong Chinese actually negotiated higher integrative agreements across culture than within culture (see Exhibit 2.6), so the distributive outcomes in

Exhibit 2.7 suggest that the Hong Kong Chinese buyers were not able to claim a large share of the integrative value negotiated cross-culturally.

Implications of Cultural Differences in Integrative Agreements and Distributive Outcomes. The data in Exhibits 2.6 and 2.7 establish that there are cultural differences in integrative agreements and distributive outcomes, but they do not tell us why these differences occur. Why are the negotiators from Israel so successful in creating and claiming value? Why are the negotiators from Japan and Hong Kong less successful in claiming distributive value across cultures than within their own culture? Now that we have established that culture makes a difference in integrative agreements and distributive outcomes, we need to understand what negotiators from different cultures bring to the table. In the next sections, we turn to cultural differences in three negotiation strategies that may help explain cultural differences in integrative agreements and distributive outcomes. These include negotiators' motivation and the goals they set, their view of power and use of influence in negotiation, and whether and how they share information.

Goals and Motivation

Targets and Distributive Outcomes. Negotiators' goals affect their ideal settlement points or *targets*. Goals are motivational; they direct activity, increase effort, encourage the development of strategy, and facilitate evaluation and decision making.[7] Targets are standards against which negotiators can judge opening offers, *concessions*, and final offers. Targets provide an alternative point of reference to a negotiator's BATNA and the opposing negotiator's opening offer. Anchoring on either her own BATNA or the other's opening offer may lead a negotiator to agree to an acceptable but suboptimal outcome, a process known as satisficing.[8] When one negotiator has a higher target than the other, the high-target deal maker typically claims more of the outcome.[9]

If you were a buyer in Cartoon and you failed to set a target, your BATNA, $3 million (see Exhibit 2.1) would be a salient reference point for evaluating the seller's proposals. As soon as the seller makes an offer that is better than your BATNA, you are likely to relax. You may get the seller to improve his offer somewhat, but you are not likely to be motivated to search hard for something much better. If you had set a target and the seller made an offer that was better than your alternative but not as good as your target, you might say to yourself, "OK, I'm going to get a deal; now let's see if I can get one that is as good as my target."

Evidence that targets are important in negotiating distributive outcomes leads to the question of how to set targets in cross-cultural negotiations. The answer turns out to be complex and cultural. In general, you want your target to be an alternative reference point to your reservation price. You want your target to be motivating. You want your target to help you set an opening offer. This means that the target has to be sufficiently extreme to motivate you to work hard in the negotiation. At the same time, it has to be sufficiently moderate that the other side does not view your opening offer as ridiculous and walk away before serious negotiations can begin.

What is ridiculous varies by culture. Negotiators from collectivist cultures often think negotiators from individualist cultures ask for far too much or offer far too little. From the collectivist perspective, outrageous openings get in the way of building a relationship and making a deal. In any culture, it is pretty ridiculous to make an offer to buy a publicly traded company for a price that is less than what it is currently trading for. (If your analysts cannot justify the market price, your best strategy is to wait and let the market cool off, or buy your BATNA.) When you are negotiating within your own culture, industry norms and past practice provide standards for setting goals and making opening offers.

When negotiating across cultures, should you act in a culturally inconsistent way? Should negotiators from individualist cultures open with more moderate demands? Probably not, because in moderating your demands, you are also likely to reduce your distributive outcome. Furthermore, if there is one *stereotype* of Americans, Israelis, and other negotiators from individualist cultures, it is that they make high demands. If you fail to act true to the stereotype, it is unlikely you will be believed.

Should negotiators from collective cultures open with more extreme demands when negotiating with someone from an individualist culture? Probably yes, for two reasons: you can anticipate that the negotiator from the individualist culture will make self-interested demands, and even if she does not, to protect your interests, you are going to have to get the attention of the negotiator from an individualist culture. You have to make clear that she is going to have to give you something in order to get what she wants. The way to do this is to play her game, at least so far as making demands in order to protect your interests, whatever they are. You can be pretty sure that she is not going to do that for you.

Setting targets ultimately depends on having good information about what is possible in a negotiation. Negotiators are often hesitant to make the first offer because they fear that they will not ask enough relative to what the other party will pay or will offer too much relative to what the other party will take. Many years ago, an investment banker told me the following story, which may be apocryphal, but it is too good not to share. A large U.S. company decided to sell a division that was not part of its core business. The CEO hired some investment bankers and asked them to give him an estimate for the business and to find a buyer. The investment bankers came back with a valuation of $150 million and several days later set up a meeting between the CEO and a potential buyer who happened to be French and happened to have a good fit with this division. The French company offered $175 million. May this happen to you once in your life! Was the deal done at $175 million? No the offer was turned down, the investment bankers were fired, and the French company ultimately paid $200 million. Clearly, the French knew something about *synergies* associated with the acquisition that the investment bankers did not. The story, true or not, makes an important point about goals and openings in distributive negotiations. When your information is poor or flawed, it is difficult to set goals and determine reasonable opening bids.

Here is some advice for setting targets:

- Find out what is normative in the other party's culture.
- Know what is normative in your own.
- Get as much information as possible about recent deals that are similar to yours.
- Be optimistic but not unrealistic.
- Don't lose sight of your target as soon as you get an offer better than your BATNA.

Here is some advice for making opening offers:

- When your information is good, there is likely to be some benefit in opening. The opening offer can act as an anchor.[10] When you have opened, the other party now has to get you off your position, not vice versa.
- When your information is poor, there is likely to be some benefit in waiting for the other party to open. However, be sure to make an opposing counteroffer, or the other party's opening may anchor the negotiation. You will also now be in a position of trying to move the other party off its anchor. The best way to do this is make a counteroffer.
- When the other party's opening is totally unacceptable and you say so, do not expect him to make an immediate concession. Instead, give him a reason to make a concession and at the same time set a counteranchor. Make a counteroffer.

Goals and Integrative Agreements. Exhibit 2.8 shows the social motives of the negotiators in our study from the United States, Hong Kong, Germany, and Israel. *Social motives* are the type of choices people make in situations, like negotiations, in which they are interdependent with others.[11] Negotiators concerned with

EXHIBIT 2.8. Social Motives of U.S., Hong Kong Chinese, German, and Israeli Negotiators.

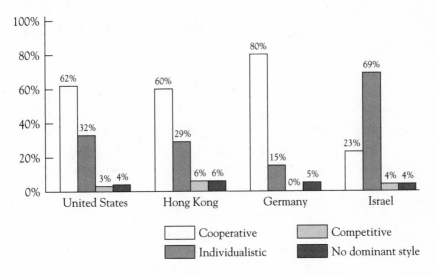

themselves are called *individualistic* and are generally unconcerned with the welfare of the other party so long as they are not affected. Negotiators concerned with their own welfare and that of the other party are called *prosocial* and are usually cooperative in their dealings with others. Negotiators who are concerned with benefiting themselves at the expense of the other party are called *competitive*.[12] Exhibit 2.8 shows significant differences in the proportions of prosocial and individualistic negotiators in the U.S., Hong Kong Chinese, German, and Israeli cultures. The Israeli negotiators are predominantly individualistic, the German negotiators predominantly prosocial, and the U.S. and Hong Kong Chinese negotiators mixed 60 percent prosocial and 30 percent individualistic. Given their social motives to do well for themselves, it is no surprise that the Israelis negotiated the highest distributive outcomes and integrative agreements.

Negotiators who, like many of the Israelis in our study, are concerned about self-interests are classic cultural individualists. They achieve highly integrative agreements because they search for outcomes that fulfill their interests and because they are pragmatic. They recognize that to get, you have to give, and they are unconcerned if an outcome that is good for them is also good for the other party. In short, they are willing to trade off.

The German negotiators in our study were also able to achieve highly integrative agreements. Their prosocial social motives actually direct them to consider the interests of the other party as well as their own. Negotiating within their own culture, the Germans were very likely to be paired with another prosocial negotiator. Even negotiating across cultures, the prosocial German negotiators were quite likely to encounter a prosocial U.S. negotiator. The cooperative behavior of a prosocial negotiator stimulates a cooperative response on the part of the other negotiator, that cooperative response is reciprocated, and joint gains result.

There were too few competitive negotiators in our study to see if their integrative agreements were low, forcing down their distributive outcomes, as theory would predict.[13] The reasoning goes like this: A competitively oriented negotiator is focused on claiming value from the other party and so is not likely to negotiate an integrative agreement. Although the competitive negotiator may claim the largest proportion of the fixed resource pie, if there is no integration, the resource pie will not be maximized, and the competitive negotiator will have less to claim than the individualistic or prosocial negotiator who claims from an integrative agreement.

The social motives data indicate that no single social motive results in integrative agreements and high distributive outcomes. In Israel, the individualistic social motive dominates, and integrative agreements result from high self-interests, the willingness to work hard to achieve those interests, and the willingness to let the other party do well too. In Germany, the prosocial motive dominates, and integrative agreements result from working together cooperatively to meet both parties' interests.

Social motives are not something that you can go out and change, either your own or the other party's. Negotiators who cross cultural boundaries need to be prepared to work with negotiators who are individualistic, negotiators who are prosocial, and negotiators who are competitive. Here is some advice:

- Push the individualistic negotiator hard to accommodate your interests while realizing his own.
- Reciprocate the prosocial negotiator's initiatives. If you initiate cooperation yourself, it is likely to be rewarded.
- Treat a competitive negotiator like an individualist. Push hard to get what you want in return for making concessions. Refuse to join the competitive negotiator's strategy. Make a proposal incorporating all the issues.

Of course, the advice assumes that you know the other negotiator's social motives, and you cannot open negotiations by asking the other party to complete a questionnaire. You also cannot rely on cultural stereotypes because as the data in Exhibit 2.8 indicate, even in the most homogeneous culture, there is substantial variance among individualistic and cooperative social motives. What to do?

- See what you can find out about the other negotiator from people who have negotiated with him in the past.
- Do an experiment. Initiate a cooperative move (more about what you might do when we get to the section on information) and see what happens. If it is reciprocated, do it again, and you will be well launched on a path of cooperation.
- Don't make concessions without getting something in return. The individualist will trade when pushed.

Power and Influence

Sources of Power. When we ask negotiators, "What do you think makes you powerful in a negotiation?" we get a variety of answers, depending on culture. Negotiators from cultures like the United

States where the social structure tends to be egalitarian invariably talk about information, and when pressed, they talk about their perceptions of their own and the other party's alternatives; in short, they talk about BATNA. Negotiators from cultures where the social structure is hierarchical, or differentiated into ranks, typically engage in influence attempts in negotiation.[14] They understand BATNA and recognize it as a source of power, but status is also an important source of power for them.

Status is a standard of fairness that can be used to distribute value. There are many bases for status standards—for example, role, age, history. There are also nonstatus fairness standards, such as equality, equity, need, and cultural differences, in the likely appeal of these norms. Equity implies that a distribution should be proportional to contribution; equality, that the distribution should be split evenly. Negotiators from cultures where self-interest is legitimate may be more likely to espouse an equity norm because it is consistent with self-interest. Negotiators from cultures where collective interests supersede self-interests may be more likely to espouse an equality norm because it is consistent with the collective interest and preservation of harmony.[15]

Use of Power and Influence. Negotiators try to influence each other to make concessions by talking about their power. There are many different types of influence strategies. Separating them into *direct influence strategies*—persuasion, argument, substantiation, and threats—and *indirect influence strategies*—appeals to sympathy, references to personal stakes in the negotiation, and references to status—helps illustrate cultural patterns in the use of influence. The difference between direct and indirect influence strategies is subtle but important. A direct strategy focuses on the other party's interests: "You should make this concession because if you do not, you will be hurt." An indirect strategy focuses on yourself: "Make this concession because if you do, it would be a big help to me—I will be able to make my quota for this year."

There are cultural differences in the frequency of use of direct and indirect influence strategies in the negotiations we studied. We audiotaped negotiations, transcribed the audiotapes (Japanese same-culture tapes were translated and transcribed), divided the speech into subject-verb phrases, and then compared how frequently different influence tactics were used by negotiators from different cultures. Exhibit 2.9 provides the definitions and some examples of the influences tactics and other codes discussed later in the chapter.

Direct Influence Strategies. When you use a direct influence strategy, you are telling the other party what you want her to do and why doing so is in her own best interest. When you argue, you try to persuade the other party to make a concession. You give her all kinds of reasons for why she should do what you want. Arguing is different from bargaining because in bargaining you offer to give the other party something in return for getting what you want. In arguing, no trade-off is implied.

Another direct influence strategy is to make explicit or implicit threats. A *threat* is an if-then statement, usually referring to your BATNA. An explicit threat might be if in the Cartoon negotiation, the seller says to the buyer, "If all you will offer is $35,000 per episode, I can do better with an alternative buyer." Threats can be implicit, too: "I'd like to do a deal with you, but of course there are other potential buyers for the *Ultra Rangers* series."

Exhibit 2.10 shows cultural differences in the use of direct influence strategies, including argument, persuasion, threats, and substantiation, in same-culture negotiations. The data in the exhibit are standardized residuals. They are easy to interpret. If negotiators in a cultural group are using direct influence as frequently as expected, given what else they are talking about, the residual will be zero. If they are using this strategy more than expected, the residual is positive; if less than expected, the residual is negative. Where the expectation comes from is a little more complicated.[16]

The data in Exhibit 2.10 show that the Japanese negotiators used direct influence more than expected given what else they talked about. The Israelis and Germans used direct influence less than expected given what else they discussed.[17]

EXHIBIT 2.9. Coding Scheme for the Cartoon Study.

INFORMATION

Definition	*Example*
Preference for a negotiable issue, option, relative importance of issues; assertion of interest	"We prefer to have the money up front." "Runs are really important to us."
Reference to minimal acceptable price or conditions (reservation price) [implicit offer here]	"If you could provide us with the product at $45,000, that is the limit we can afford to spend."
Reference to BATNA—what we do if we don't reach an agreement; general other offer, or specific numbers [implicit threat here]	"We've received an offer from one of your competitors." "We already have an offer with a price better than what you are offering."
Reference to or preference for multiple issues with or without trade-offs; usually "if-then" or "and"	"Runs are more important to us than financing." "We'd like to propose *Ultra Rangers* and *Strums* in a package."
Information about product or nonnegotiable issue (ratings, number of episodes, time slots, story, characters, sponsors, tie-ins, *Strums,* profitability)	"Our cartoon show stars Indiana Smith, a twelve-year-old boy." "Based on the U.S. ratings, we forecast at least a 10." (if ratings haven't become negotiable issue) "We're looking for a Saturday morning show."
Information about competitors (other stations, other cartoons or shows, other suppliers)	"We are looking for programs from other companies as well."
Information about own company (strategic plan, profitability, long-term relationships, reputation, power)	"We are planning to introduce some other cartoons in the future." "Hollyfilm is a leader in the industry."

Definition	*Example*
Reference to personal stake of negotiator in transaction	"This arrangement is very important to me. I would like to go back with a good deal."
Other information outside of case information (ratings of current show in time slot)	"Our current show has 11 points." "Have you ever negotiated this kind of deal before?"

QUESTIONS

About preferences for negotiable issue, option, relative importance of issues, offers	"How many runs do you want?" (with specifics–for example, "What do you think about five runs?") "What kind of payment range were you thinking of?"
About minimium or maximum acceptable price of conditions (reservation price)	"Is that the best offer you can make?"
About BATNA	"What will you do if you don't buy our program?"
About product or nonnegotiable issue (ratings, number of episodes, story, characters, sponsor, tie-ins, profitability)	"What sort of profits have you seen from tie-ins?" "Am I right in assuming you are looking for an afternoon show?"
About competitors (other stations, other cartoons or shows, other suppliers)	"Can I ask whose other programs you are considering?"
About company (strategic plan, profitability, long-term relationships, reputation, power)	"Do you see additional programming needs in the future?"

Continued

Exhibit 2.9. Coding Scheme for the Cartoon Study, *continued.*

QUESTIONS

Definition	Example
About personal stake of negotiator in transaction	"Will it reflect poorly on you if you don't stick to the 50 percent down?"
About external information	"What is your current rating in this time slot?" "Are you afraid people will be reading instead of watching TV?"

SUBSTANTIATION, ARGUMENT, PERSUASION

Substantiation ("you do this"/ "good for you"/"because how it affects you/your company")	"This is a good opportunity for your company to get in the market."
Argument/persuasion ("we need"/ "because "why"; informational persuasion) [reference to something positive for me, you, or us]	"We're confident that there's a worldwide appeal." "We really think Indiana is worth $80,000 a show. It has strong, proven demographics."
Sympathy ("you do this"/"good for you"/"because how it affects me/ my company") [reference to something negative for me]	"We cannot exceed our budget. Right now, it's really tight—if you could find a way to share the risk, it would be very helpful for us." "We've got to make a profit." For seller: "We need to have cash up front because of all of our expenses."

OFFERS

Single-issue offer or counteroffer	"We're offering to pay 40 percent up front."

Definition	*Example*
	"What do you think about five runs?"
Multiple-issue offer without trade-off (often phrased using *and*)	"Would you consider eight runs and $50,000 per title?"
Multiple-issue offer, with trade-off (often phrased using *if-then*) *or* Counteroffer in response to an offer	"With that type of payment schedule and for a six-run deal, I really think I still need to ask you for $70,000 per episode." "If you give us $50,000 per title, then we'll only take 50 percent up front." In response to offer: "I'm OK with the eight runs, but I can only pay $55,000."

REACTIONS

Positive or neutral reaction (vague ideas, arguments); positive acceptance of offer; affirming what other said	"If possible, we'd like to broadcast your show." "We think that this is a nice line-up." "We may be able to do that."
Negative reaction	"That is too risky for us." "We're still not sure how well the show will be received."

MUTUALITY

Noting common or mutual interests (this is a tactic, likely at beginning of negotation)	"We need a new show in our line-up and you need to sell this contract, so this deal can have benefits for both of us."

Continued

EXHIBIT 2.9. Coding Scheme for the Cartoon Study, *continued*.

MUTUALITY

Definition	*Example*
Noting differences	"We don't see the rating at 10 but at 7."

PROCEDURAL COMMENTS

Comments regarding procedures to be used or in use *except* reciprocity (issue-by-issue packaging, moving on without resolving issue, reopening issue already resolved, making compromises) Threat to terminate without refer-to BATNA	"We can argue about number of runs all afternoon. Let's move on to price." "If you keep yelling at me, I'm not going to negotiate with you." "I must talk to our management" (when it means "let's put this issue aside for now"). "Let's hear your offer."
Comments regarding *process* of reciprocity (must be an explicit statement of concessionary behavior or procedure)	"I made the last concession; now it's your turn."
Positive expectations about negotiation process or outcome	"I am sure we will be able to negotiate an agreement suitable to both of us."
Limits of case information; sources of case information	"We weren't provided with that information." "Where did you get that information?"
Time out to calculate, think, or break	"Let me stop and make some calculations."

Definition	*Example*
	"Do you need to take a break?" At end of speaking turn: "Gimme a second; I need to talk to our management."

JUNK

Junk; uncodable	"Of course, if this were real life, we would be . . ." "Well . . ." "But . . ."

CONFIRMATION/QUALIFICATION

Question or response to question for clarification, repetition; clarification of offer; summarizing or paraphrasing; stating "that's not what I meant"	"It's a six-run series." "Six-run series?" "Yeah, I'm sorry." "OK, not five runs." "My offer was based on six runs" "Six runs?" "Sorry, five runs."

Source: Adapted from W. L. Adair, T. Okumura, and J. M. Brett, "Culturally Bound Negotiation Scripts and Joint Gain in U.S. and Japanese Intra- and Intercultural Dyads," *Journal of Applied Psychology,* in press.

EXHIBIT 2.10. Direct Influence Residuals from Expected Values in Same-Culture Negotiations.

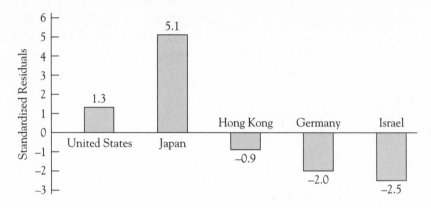

Indirect Influence Strategies. When you use an indirect influence strategy, you are basing your appeal on your own interests by asking for sympathy or referring to personal stakes in the negotiation. References to status are a little different but still indirect. An obvious appeal to status would be "We are the premier developer of action cartoons, and so we are asking top dollar for this series." In this type of appeal, there is an implied and hence indirect threat: "If you don't give us top dollar, your competitors will." But sometimes talking about status can be an appeal to sympathy: "You know, we have just been released to begin purchasing programming again after a financial reorganization. We really like *Ultra Rangers*, and we think we can position it very well in this viewing area for you, but our budget is limited."

Exhibit 2.11 shows cultural differences in the use of indirect influence, including appeals to sympathy, references to personal stake in the negotiation, and references to status. Hong Kong Chinese negotiators used indirect influence more than expected, as did German negotiators. Israeli negotiators used this form of influence much less than expected.

Direct and Indirect Influence and Integrative Agreements. Cultural patterns of use of direct and indirect influence and cultural dif-

EXHIBIT 2.11. Indirect Influence Residuals from Expected Values in Same-Culture Negotiations.

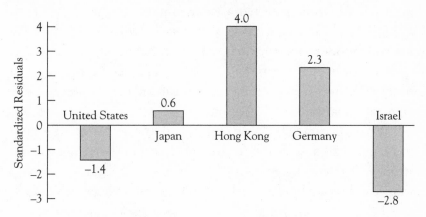

ferences in integrative agreements do not match. Review Exhibit 2.6. Israeli and Japanese same-culture negotiators have the most integrative agreements, then the Germans, the U.S., and Hong Kong Chinese. Now review Exhibits 2.10 and 2.11. There are clearly cultural patterns in integrative agreements and cultural patterns in the use of direct and indirect influence, but there is not a direct correlation between influence use and integration.

When U.S. negotiators use influence, they are likely to use direct influence and somewhat less likely to use indirect influence. Japanese negotiators, in contrast, use a lot of direct influence and some indirect influence. Direct influence and integration go together in Japanese culture relative to other cultures. The Hong Kong Chinese negotiators use influence too, but they rely on indirect influence, and their level of integration is low. The Germans use indirect influence, and their joint level of integration is relatively high. Finally, the Israelis do not rely on either direct or indirect influence strategies, and their level of integration is the highest among all the cultures studied.

The different patterns of influence use and integration are important and puzzling. The same strategic behavior appears to lead to different outcomes, depending on the culture in which it is employed.[18] Avoidance of influence can be associated with negotiating integrative value in some cultures (Israel) and engagement in influence attempts with integrative value in others (Japan). U.S. negotiators do not integrate when they use influence strategies.[19] They may get caught in reciprocal conflict spirals.[20] We thought the Japanese might not reciprocate influence strategies and so avoid conflict spirals. However, this was not the case.[21] Japanese negotiators, like negotiators from other cultures, reciprocate influence strategies. Reciprocation is not the explanation.

What appears to be going on is the following: negotiators need to be motivated to search for the information they need to construct integrative agreements. One factor that clearly motivates that search is goals, either self-interest goals or cooperative goals. The behavior of the Japanese negotiators suggests that another factor may motivate search in their culture: uncertainty about power and influence. When two parties are engaged in an influence contest, each is trying to persuade the other to concede. If they integrate and expand the resource pie, each may receive what he wants. We have speculated that trying to influence each other motivates the search for integrative agreements in Japanese negotiations.[22] When neither party is willing to make concessions, the only strategy available that will lead to an agreement is to try new proposals. As we will see in the next section, the Japanese negotiators use a lot of proposals. Proposals are probably the ultimate key to their success. However, it is important to note that the Japanese negotiators, unlike negotiators from other cultures, are able to identify integrative value despite using and reciprocating direct influence. The Germans, too, are able to integrate and use and reciprocate indirect influence.[23]

Advice and Cautions About Power, Influence, and Culture. Our research shows that the use and the effects of using power and influence in negotiations varies by culture. The patterns, just among the five cultures we studied, are complex and not easy to remember—and these are just five out of hundreds of cultures that you might meet at the negotiating table. Here are some truths to keep in mind:

- Power is a perception. It can be based on a party's alternatives, or it can be based on a party's status. Because power is perceptual, my view of your power and your view of your power may be quite different.

- Discussion about alternatives, status, and appeals to sympathy are all influence attempts, no matter how direct or indirect. The focus may be different in different cultures, but the intent to influence is the same. Reciprocating influence attempts is normative in all the cultures we have studied. On the one hand, by not reciprocating, you may appear weak. On the other hand, refusing to reciprocate an influence attempt is not the same as making a concession. (Chapter Three discusses the leverage that not reciprocating provides in a disputing context.)

- Engaging in an influence contest to determine who is more powerful may in some cultures reduce the probability of an integrative agreement.

- When one negotiator is very focused on status, it may be helpful to affirm that status. One way to do so is by distributing more of the resources to the high-status party. But affirmation of status may take other forms—for example, recognition—that are not reflected in the distributive outcome.

Finally, a caution about the use of power and influence across cultures. Do not assume that great deference should always be paid to buyers and that as a result they will claim more value than sellers, particularly in collectivist cultures, where status implies power at the bargaining table. There is quite a lot of research showing that buyers gain more than sellers in many different cultures, including the egalitarian United States.[24] There is an explanation for buyers' distributive outcomes that may also be cultural but has little to do with status. Buyers may frame deals in terms of losses and consequently be more willing to take risks, while sellers may frame deals in terms of gains and be more risk-averse.[25] This suggests that buyers are more willing to hold out and risk impasse, while sellers are more eager to close the deal. However, this orientation toward risk may interact with culture. In our own research, buyers from individualist cultures gained more than sellers, and sellers from collectivist cultures gained more than buyers.[26]

Information

Negotiated agreements are constructed from information. Negotiators create integrative value when they make trade-offs based on information about differences in interests and priorities and take advantage of information about compatibilities. Negotiators claim distributive value when they acquire information about the other party's reservation price. Negotiators want full information about the other party's interests and priorities and reservation price, but they do not want to reveal the same information about themselves. Sharing information in negotiation makes you vulnerable. When you share information about your reservation price, the other party knows that you will accept an offer just slightly better than your reservation price. When you share information about your interests and priorities, the other party knows what you are willing to give up and what you must have.

Given these incentives against sharing information, it is quite surprising that negotiators ever reach agreements. Cartoon negotiators who reach agreements that are not fully integrative—for example, alternative A in Exhibit 2.2—typically have only the vaguest idea about the other party's interests, preferences, and reservation prices. They agree because the offer is better than their BATNAs, but despite their agreement, they are in a state of uncertainty about whether the agreement is as good as it could be. They typically have difficulty explaining the choices they made for runs and financing.

Cartoon negotiators who reach integrative agreements have two characteristics in common. They are very interested in information in negotiation, and they have a strategy for getting it. There are three strategies for acquiring the necessary information to reach integrative agreements. All appear to be equally effective. Like influence strategies, they are not used with the same frequency in all cultures. Negotiators can share information directly with a series of questions and answers, comments on mutual interests and differences, and feedback. They can share information indirectly via a series of proposals, particularly multi-issue proposals. Negotiators can also agree to search for a second agreement after a first agreement has been reached.

Sharing Information Directly. Direct information sharing could be a series of questions and answers, comments on mutual interests and differences, or feedback about the correctness of a negotiator's inference.[27] One party asks a question about the other party's preferences; the other party answers honestly and asks her own question in return. Negotiators might comment on what issues seem to be in their mutual interest and what issues are more important to one party than the other and correct erroneous conclusions. In the Cartoon negotiation described in Exhibit 2.1, a series of questions about preferences and priorities might reveal that runs are more important to the buyer and financing more important to the seller. Further questioning might reveal that both parties were also interested in the sale of syndication rights for the second cartoon, *Strums*. Exhibit 2.2 illustrates that the trade-off between runs and financing adds $1.7 million in integrative value to the deal. Adding *Strums* at a price between $10,000 and $20,000 per episode adds another $1 million, as shown in Exhibit 2.5.

In our study, the German negotiators were particularly likely to share information directly. Japanese and Israeli negotiators were not likely to engage in direct information sharing. Exhibit 2.9 features definitions and examples of direct information sharing. Exhibit 2.12 shows the data again as differences from expectations. Recall that a zero residual indicates that the amount of direct information sharing in negotiations within that culture is about what would be expected given what else was discussed and how frequently direct information sharing occurred across cultures.

EXHIBIT 2.12. Direct Information-Sharing Residuals from Expected Values in Same-Culture Negotiations.

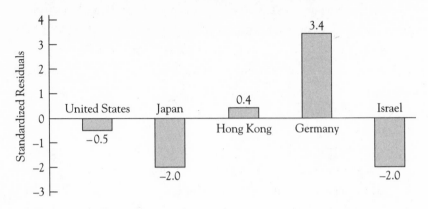

Why did the German negotiators in our study share information directly? Disclosing information about preferences means telling each other what is less important—what you are willing to give up—and what is more important—what you must have. Revealing preferences signals the structure of the deal you will accept. Recall from Exhibit 2.8 that more than 60 percent of German negotiators had cooperative social motives. Their motives provided a basis for trusting each other with sensitive information about preferences and priorities.

Trust gets built in cultures where negotiators are comfortable with direct information exchange, when information is given by one negotiator and reciprocated by the other. Trust grows as each negotiator recognizes that the other negotiator is using the information provided to construct an agreement that takes into account both parties' interests. As trust grows, negotiators share more information and improve their joint agreement. Reciprocity is key to building trust.[28] Just as trust blooms with reciprocal information sharing, trust fades when information is not reciprocated. Here is some advice for direct information sharing:

- Ask questions about interests or priorities. In general, ask questions about things that you would be willing to share information about in return. Asking questions has two purposes: getting information and building trust. Ask questions about reservation price or the absolute value or cost of an issue to the other party cautiously. If he answers such a question, he is likely to turn the question around and ask you to share your reservation price, which you may not want to do. When you fail to answer, trust is broken; you did not reciprocate.

- Give a little information about your own interests or priorities and then ask the question. This gives the other party something in advance of answering the question.

- Be sure to reciprocate information with information.

- When you cannot answer a question because it would give away too much strategic information, be honest about it and give some other information that you can share: "I'm sorry, I cannot give you that information at this point, but I can tell you . . ."

- Build trust by meeting expectations.

Negotiators from cultures where direct information sharing is not normative scoff at asking questions. Chinese managers in Beijing said to me, "Why should we bother asking the other party questions? We won't believe his answers, and he won't believe ours!" To be effective, direct information sharing requires truth telling, and truth telling requires trust. When there is no basis for trust, a different information-sharing strategy is needed.

Another risk with direct information sharing is that it separates the integrative and distributive aspects of the agreement. When negotiators trust each other and share information about interests and priorities, they can integrate, but they still have to divide the integrative value. Sometimes when negotiators realize just how large this value is, they get greedy and change their target, which is

OK, and change their reservation price, which is not OK. Recall that reservation prices are based on BATNA information. New information about integrative value does not change negotiators' BATNAs and so should not change their reservation prices. Changing your reservation price because of new information about what is attainable risks impasse. One solution is to agree to a distributive outcome before you search for the integrative value. This is sometimes difficult to do because negotiators are reluctant to agree to a distribution without knowing how much they will get and whether their distributive share will be better than their BATNA. Another solution is to use an indirect information strategy that links integration and distribution.

Sharing Information Indirectly. Indirect information sharing is a series of proposals and counterproposals.[29] Information gets shared in the following way. If you assume that the other will only make a proposal that is favorable to her interests, then you can infer the other party's priorities by noting how she changes your proposal in making a counterproposal. Consider a series of proposals that might be made in the Cartoon negotiation illustrated in Exhibit 2.1. The seller might propose $70,000 per episode, six runs, and up-front payment. The buyer might counteroffer $30,000 per episode, eight runs, and equal payments over the five-year contract. The first round of proposals does little more than provide a distributive picture for each party. The second round of proposals may be a bit more revealing. The seller might counter by saying, "If you want eight runs, I want payment up front." Multi-issue proposals force negotiators to link issues. When negotiators link issues, they build trade-offs into their deal. If the seller had linked price into a multi-issue proposal—"If you want eight runs, I want $60,000 per episode up front"—his proposal would have specified both the distributive outcome and the integrative agreement.

The Japanese negotiators in our study stand out in their use of proposals. Exhibit 2.13 shows that they use proposals much more than expected. When you read through the transcripts of the Japa-

EXHIBIT 2.13. Indirect Information-Sharing Residuals from Expected Values in Same-Culture Negotiations.

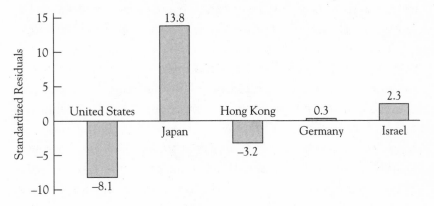

nese negotiations and the U.S. negotiations, the difference in use of proposals is immediately noticeable. The Japanese negotiators might open the negotiation with a proposal. They are busy making proposals and counterproposals from the very beginning of the negotiation. The U.S. negotiators tend to begin by asking questions and wait to make proposals until after they have run out of questions.

The size of the Japanese residual in Exhibit 2.13 tends to hide the size of the residual for Israel. The Israelis, too, used proposals more than expected. Negotiators from both of these cultures were comfortable using proposals. Note that negotiators from both cultures also negotiated the most integrative agreements.

When negotiators, like many of the Israelis in our study, are motivated to be self-interested (maximize their own outcome), the exchange of multi-issue proposals can result in an integrative agreement.[30] Self-interested negotiators can infer each other's priorities from the exchange of proposals. The proposal format keeps issues linked and forces concessions on low-priority issues in return for gains on high-priority issues.

When negotiators, like many of the Germans in our study, are motivated to be cooperative (maximize their own and the other's outcome), they do not need to link all issues into a proposal to reach an integrative agreement.[31] They can reach agreements one issue at a time and reach an integrative agreement. They do so because they share information about priorities and engage in extended reciprocity. They concede on a low-priority issue because they expect a reciprocal concession from the other party on a subsequent issue that has high priority. This may seem farfetched in a business context, but put it in a family context. Isn't this what you do with your spouse or significant other with whom you have a cooperative relationship? Of course, at the cross-cultural bargaining table, you cannot assume that the other party will be cooperative, so even negotiators from cultures where direct information sharing is preferred should know how to use multi-issue proposals.

Equivalent Proposals. Equivalent proposals are a particularly effective indirect information-sharing strategy when the other party is not forthcoming about preferences, refuses to make a counterproposal, or may be lying about her priorities and interests. Note the almost equivalent proposals in the context of the Cartoon negotiation appearing in Exhibit 2.2. Option A: price $46,000 per episode, six runs, and 25 percent up front and 25 percent in years 1–3 nets the buyer $1.5 million and the seller $0.9 million. If the seller turns down the offer, refusing to say more than "not good enough," the buyer could put a second offer on the table, for example, B in Exhibit 2.2: $55,000 per episode, eight runs, and 100 percent up front. The buyer then asks the seller whether he likes A or B better. If the answer is B, the buyer, knowing that the two proposals are almost equivalent from his own perspective, can then infer that the seller must be extremely sensitive to financing.

Be careful when making equivalent proposals that the value gained from the trade-offs does not all go to the other party. In the example in Exhibit 2.2, the buyer's proposal B created $1.7 million in additional value, all but $100,000 of it going to the seller. Proposal C generates the same $1.7 million in additional gains with all but $100,000 going to the buyer. Other proposals along the B–C line in Exhibit 2.2 will split the value created more evenly.

Since there is no way to keep from directing all the gains created by the equivalent proposals to the other party, construct them with your target carefully in mind. For example, instead of offering alternatives A and B in the chart in Exhibit 2.2 that net the buyer $1.5 million and $1.6 million, respectively, the buyer might offer

> ALTERNATIVE J: $45,000 per episode, eight runs, 80 percent up front and 20 percent the first year (buyer's net value, $2.6 million; seller's net value, $1.3 million)

versus

> ALTERNATIVE K: $44,000 per episode, eight runs, 100 percent up front (buyer's net value, $2.68 million; seller's net value, $1.4 million)

Alternative K distributes more of the additional gains to the seller than the buyer, but the buyer has anchored the equivalent proposals so that the buyer's distributive gain at $2.6 million is far better than the $1.5 million with alternative A or the $1.6 million with alternative B in Exhibit 2.2.

Dealing with Negotiators You Think Are Lying About Preferences. Equivalent proposals are also an extremely useful way to manage a negotiator whom you think is lying about her preferences or a negotiator who puts a new issue on the table after you thought you had an agreement. In either case, make one proposal that you think should be acceptable and another that integrates the new issue or gives more on the issue you think has a false priority. Make sure the proposals are equivalent to you and anchored to give you as high a distributive outcome as you think is possible.

Alternatives J and K provide an example of using proposals to learn priorities when you think the other party is being less than

forthright. Suppose the seller is suggesting that price is more important than receiving 100 percent of the money up front. The buyer
could propose alternative J, which gives more on price and less on
financing, and alternative K, which gives less on price and more on financing. The seller is now faced with deciding just how important
price is in the context of financing. With alternatives J and K in
front of her, the seller should prefer K to J. Armed with that information, the buyer can now infer that financing just 20 percent of a
deal worth $4.5 million costs the seller more than $100,000, since
a $4.4 million deal with no financing is preferable to the seller.
Whether the seller did not understand her own priorities or was
lying about them is really irrelevant because the buyer understands
the seller's priorities. Perhaps one reason why the Chinese managers
with whom I worked in Beijing like using proposals is their concern
with truth telling. Proposals, especially equivalent proposals, act
like a truth serum.

Making Proposals and Equivalent Proposals. Here is some advice
about proposals and equivalent proposals:

- Multi-issue proposals are more efficient in getting information
  about preferences and priorities than single-issue proposals.
  Multi-issue proposals also link integrative and distributive
  outcomes; single-issue proposals do not.

- Do not make proposals that are unacceptable to you. First, the
  other party will assume that the proposal is acceptable to you,
  or you would not have offered it. Second, when you back away
  from a proposal, you lose credibility. Sometimes this happens
  because the proposing party has made a mistake. Take time to
  construct and check your proposals. Once you have offered
  something, it is hard to take it away unless you link the retrac-
  tion to a concession elsewhere.

- Anchor proposals so that you receive an adequate distributive
  outcome. This is especially important for equivalent
  proposals because they give all the additional integrative

value to the other party. Make sure you are claiming adequate distributive value.

- Post proposals visually on a flipchart or chalkboard, or write them on paper that you can hand to the other party. Make it easy for the other party to understand what you are proposing.

- Make two or at most three equivalent proposals at a time. Don't overwhelm the other party.

- Have a computer and spreadsheet handy so that you can analyze proposals quickly. Once you introduce proposals, the other party is likely to do so too.

- Once you have offered a proposal and the other side understands it, leave the room and allow time for running numbers. You want the other party to understand the differences between the proposals.

Second Agreements or Postsettlement Settlements. A third way to get the information necessary to reach an integrative agreement is to agree that once a first agreement has been reached, the parties will share information fully and try to move to a second more integrative agreement, in effect a postsettlement settlement. If the negotiators who reached outcome A in Exhibit 2.2 had agreed to keep searching, they could have improved their distributive outcomes by reaching a second agreement somewhere within the triangle formed by A, B, and C. The rule for negotiating second agreements is that the first agreement stands unless the parties identify another agreement as good or better for each of them.[32]

Second agreements have some negative characteristics. One problem is that as full information is shared, the parties may learn that one of them was more forthcoming or more honest than the other was. The party who shared naturally feels taken advantage of and mistrustful. Had there been no provision for a second agreement, the level of differential disclosure might never have surfaced. If you have interests or information that you do not want the other party to know, a second agreement is not a wise strategy. This sometimes occurs during acquisitions. The seller, anxious to get the best price, presents his financials in the best possible light. An agreement is reached, the seller gives the buyer full access to information in the expectation that new synergies between the merged companies will be revealed, and a second agreement can be reached. Instead, the buyer is surprised and unhappy when given full access to the seller's financial information. Not only does the buyer see no further synergies, but he believes he has overpaid for what he is getting.

Another problem with second agreements is how to distribute the additional value found by full information sharing. If negotiators in Cartoon shared their confidential information, essentially making all the information in Exhibit 2.1 available to both negotiators, they would see that there is an additional $2 million to be gained and distributed by integrating runs and financing and adding *Strums* to their agreement. How should that additional value be distributed? Negotiators sometimes reach impasse over this problem because second agreements separate the integrative and distributive outcomes of negotiation. A better strategy is to agree to the distribution of integrative value before going looking for it in a second agreement.

Sharing Information About BATNA and Reservation Price. Negotiators are understandably reluctant to share information about their reservation prices, and there is nothing particularly cultural about this reluctance. When the other party knows what you will settle for, why should she offer you anything more? If a buyer in Cartoon shared her price limit of $60,000 per episode and the seller did not share his price limit of $35,000 per episode, the seller is very likely to insist on $60,000 per episode. Sharing information about reservation prices gives the other negotiator an alternative reference point besides his BATNA, own reservation price, and target. The negotiator who shares reservation price information unilaterally is unlikely to claim high distributive value. When both negotiators share their reservation prices, they may have difficulty reaching an agreement. A large bargaining range like the $35,000 to $60,000 range on price per episode in Cartoon may make nego-tiators focus on the other party's limit and their own gains. In such a situation, negotiators may find it very difficult to distribute value and may even reach impasse, unless they are willing to compromise at the midpoint between their respective limits.

There are times when sharing information about BATNA and even about reservation price is appropriate in negotiation. One time is when you cannot get the other party to the table. You have little to lose in this situation, since there are no negotiations. The other time is when deal-making negotiations have broken down and impasse is imminent. At this point in the negotiation, informa-tion about your BATNA should probably be framed as a threat. The seller in Cartoon might say, "If you do not offer me a deal that is at least as profitable as the one offered by your competitor, I am going to have to deal with him." A common response to such a statement is the question, "Well, how much is my competitor offering?"

When announcing your BATNA in a deal-making negotiation, be prepared for a question about your reservation price. If you answer truthfully and reveal your reservation price, you are not likely to get an offer that is much better. But if before revealing your BATNA, you had no offer better than your BATNA, revealing your reserva-tion price at that point in the negotiation risks little.

Some negotiators may be tempted to answer the question about reservation price untruthfully, construing a nonexistent alternative offer that is much better than their BATNA. Sometimes this strat-egy works. The other party increases his offer, and you get a deal that is better than your BATNA. But when the strategy does not work, you have a problem: impasse and no BATNA. The other party expects you to close a deal with his competitor, but you don't. He wonders why not and concludes you lied about your BATNA, and he is right, you did. Not only has your strategy left you without a deal, but it has also left you with a damaged reputation.

Reputation in negotiation is important. Negotiators in our classes at Kellogg who acquire a reputation for lying early in the ten-week course find themselves having trouble getting a deal at all, much less an integrative deal, in subsequent weeks. Their class-mates, afraid of being taken advantage of, will not share informa-tion. Some, believing that the liar's reputation frees them from the norms of honesty, will lie preemptively to the liar. A classroom is not unlike an industry in which parties know each other by reputa-tion and have repeated encounters over time. Think twice before lying about your BATNA.

Contingent Contracts: Distributive Outcomes That Require Integrative Skills

A *contingent contract* is an agreement to change the negotiated out-come in a specific way based on the occurrence of a future event. An example of a contingent contract in Cartoon is based on the buyer's and seller's different expectations of the ratings the series will have in the buyer's selling area. The ratings information at the bottom of Exhibit 2.1 shows that the seller is optimistic about the ratings, anticipating with a 50 percent likelihood that the ratings will be on the order of 9 to 10. The buyer is more pessimistic, antici-pating with a 50 percent likelihood that the ratings will be between 7 and 8. The buyer anticipates that it can sell $1 million of adver-tising for each rating point. Exhibit 2.14 shows that the buyer's overall estimate of the net advertising revenue for the series is $8.4 million. This is simply an expected value calculated as shown in the exhibit. If we used the same math but inserted the optimistic seller's estimates of the likelihood of each rating category, the expected revenue using the seller's expected ratings is $9.6 million. If the seller is correct, the buyer's revenue will be $1.2 million greater than was anticipated at the time of the negotiation. The seller would like to share this additional revenue if it materializes. The seller proposes a contingent contract: if the ratings are 9 or greater, the buyer will pay the seller an additional $1 million. The buyer, still conservative and not expecting to have to pay, agrees, if the seller is also willing to provide a $1 million rebate if the ratings come in below 8.

EXHIBIT 2.14. Net Advertising Revenue Calculations in Cartoon.

Ratings	Likelihood	Net Advertising Revenue
6–7	20%	$7 million
7–8	50%	$8 million
8–9	10%	$9 million
9–10	10%	$10 million
10–11	10%	$11 million

Expected-value calculation: Assuming that each episode will be run six times, your overall estimate of the net advertising revenue from the series is calculated as follows:
(0.20 × $7 million) + (0.50 × $8 million) + (0.10 × 9 million) + (0.10 × $10 million) + (0.10 × $11 million) = $8.4 million

 This example is only one of many possible contingent agreements that could be made on the buyer's and seller's different expectations of ratings in Cartoon. The risk in negotiating contingent contracts is that the factor on which the contract is contingent is not objective. (Ratings in our example are reported by a third party.) When negotiations are cross-cultural and companies have different accounting methods, finding an objective factor on which to make contracts contingent may be difficult. When contingent factors are not objective, parties can legitimately have different opinions on whether or not the contract has been met, and a dispute can ensue. In general, it is unwise to negotiate a deal that you fear may generate future disputes.

 Contingent contracts generate distributive outcomes. In the example from Cartoon, no new value was created. The contract just shared with the seller value resulting from greater demand for *Ultra Rangers* than the buyer anticipated. Without the contingent contract, if the ratings came in at 9 or above, the buyer would have kept all the additional advertising revenue. Why, then, would the buyer enter into such a contract? Possibly because the buyer could negotiate a lower price per episode, if he were willing to share advertising revenue upon achieving 9 ratings with the seller. If the seller really believes his analysts, the contingent contract would be equivalent to receiving $50,000 per episode rather than the $40,000 per episode in, for example, alternative C.

Negotiators from some cultures in our study are much more comfortable negotiating contingent contracts than negotiators from other cultures. Not only do the Israelis generate the highest integrative value, but they are also the most likely to negotiate contingent contracts in Cartoon. A contingent contract is a creative way to avoid impasse when the buyer and the seller are extremely self-interested, as is characteristic of many of the Israelis in our study, and have set high targets. The buyer uses her ratings and is pleased with her outcome; the seller uses his ratings and is pleased with his outcome.[33]

Because contingent contracts are built on differences, the same information search skills needed to generate integrative agreements are needed to negotiate contingent contracts. Negotiators can search for differences on which to build contingencies using direct and indirect information strategies and second agreements.

Excellent Cross-Cultural Deal Makers

What does it take to negotiate high-net-value integrative and distributive deals across cultures? Our studies suggest three negotiator types or models that are culturally linked. Many of the Israeli negotiators we studied could be characterized as *pragmatic individualists*; many of the Germans, as *cooperative pragmatists*; and many of the Japanese, as *indirect strategists*.

The pragmatic individualist sets a high target, is motivated to search for information, is willing to make trade-offs, and avoids getting distracted about who is more powerful. Israeli negotiators were the premier practitioners of this strategy, and many used it regardless of the culture of the person on the other side of the table. The Israelis relied heavily on proposals for information search, and those proposals allowed them to integrate and distribute value simultaneously. Another indicator of the Israelis' individualism and pragmatism was their use of contingent contracts that allowed buyer and seller to reach an agreement based on their different views of the future.

The strategy of pragmatic individualism potentially has a downside. Our research does not follow relationships over time. Negotiators from other cultures sometimes feel rather overwhelmed or steamrollered when coming out of a negotiation with an Israeli colleague. Those feelings are somewhat but not entirely dispelled when they realize how well they did as a team or as an individual with an Israeli partner. The longer-term issue is whether the outcome is worth the discomfort some negotiators clearly feel with the process. Negotiators following this strategy may be limiting their future options by using the negotiation to reap short-term gains and failing to build long-term relationships.

The cooperative pragmatist is concerned about his own goals and the other party's goals, builds trust by asking questions and answering them, and deals with power indirectly. The German negotiators were the quintessential practitioners of this approach. They used this strategy to negotiate integrative deals and to realize distributive outcomes.

The potential downside of this strategy is that a cooperative pragmatist might be taken advantage of by a pragmatic individualist. However, trust, the core of the cooperative pragmatist's strategy, is hard won and easily lost. So long as the cooperative pragmatist monitors the level of trust in the relationship, he should not be giving information without receiving it in return. He will not be taken advantage of, but he may not be able to lead the negotiation to an integrative agreement if he cannot use the direct information-sharing strategy with which he is most comfortable. As our research program continues, we look forward to monitoring negotiations that cross the cultural boundary between these two types of negotiators.

The indirect strategist may rely on uncertainty about power to motivate an indirect search for information. Japanese negotiators were practitioners of the art of blending direct use of influence and indirect search for information. This model was quite successful within their culture but was problematic across cultures. Japanese negotiating with U.S. deal makers did not maintain this cultural style. The level of integration in Japanese-U.S. cross-cultural agreements was the lowest of any cross-cultural group we studied (see Exhibit 2.6). Japanese cross-cultural negotiators were less likely than same-culture negotiators to use indirect information strategies and direct or indirect influence strategies. Japanese negotiators moved away from normative Japanese negotiation strategies and toward normative U.S. strategies, but the result was not very effective in terms of either integrative agreements or distributive outcomes[34] (see Exhibits 2.6 and 2.7).

Negotiators who maintain the indirect strategist model may have difficulty negotiating across cultures. Indirect information sharing may be too subtle for negotiators from cultures where direct strategies are normative. Direct influence may lead negotiators from cultures where such behavior at the negotiating table is not normative into a conflict spiral and away from integrative agreements.[35]

Given that these rather different models of negotiation are normative in different cultures, effective cross-cultural negotiators need to be able either to adapt to another model or to force their model on negotiators from other cultures. What is common to all three models is clarity of purpose, a thirst for information, facility with a strategy to seek it, and an understanding of how to manage influence attempts. What is different is how negotiators using each of these different models set goals, seek information, and use influence.

Although forcing your preferred model of negotiations on others may be an effective strategy in the short-term, negotiators who are most effective crossing all sorts of cultural boundaries are likely to be the ones who are fluent in all aspects of negotiation strategy. These excellent cross-cultural negotiators understand their own goals and respect that the other party has goals that it must also meet. They are intent on searching for information about differences and compatibilities to use in constructing integrative agreements. They are equally adept at building trust through direct questioning and extracting information from proposals. They understand that power influences the distributive outcome of the negotiation. They recognize direct and indirect influence attempts as power plays and parry them effectively.

3

Resolving Disputes

Conflict is a perception of opposing interests, involving scarce resources, goals, or procedures.[1] For example, in a U.S. Chinese joint venture, the Chinese partner wanted access to the U.S. partner's state-of-the-art technology, and the U.S. partner wanted to protect its intellectual capital while gaining access to the vast Chinese marketplace. In negotiating the joint-venture agreement, a transfer of technology was agreed on in principle, but once the venture began to operate, the Chinese partner was not satisfied. At this point, the conflict was expressed as a claim: "You promised to transfer technology to us." When the claim was rejected—"There's nothing in the contract that says we have to share our patents and systems with you"—the conflict became a dispute. Where conflict is a perception of differences, a dispute is a rejected claim.[2]

No culture is immune from conflict. People everywhere in the world experience conflict, make and reject claims, and try to resolve disputes. How they do so varies systematically with culture. Culture affects why claims are made and rejected, how claims are made and rejected, how disputes are resolved, and what procedures people use to resolve them. The cross-cultural negotiator, armed with an in-depth understanding of how conflict is managed in different cultures, should be prepared to negotiate the resolution of disputes regardless of where in the world the dispute occurs.

Why Claims Are Made and Rejected

Not all conflicts turn into disputes. In the U.S. culture, for example, contracts are carefully drafted to minimize misunderstandings that lead to disputes. If the joint venture had been between two U.S. companies, the contract would likely have been explicit on the issue of technology transfer, stating what technology was to be transferred and when. If the joint venture had been between two Chinese companies, there may have been no contract at all, just a memorandum of principles, and a relationship that was expected by both sides to be able to deal with claims about technology transfer or anything else.

Neither the contractual nor the relationship approach to minimizing disputes is foolproof within cultures, much less across cultures. Claims are made and rejected because not every contingency can be anticipated at the time a contract is signed and not every difference in interpretation can be identified and resolved. Likewise, claims are made and rejected because not all relationships are strong enough to overcome the cost and disappointment of an unfulfilled expectation and a rejected claim.

Disputing is often emotional. People tend to take rejections personally. Deal making can become emotional, but deal-making negotiations do not normally start out with outraged, angry, hurt, unhappy negotiators. Dispute resolution negotiations often do. Disputes over goals and resources (called *task conflict*) and disputes over means, including the dispute resolution process itself (called *procedural conflict*), may easily spill over into *interpersonal conflict*, with each party blaming the other. When claims are made and rejected, people's self-respect is affronted—"How dare he claim that I was unfair!" "The nerve of her, rejecting my legitimate request!" Once an incident is framed as an insult, emotions are engaged and dispute resolution negotiations may not only have to resolve the issues in dispute but also restore the honor and self-respect of the disputants.

How Claims Are Made and Rejected

Consider another incident that occurred in our U.S.- Chinese joint venture, one that was mentioned in Chapter One. When a U.S. manager had a problem with a report that was not generating the information he had expected, he phoned the Chinese manager who was responsible for the report to ask for a meeting to discuss his needs. She politely put him off. A day later, he was called into her manager's office and told that there was no problem with the report: it was exactly as it had always been, and it would not be changed. The U.S. manager, who had not been angry at his Chinese counterpart, is now furious. From his perspective, her behavior—refusing to meet with him and then getting her superior involved, stimulating a reprimand from the superior—was inappropriate. He had wanted to talk about his interests; she had turned the situation into a power play that he lost. From her perspective, she would lose face having to deal with his dissatisfaction with her department's report in a face-to-face meeting. She knew that she did not have the authority to change the report. So involving her superior, who did have the authority to change the report, was the right approach. She is content with this approach. She has maintained harmony. He is offended, worried about always having to work through her boss to work with her in the future, and concerned that if his U.S. superiors learn that he cannot manage conflict with his joint-venture peers, his career will be affected. From her perspective, the conflict is resolved; from his, it is ongoing.

This dispute began as a task conflict that had no particular cultural basis. The U.S. manager's goals were in conflict with those of the Chinese manager. His interests were in getting the data he needed; hers were to produce the reports that were her responsibility. The dispute intensified as it expanded to encompass procedural and interpersonal conflict. He actually made a procedural claim for direct negotiation: "Let's sit down and talk about the data in the report." Her rejection was indirect in two ways. She involved a third party, her boss, and she let the boss reject the task-based claim.

Ultimately, the dispute became interpersonal as the American manager blamed the Chinese manager for avoiding him and involving her superior.

Task, procedural, or interpersonal conflict can cause disputes. A dispute that begins in one domain easily spills over into other domains. Disputes like the one between the Chinese and U.S. managers take on a life of their own and seldom stay compartmentalized. The degree of spillover may also be cultural. In Chapter Two, I talked about the German, Israeli, Hong Kong Chinese, and American M.B.A. students who come to Kellogg for a week of negotiation training each year. Many of the Israeli negotiators are very good at generating integrative agreements and distributive outcomes. Their style is pragmatic—they seldom reach impasses in deal-making negotiations—and it is also aggressive—they are demanding and rather unrelenting. Yet once the deal is done or the dispute resolved, they are friendly—"That was fun!" they'll say. "Let's go have coffee." Their negotiation partners from other cultures do not always appreciate the Israeli negotiators' style. Their partners are often surprised by the invitation for coffee and not sure after the negotiation that the Israeli partner is someone with whom they want to spend their break. Participants from Germany, Hong Kong, and the United States whose style, especially in disputing, is a little "softer on the people" than the Israelis' style view their own normative style as equally or more valid. Even in a simulation, task conflict expands into procedural conflict and interpersonal conflict.

The cross-cultural negotiator needs to recognize the cultural legitimacy of different styles of disputing and to learn to resolve disputes when the other negotiator's style is direct or indirect. The behavior the U.S. joint-venture manager interpreted as avoidance is behavior that is normative and therefore legitimate in the Chinese manager's culture. Labeling such behavior avoidance is not really accurate and does not lead to an effective response. The Chinese manager avoided direct confrontation, but she did not avoid dealing with the claim. It is just that her preferred approach was indirect, when his was direct. The question is how to resolve disputes successfully across cultures especially when one culture prefers direct and the other indirect means of confrontation. We next look at three ways to resolve disputes: interests, rights, and power.

Resolving Disputes Across Cultures

There are three ways to resolve disputes, regardless of whether the confrontation is direct or indirect.[3] You can uncover the interests underlying disputants' positions and integrate those interests. You can determine who is right and who is wrong according to some standard of fairness, contract, law, or precedent. Or you can determine who is more powerful and therefore who should concede. In making a claim for different data, the U.S. manager in the joint venture wanted to talk about interests: why he needed the requested data. The Chinese manager, in taking the claim to her boss, escalated to power. The boss's response—"This is what is always in the reports"—relied on precedent, a *rights*-based argument. His decision—"This is all you are going to get"—relied on power. Some procedures for resolving disputes focus primarily on interests, others on rights, and others on power. When bosses get involved in disputes, they frequently, though not always, use their authority (power) to impose a resolution on disputants. (Some bosses will try to get to the interests underlying the dispute and facilitate an interest-based resolution. We will return to this later in the chapter.) Negotiation, however, can switch from interest-based to rights-based to power-based all within a short span of time. If you watch disputants negotiate, you will frequently see a shifting focus rather like the shifting patterns when you turn a kaleidoscope.

Interests and Culture

Interests are the reasons why claims are made and rejected. They are the needs and concerns underlying parties' positions on the issues in dispute.

Culture affects the relative importance of self-interests versus other interests.[4] People all over the world are concerned with realizing their goals and being respected by others, as well as achieving the goals of the social groups to which they belong and acting in ways that reflect positively on those groups. In individualist cultures, self-interests generally take precedence over collective interests. In collectivist cultures, collective interests generally take precedence over self-interests. Of course, people from collectivist cultures have self-interests and people from individualist cultures have collective interests; it is just that when in their own culture, values, norms, and institutions cue culturally consistent behavior. When one disputant is from a collectivist culture and the other is from an individualist culture, there may be an opportunity to trade self-interests off against collective interests. But there may also be frustration and misunderstanding, because a primary focus on self- versus collective interests can lead to different outcomes.

In one of our studies, we compared the way Hong Kong Chinese and U.S. managers resolved a dispute between the director of human resources and the director of engineering for a heavy construction company.[5] The dispute was over the hiring of summer interns. Companies in many cultures hire university students as summer interns. The primary purpose of these programs is long-term recruiting. Summer internships provide both students and companies with information on which to base a postgraduation offer of permanent employment. A secondary purpose of summer internships is low-cost temporary labor, if the human resource department's budget, and not the budget of the project to which they are assigned, is paying for the internship. In our Summer Interns scenario, Engineering asked for summer interns early because Engineering had work for them. HR was not able to supply the interns, and Engineering went out and hired two on its own. HR then claimed that the two interns hired by Engineering would not be part of the summer interns program and that Engineering would have to pay for them itself. Thus there were two interrelated issues that needed to be resolved immediately: who was going to pay for the two summer interns that Engineering had already hired and whether these two employees were going to be participating in all of HR's summer interns programs, such as orientation and mentorship. There were numerous other issues, including how future interns would be hired and when they would be hired. Most of the Hong Kong Chinese managers were uncomfortable in the role-play. They told us they would prefer to discuss the problem with their boss. But since we did not provide a boss, they tended to resolve the two immediate issues and direct the other issues to a committee of peers who also used summer interns in their departments. Most of the U.S. managers negotiated fairly elaborate agreements, often resolving how they were going to interact with each other in the future over summer interns first and then deciding what to do about the immediate problem.

Different patterns of interests generate different outcomes. Which outcome do you prefer, the Hong Kong Chinese managers' agreements that took into account the interests of those not at the table or the U.S. managers' agreements that resolved all the issues at one meeting? It depends a little on your perspective, doesn't it? If you were the Engineering manager and your interests were met, the multifaceted U.S. solution would be both expedient and best. If your interests were not met, involving your peers in other operating departments in a thorough evaluation of the program might result in a better, if less expedient, outcome. If you were one of these managers' peers and the resolution of their dispute would likely set a precedent for your future summer interns, would you prefer the U.S. or the Hong Kong Chinese model?

Where disputants from individualist cultures negotiating with disputants from collectivist cultures are most likely to err is in underestimating the importance of concerns for the collective. Disputants from individualist cultures need to keep in mind that managers in collectivist cultures share many similarities to union leaders and political leaders whose continuity in office depends on their ability to deliver value to their constituency. In collectivist cultures, future social status depends on the maintenance of relationships and harmony within the social group. When a negotiation process or outcome imperils relationships or harmony, social well-being is threatened. No wonder disputants from collectivist cultures are so concerned about the collective interest.

One useful tool for thinking about interests is to prepare a "positions and interests chart" like the one in Exhibit 3.1. Usually, positions and interests charts have a row for every issue and a column for every disputant, and this may be sufficient when disputants are from individualist cultures. When one or the other disputant is from a collectivist culture, it is wise to add a column representing the positions and interests of the collective, as in the exhibit. Positions go in the triangle above the diagonal line, and interests go below it. You can tuck priorities into the little box inside the interests triangle. The positions and interests chart displays all the information needed to create integrative agreements.

Interests are not quite the same as priorities, which are so important for making trade-offs. Interests explain *why* one issue is relatively more important than another or *why* a position has been taken. Priorities, as discussed in Chapter Two, explain the relative importance of issues. You do not have to understand interests to use

EXHIBIT 3.1. Positions and Interests Chart.

Issue	Self	Other	Collective
BATNA			

priorities to make trade-offs. But knowing interests may help identify creative ways to resolve disputes. For example, if the Chinese manager in our joint-venture dispute had understood why the U.S.
manager wanted the new data, she might have seen a way for others to use the same data and have suggested how he might generate
consensus around a new reporting format.

It is often difficult to guess negotiators' interests. When I was
negotiating for pumpkins with Madame Petit, it never would have
dawned on me that she was reserving some pumpkins to save the
seeds. In my experience, vegetable garden seeds came from pack-
ages! Luckily for me, Madame Petit was willing to respond to my direct question, and the key to identifying interests: *why*. Negotiators
resolving disputes should be prepared to use both direct information
strategies—asking questions, and answering them in a reciprocal
fashion—and indirect information strategies—offering multi-issue
proposals for settlement—to uncover interests. Using proposals to
infer interests is even more challenging than using proposals to infer
priorities. I can think of proposals that would rule out hypotheses
about Madame Petit's interests—for example, offering her more
money for all thirty of her pumpkins—but I'm doubtful I would
ever have guessed her interest in the seeds.

Sometimes historical and cultural information can help uncover
interests. Ultimately, my failure to guess Madame Petit's interests can
be traced to my social-cultural upbringing where seeds come from
packets. Had I grown up in a farming community, I might have
known that farmers often reserve seeds from one crop to plant the
next season, and so I might have guessed Madame Petit's true interests. Historical and cultural information, for example, is widely available to explain why rice farmers are continuing to block the
proposed construction of a second runway at Narita airport in Japan
and why French farmers initially opposed the construction of Euro-
Disney (now Disneyland Paris). Both groups of farmers would be
compensated for the loss of their land to development. Both groups
would ultimately benefit from the economic development that these
projects promised. But both groups are concerned about preserving

the past and handing down their cultural heritage to their children, not economic development. Cultural knowledge is often helpful in understanding interests in cross-cultural dispute resolution.

Once you know the other disputant's interests, there are a number of ways of identifying integrative solutions to disputes in addition to trading off low-valued interests for high-valued ones. Some disputes can be resolved if the party rejecting the claim would take a onetime, non-precedent-setting step. The Chinese manager might have been willing to provide the requested data on a onetime basis, so that the U.S. manager would have time to look for other sources for the information he needed. Sometimes claims are rejected because of skepticism. The Chinese manager may have been convinced that the data requested would be unreliable and hence of little value. A limited-duration experiment with criteria for evaluation meets such an interest quite nicely. Often disputes uncover fundamental problems, and disputants are satisfied with a plan to work on those problems. The Chinese manager might have said, "I'd be happy to give you that information if I could get it using the software that we've got, but I can't. Can you help me make a case for purchasing a new software package so we can get the information you need?" Finally, sometimes a short-term fix is enough. The Chinese manager might have offered, "I can't give you exactly what you want, but I could give you something similar." Exhibit 3.2 identifies six different types of integrative agreements.

A settlement between a U.S. computer manufacturer, High Tech, and its Argentine distributor, Prosando, illustrates another interest-based way to resolve disputes. These two parties, with the assistance of a *mediator*, agreed to a future business relationship as part of an effort to resolve a dispute over their prior business relationship. Commercial disputes are often about who pays how much for damages incurred when the relationship between two parties does not work out. High Tech terminated its contract with Prosando because Prosando was not generating expected sales. Prosando claimed that the termination was improper under the contract and sued for $10 million in damages. The dispute was ultimately resolved with High

EXHIBIT 3.2. Types of Integrative Agreements.

Type of Agreement	Description
Trade-off agreement	Agreement in which parties make concessions on low-priority issues in order to gain more on high-priority issues.
Narrowly focused agreement	Agreement that focuses on the particular circumstances of the dispute, as opposed to the general principle underlying the dispute.
Limited-duration agreement	Agreement to try something for a limited time and then evaluate before continuing.
Contingent agreement	Agreement that depends on another event, usually in the future.
Broadly focused agreement	Agreement that focuses on the interests underlying the dispute.
Future-based agreement	Agreement that deals with the future before dealing with the past.

Tech paying some damages but also entering into a new and more realistic relationship with Prosando.[6]

In thinking about interests and culture, keep the following thoughts in mind:

- Culture affects the relative importance of self- versus collective interests, and the relative importance of these two different types of interests can lead to different outcomes.

- Do not underestimate the importance of collective interests when negotiating with a disputant from a collectivist culture or the importance of self-interests when negotiating with a disputant from an individualist culture.

- *Why* is the fundamental question for uncovering interests across cultures. Negotiators from high-context cultures, however, may be uncomfortable with direct questions, and you may be better off making proposals to uncover their interests.

- When interests are understood, many types of agreements may be created in addition to ones that trade low-priority interests for high-priority ones. Knowing interests may lead to non-precedent setting solutions, limited-duration experiments, or the discovery of fundamental problems that both parties agree need to be managed more effectively.

Rights and Culture

Rights are standards of fairness, contract, law, or precedent. Disputants justify making and rejecting claims with a variety of rights standards. The U.S. manager requesting new data used a needs standard: "I need these data to . . ." The Chinese boss, in rejecting the claim, relied on precedent: "The report contains what it has always contained." He could have used a fairness justification: "You should have asked for what you wanted before the report was compiled. It's not fair that she be asked to rerun the report for some after-the-fact notion of yours." In the dispute between Prosando and High Tech, the claim and its rejection rested on differing interpretations of the contract. Prosando claimed that High Tech had terminated the contract wrongfully; High Tech disagreed.

Rights standards endow claims with legitimacy, and in principle, legitimate claims should be easier to accept. In fact, two characteristics of rights standards make rights-based dispute resolution problematic. First, there are many different potentially relevant rights standards. Second, imposing a rights standard on a dispute generates a distributive outcome, and different standards generate different distributions. When a rights standard is imposed on a dispute, one party usually wins and the other loses. People resist negotiating losses.

Some rights standards are explicit, like laws and contracts that result from negotiations in which parties agree to terms and conditions to govern their interactions. Other rights standards are implicit, as in the case of norms, like deference to status or age, and standards of fairness, like equity and equality. Explicit standards are codified and enforced by social institutions such as the police and the courts. Implicit standards are embedded in the cultures of social groups and enforced by social acceptance and social ostracism.

The basic principle of fairness as a justification for making claims, rejecting them, and using them to resolve disputes extends across cultures. However, reliance on one versus another standard of fairness varies with culture because values and norms extend only to the boundaries of social groups.[7] Catherine Tinsley audiotaped and transcribed managers from Germany, the United States, and Japan trying to resolve the Summer Interns dispute.[8] She coded every argument and justification used during the forty-five minutes allowed for negotiation. Exhibit 3.3 shows her definitions and some examples of explicit rules, implicit rules, future rules, and precedent. Exhibits 3.4 through 3.7 illustrate her findings with respect to various rights standards. The data in these figures are standardized residuals, the same as in Exhibits 2.10 through 2.13 in Chapter Two. Recall that if managers in a cultural group are using a behavior as frequently as expected, the residual will be zero. If they are using it more than expected, the residual is positive, and if using it less than expected, the residual is negative.[9]

Exhibit 3.4 shows that German managers were relatively more likely to refer to procedures and regulations (explicit rules) than U.S. or Japanese managers. They were also more likely to talk about "right" and "wrong" and fairness (see Exhibit 3.5). The U.S. managers, in contrast, were more likely than other managers to set up rules to govern future interaction (how the summer interns would be hired in the future) (see Exhibit 3.6). Exhibit 3.7 shows that the

EXHIBIT 3.3. Coding Scheme for the Summer Interns Study.

Category	Definition	Example	Key Words or Phrases
INTERESTS			
Self or department	Wants, needs, or concerns of negotiator.	"My objective is to get the two interns." "We don't want interns just running around wildly."	I want, My objective
Company	Wants, needs, or concerns of company.	"We like people to return for our company." "It's for everyone's benefit."	Good for the company
Other side	Wants, needs, or concerns of the other party.	"You just needed to get this going?"	You want, Your goal
RIGHTS AND STANDARDS			
Explicit rules	References to explicit rules procedures, and regulations. Discussions of due rights, jurisdiction, or violations of rules and policies.	"You followed the GPA requirement?" "Did you post the job for 48 hours?" "Students must go through the orientation sessions."	GPA requirement 48-hours procedure Orientation session

Continued

EXHIBIT 3.3. Coding Scheme for the Summer Interns Study, *continued.*

Category	Definition	Example	Key Words or Phrases
		"The mentorship sessions are not necessary."	Mentorship session
		"We should come up with the hiring criteria."	Hiring criteria
		"I consider that I'm due to have two interns."	I'm due
		"I just wanted a special case granted this time."	Special case
Implicit rules	References to implied rules, standards, and norms. Statements about fairness or "rightness or wrongness" of actions.	"Wrong to rely on personal judgment."	Wrong
		"Not supposed to hire randomly."	Not supposed to
		"What kinds of tasks do engineer interns have?"	
		"You're setting a bad example."	Bad example
		"It cannot happen that you hire on your own."	Cannot (should)
		"I don't think that is a fair distribution."	Fair
Precedent	Salient actions that occurred in the past.	"Similar to last year's case."	Last year

	Trends, traditions, past conflicts, asking and telling.	"SIP always starts in June." "The previous time, he was just book smart." "Are they too slow?"	Always (usually) Previous
Future rules	Proposals to create future rules and for resolution of this conflict.	"Next year, how about if I come to you?" "From now on, I guarantee interns within three weeks."	Next year, I will

POWER STATEMENTS

Attacks, blame, scolding	Uncooperative statements: accusatory, disapproving. Used to bait, incite other.	"You make a sham out of this process." "I would like to know whether you've planned appropriate manpower to finish this project."	Blame, fault Condescending tone
Threat, ultimatum	Uncooperative statements to intimidate, suggest negative consequences.	"He cannot do it, there's no discussion." "If it doesn't go as quickly as it should, then we are forced to take things into our own hands."	There's no discussion We are forced to . . .
Powerful people	Mentioning people of status and suggesting they support your position.	"Why don't we ask the board what it thinks?" "Besides us, many other departments are unhappy."	(Boss's name) Other directors

Source: Courtesy of Catherine H. Tinsley. See also Catherine H. Tinsley, "How We Get to Yes: Predicting the Constellation of Strategies Used Across Cultures to Negotiate Conflict," *Journal of Applied Psychology,* forthcoming.

EXHIBIT 3.4. References to Rules, Procedures, Regulations, and Jurisdictions in the Summer Interns Study.

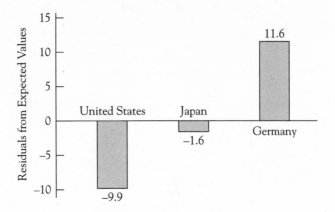

Source: Courtesy of Catherine H. Tinsley.

EXHIBIT 3.5. Statements About Fairness and Norms in the Summer Interns Study.

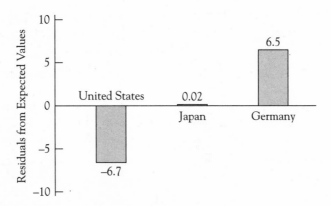

Source: Courtesy of Catherine H. Tinsley.

EXHIBIT 3.6. Concern for Establishing Future Rules for Resolving Conflicts in the Summer Interns Study.

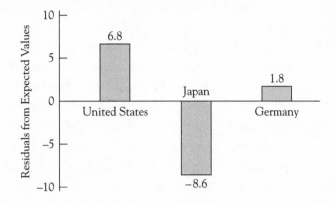

Source: Courtesy of Catherine H. Tinsley.

EXHIBIT 3.7. Reliance on Precedent in the Summer Interns Study.

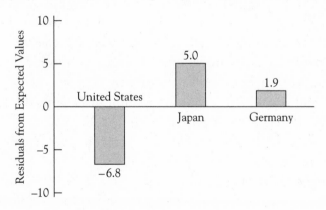

Source: Courtesy of Catherine H. Tinsley.

Japanese managers were more likely to rely on precedent than managers from other cultures.

Trying to use rights standards to resolve disputes can be extremely frustrating. Often one standard is used to justify a claim and another to justify rejecting it. Which standard should prevail? If the two parties agreed on the rights standard, they would not have a dispute in the first place. The process of rights-based dispute resolution is one of searching for an acceptable rights-based standard. But any standard suggested by one party will be viewed as self-serving by the other party. The U.S. manager in the joint-venture dispute made his claim on the basis of need. The Chinese manager might have rejected his claim based on equity: "It's not fair for me to have to rerun the report."

Cultural differences in preferences for rights standards added to normal differences over which rights standard applies make the rights approach to dispute resolution even more frustrating and confusing. Different cultural characteristics seem to fit with different fairness standards, making it difficult to know what rights standard would be most acceptable in what culture. For example, the major cultural influences on Chinese negotiating style suggest that equality, need, and equity standards are all normative in China.[10] The Confucian legacy in China, which emphasizes hierarchy and tradition and teaches social responsibility, supports the need standard. Chairman Mao's vision of communism supports the equality norm. Sun-Tzu's ancient principles in *The Art of War*, which emphasize strategy, deception, and taking advantage of an adversary's misfortune, support an equity principle.[11]

What to do?

- Realize that you are unlikely to suggest a rights standard for resolving a dispute that does not result in a beneficial outcome to you, and neither is the other party.
- When weighing potential rights standards, think about what the other party might consider fair.

- Recognize that using a rights standard to resolve a dispute ordinarily means that one party will win and the other will lose. This makes it difficult for disputants to agree on what standard to apply.

Rights-based settlements do occur in certain circumstances. Disputants may change their positions when new credible information becomes available to interpret a situation or a rights standard. Lawyers, for example, seek evidence and search for legal precedents. New evidence that is credible and clear may encourage disputants to withdraw claims or grant them. When new credible evidence makes the basis for claims uncertain, disputants may compromise, shift their dispute resolution focus and seek an interests-based settlement, or seek to clarify the rights standard. Rights-based settlements may also occur after disputants consider their BATNA—what will happen if no agreement is reached. If a third party is likely to get involved, disputants may consider how persuasive their rights standard is likely to be with that third party. Concluding that your argument is not very persuasive may motivate conceding to the other party's rights standard.

Intuitively, argument and persuasion would seem to be the appropriate way to convince the other party that you are right and he is wrong under some rights standard. In fact, argument that does not contain new credible information is widely perceived as self-serving and is consequently ineffectual. When one party withdraws or grants a claim after a fierce argument in which no new information was exchanged, the concession is as likely motivated by a decision that pursuing the claim was not worth the costs or by a desire to restore harmony as by enlightenment.

In thinking about rights and culture, keep the following thoughts in mind:

- Culture affects how strongly disputants rely on rights standards and the rights standards they prefer to use.

- Because there are so many different rights standards and because different aspects of culture support different standards, it is difficult to know which standard will be acceptable to the other disputant.

- Because a disputant is unlikely to propose a rights standard that does not benefit him, rights standards are suspected and discounted.

- The key to success in using rights standards to resolve disputes is either to propose one that the other disputant will agree is fair or to provide new credible information that makes the proposed standard appear fair. Without new credible information, argument is unlikely to be effective.

Power and Culture

Power is the ability to get what you want from a dispute—to have your claim granted or your rejection upheld. Figuring out who is more powerful in a cross-cultural dispute is complicated by the fact that power is a perception and perceptions are filtered through cultural lenses. It is easy to see after the fact that the U.S. manager in the joint-venture example was not powerful. He did not get what he wanted. But what about before he made the claim? Had he known in advance that his request was not only hopeless but also risked censure, he might not have made the claim in the first place. Surely he did not view his claim as without merit or himself as powerless to promote the claim.

Power is an assessment or judgment of dependence.[12] In general, the more dependent you are, the less powerful you are. If you have good alternatives, you are less dependent and therefore more powerful.

Deal-making negotiators' BATNAs are usually not linked. If no agreement is reached, each negotiator turns away and starts negotiating with a new partner. Disputing negotiators also take stock of their power by considering their alternatives. They too do the negotiation dance. But if they do not reach agreement, they cannot turn their backs on each other and walk away. Their wrists are tied together. Just saying no in dispute resolution negotiations does not make the claim go away. The other party can continue to press the claim, and you have to deal with it.

In dispute resolution negotiations, BATNAs are linked. Consider a few examples. When Mitsubishi Electric refused to negotiate a settlement of Fusion Systems' claim that Mitsubishi was violating Fusion's patent rights in Japan, Fusion Systems stepped up its embarrassing negative publicity campaign. When Disneyland Paris was under construction, local farmers used their hay wagons to block access to the site from public highways. They were piqued because their claims had been ignored. In some cultures, it would be reasonable to expect that national police would be called in to open routes, and perhaps that was Disney's expectation. In France, at least during the late 1980s and the 1990s, the government has not acted against similar demonstrations by farmers and truckers. Disney failed to recognize that its BATNA was to stop construction while its partner, the French national government, tried to resolve the local disputes. The French farmers could and did shut down construction. Disney's BATNA was the farmers' BATNA: suffer construction delays and negative publicity due to the farmers' actions. In our joint-venture example, the U.S. manager's claim went up the hierarchy to the Chinese boss. Presumably, if the U.S. manager had wanted the Chinese boss involved, he would have started the dispute there.

In deal-making negotiations, it is wise to consider the other party's BATNA in order to understand his reservation price. In dispute resolution negotiations, it is critical to understand the other party's BATNA. Instead of thinking about the best alternative if no agreement can be reached, think about the worst thing the other party can do to you. That is your BATNA in a dispute resolution negotiation. This failure to understand how BATNAs are linked is probably the most common mistake dispute resolution negotiators make. My students, after making this mistake once, prepare for their next dispute resolution exercise with new acronyms: LATNA for "least (desirable) alternative to a negotiated agreement," and WATNA, for "worst alternative to a negotiated agreement."

Power does encourage people to resolve disputes. When disputants recognize that their worst-case scenario is bad, they may be motivated to compromise principles and settle. The problem with disputing is that emotions get engaged, often making people not very rational in assessing their options. When people really get emotional about disputing, they may lose sight of the dispute and focus instead on revenge. Because emotions are often high in disputing, because focusing on power often escalates emotional involvement, and because emotions cloud rational thinking, it is not easy to resolve disputes on the basis of power unless authority is clear.

Disputants from egalitarian cultures tend to be less deferent to status and authority than those from hierarchical cultures. They may be willing to make claims across status boundaries that people from hierarchical cultures would not make out of fear of failure or fear of revenge or even fear of making the respondent lose face. A Canadian manager described his experience with an outstanding Chinese woman who worked at his company as a computer programmer as part of a two-year government program.[13] As the end of the two years approached, she became more and more angry as aspects of the program that she believed had been promised were not delivered. He knew she was unhappy, but she would not tell him why. He ultimately decided that if she could not talk about it, he could not do anything about it. Both parties were trapped within the norms of their respective cultures. Coming from a hierarchical culture, she could not make claims against the boss and head of the international program without making him lose face. Coming from an egalitarian culture, he relied on her to tell him what the problems were. The solution? Probably, a third party. One of her Canadian peers might have gained her confidence and then brought the problems to the attention of the boss. Behavior that might be labeled tattling in an egalitarian culture is the way information gets conveyed in a hierarchical culture.

When people from hierarchical cultures do make claims in situations in which they recognize their lack of status, they are likely to appeal to sympathy, reminding the high-status respondent of the responsibility to take care of the needs of the low-status claimant. When Westerners or other disputants from egalitarian cultures make claims in situations in which they lack power, they will frequently avoid talking about power and focus on interests.

When power is uncertain, disputants from egalitarian cultures talk less about power than disputants from hierarchical cultures. In the study comparing the way German, U.S., and Japanese managers negotiated Summer Interns, the Japanese managers were more likely than either German or U.S. negotiators to use power-based strategies.[14] Exhibit 3.8 shows that the Japanese were more likely than the Germans and especially U.S. negotiators to engage in attacks, defined as uncooperative, accusatory, and disapproving statements. Exhibit 3.9 shows the same pattern with respect to threatening behavior, defined as ultimatums, attempts to intimidate, and suggestions of negative consequences.

Involving a boss or another higher-level manager in disputes is more characteristic of disputants from hierarchical cultures than egalitarian ones. In the study comparing the way Hong Kong Chinese and U.S. managers resolved the Summer Interns dispute, we found that the Hong Kong Chinese were significantly more likely than the U.S. managers to "resolve" one or more issues by involving upper management.[15] Exhibit 3.10 shows that Japanese managers negotiating the Summer Interns dispute were much more likely than either German or U.S. managers to allude to powerful people.[16] By involving a third party in the resolution of a disputed issue or by alluding to powerful third parties when negotiating an issue, disputants are trying to acquire power via association with others. This is a very political way of thinking about power. It happens in egalitarian cultures, but interestingly such behavior might be sanctioned more quickly in an egalitarian than a hierarchical culture if it is viewed as an overt display of power grabbing.

EXHIBIT 3.8. Use of Attacks in the Summer Interns Study.

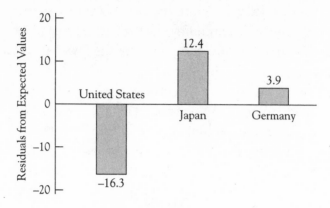

Source: Courtesy of Catherine H. Tinsley.

EXHIBIT 3.9. Use of Threats in the Summer Interns Study.

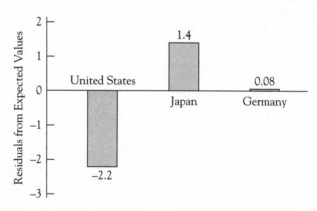

Source: Courtesy of Catherine H. Tinsley.

EXHIBIT 3.10. Allusions to Powerful People in the Summer Interns Study.

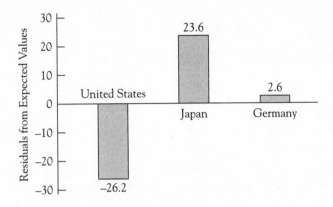

Source: Courtesy of Catherine H. Tinsley.

In thinking about power and culture, keep the following ideas in mind:

- Power in disputing is different from power in deal making in one key respect: disputants' BATNAs are linked. Instead of considering the best alternative for you if no agreement can be reached, it is important to consider what the other party can do to you if no agreement can be reached. Instead of your best alternative, consider your worst alternative to a negotiated agreement.

- Culture affects the degree to which status is used as a basis for power and the likelihood that a third party will be called in.

Procedures for Resolving Disputes

There are cultural differences in how people prefer to resolve disputes. Some cultures use direct confrontation more than indirect confrontation. Other cultures use indirect confrontation more than direct confrontation.

Direct Versus Indirect Confrontation and Culture

Direct confrontation is a face-to-face verbal interchange between principals. Confrontation becomes less direct when it is no longer face to face, as when negotiations are carried out over the telephone or by e-mail; when it is nonverbal, as when one party withdraws from interacting with another; or when it is conducted by agents, such as lawyers or intermediaries, or through mediators.

Characteristics of Asian cultures—high-context communications, collective interests, hierarchical power distributions—encourage disputants, like the Chinese woman who went to her boss with the request for data, to deal with conflict indirectly. Characteristics of Western cultures—low-context communications, self-interest, and egalitarian power distributions—encourage disputants to confront directly. As with all cultural divides, this one is of relative emphasis, and no randomly selected disputant from a given culture is likely to have a preference structure that perfectly matches the cultural prototype. Still, it is well worth understanding these cultural differences in preferences for dispute resolution procedures. When the other party uses a procedure that is not normative in your culture, the tendency is to take the procedural choice personally—"She went to the boss because she wants to get me in trouble." Personal attributions about procedural choice escalate task conflict by extending the scope of the conflict from task to procedural and interpersonal. Recognizing that the other party's behavior is normative in that person's culture—"She went to the boss because that was the right thing to do in her culture"—does not resolve the task conflict. It also does not resolve the procedural differences, but it does keep conflict from becoming personal. Understanding cultural differences in preferences for procedures is the first step toward being able to resolve disputes across cultures.

Direct confrontation is consistent with the action-oriented and solution-minded communication that is characteristic of low-context cultures.[17] It typically challenges the status quo—an act that is discouraged in hierarchical cultures and a right that is protected in egalitarian cultures. Direct confrontation also disrupts harmony, a value in collectivist cultures.

Underlying the preference for indirect confrontation is a particular concern for face. Face refers to the self-image one projects to others.[18] Respect is the currency by which face is maintained. Disrespect affronts face; respect confirms it.[19] Although face is not unimportant to people from individualist and egalitarian societies, it seems to be more important to people from collectivist and hierarchical cultures.[20] Maintaining face both confirms the person's acceptance in a society (collectivism) and that person's status within the society (hierarchy). It is easier to maintain face using an indirect approach than negotiating directly, where negotiations could escalate with either or both parties becoming emotional and showing disrespect. When disputing is carried out indirectly through third parties, the disputants are buffered from each other. Third parties may also remind disputants, either directly or indirectly through their presence, of the importance of relationships and social harmony, factors that may be forgotten in the midst of emotional face-to-face negotiations.

Recent theorizing suggests that face and relationship issues are more important when conflict is between people within a social or cultural group than between people in different social or cultural groups. The disrespectful behavior of out-group members does not carry as much social identity information as the same behavior of in-group members.[21] However, commercial disputes are frequently carried out in a public forum. Publicity from an intercultural conflict may affect a party's reputation within its own culture. A good example is the dispute between Fusion Systems and Mitsubishi Electric. Fusion Systems held patents in the United States and Japan for an ultraviolet lamp that had applications in the printing and silicon chip industry. Fusion claimed that Mitsubishi Electric violated its patent rights in Japan. Mitsubishi Electric rejected the claim, pointing out that it had recently won an industry award for its own ultraviolet technology. Fusion's response was a negative publicity campaign about this dispute in the American and Japanese business press. The publicity must have been extremely embarrassing to Mitsubishi Electric, because it appears to have brought Mitsubishi Electric back to the negotiating table, though not to resolution.[22] Finally, after ten years, Fusion and Mitsubishi resolved their dispute privately. Their joint press release dated July 9, 1993, announced an agreement, but no terms were ever released—a face-saving decision.

With this understanding of East-West differences in preferences for direct and indirect confrontation, what could the U.S. manager in the joint-venture example have done differently? Since the U.S. manager was the party making the claim, he might have gone directly to the Chinese manager's superior. Alternatively, knowing the Chinese cultural preference for indirect confrontation but not exactly how his Chinese counterpart would react to a claim, the U.S. manager might have put the procedure on the table. He could say to his Chinese counterpart that he would like to talk about the data in the report and ask if it would be appropriate to talk with her about the data or if he should speak with her superior.

Making the choice of direct versus indirect confrontation is just not easy when different cultures are involved. What if the cultural backgrounds of the two negotiators had been reversed and the party making the claim for data was the Chinese manager and the party with access to the data was the U.S. manager? Going to the Chinese boss to ask for the data would be indirect and normative for the Chinese manager. It would be offensive to the U.S. manager. Making the claim for data directly to the U.S. manager and being turned down would have caused the Chinese manager to lose face. But if she was turned down, the Chinese manager still had the option of going to her superior.

Managers resolving disputes cross-culturally need the strategic flexibility to do so directly and indirectly. Claimants should be particularly sensitive to cultural preferences for direct versus indirect confrontation, because choosing an approach that is culturally offensive to the other party may cause the dispute to expand from the task and become procedural and interpersonal.

Nonconfrontation: Not Really an Option

Deciding to take a direct or an indirect approach to dispute resolution presumes that unless dealt with somehow, the dispute will have dysfunctional consequences. In the example of the rattling bicycles mentioned in Chapter One, the claimant, the U.S. buyer, feared that if he did nothing, his Chinese partner would ship the rattling bicycles and his German buyer would reject them. The U.S. manager judged the cost of doing nothing as greater than the value of the likely outcome of doing something. He confronted, although indirectly.

Some claims, however, are not worth pursuing. In the example of the U.S. manager seeking different data from his Chinese counterpart's report, the U.S. manager might never have made the claim if he thought that the Chinese boss would get involved. He would rather live with the data he was getting than risk censure from a higher-level manager. Had his Chinese counterpart just said no, he might have done nothing further. What happened instead is a classic example of how disputants often lose control over their disputes and why just walking away to embrace your BATNA, almost always an option in deal-making negotiations, is seldom an option in dispute resolution negotiation. The U.S. manager did not have the option of withdrawing his claim—what is known as *lumping it*. His Chinese counterpart took it to the boss. Although he viewed his BATNA as lumping it, she forced him to embrace her BATNA, which was his WATNA. Of course, if she had rejected the claim, she could not be sure that he would not pursue it with the boss. She may have reasoned that it was better to get there first. In short, because BATNAs are linked in disputing, lumping it is not often a viable option.

Direct Confrontation: Negotiating the Resolution of Disputes

Negotiation is a direct confrontation dispute resolution procedure. Disputants can integrate their interests and determine who is right and who is wrong under some standard of contract, law, or precedent or who is the most powerful. They can do so face to face, electronically, or through agents. Dispute resolution negotiations can change focus from interests to rights to power and change modes of communication with some aspects handled face to face, others on the telephone, and still others by agents. To be effective at resolving disputes across cultures, negotiators need to know when to focus on rights, power, facts, and interests, how to change strategic focus, and how to choose among different types of communications.

When to Use Interests, Rights, and Power. Exhibit 3.11 shows interests, rights, and power as concentric circles, with interests embedded within rights and rights embedded within power.[23] The concentric circles indicate that negotiations focused on the reconciliation of interests occur within the context of who is right and who is wrong under some standard of contract or law and of who is more powerful. Negotiations focused on the determination of who is right and who is wrong occur within the context of who is more powerful. Negotiating to resolve a dispute via integrating interests, determining rights, or relying on power is a strategic decision. Negotiators need to have clear strategic reasons for selecting a focus.

Rights. Keep in mind that focusing on rights suggests to the other disputant that you have in mind a distributive outcome in which you win and he loses. Of course, if the other party did not mind

EXHIBIT 3.11. Three Approaches to Resolving Disputes.

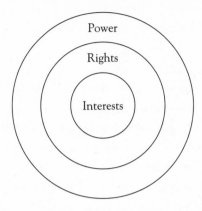

Source: W. L. Ury, J. M. Brett, and S. B. Goldberg, *Getting Disputes Resolved: Designing a System to Cut the Costs of Conflict* (Cambridge, Mass.: Harvard Program on Negotiation, 1993), fig. 1. Reprinted by permission of Jossey-Bass, Inc., a subsidiary of John Wiley & Sons, Inc.

losing, he would most likely have granted your claim in the first place. This suggests that opening negotiations by focusing on rights is unlikely to lead to a quick resolution of the dispute unless you have new credible rights information that the other party did not know when rejecting your claim. In fact, because disputants tend to reciprocate each other's rights arguments, opening with or directing the negotiation toward such arguments is likely to escalate the dispute rather than resolve it.[24]

There are three very appropriate times to use rights arguments in negotiations:

- When you think that you have a rights standard that the other party has not considered and that once she considers your standard, she will recognize the weakness of her own position and come to agreement.

- When you have a rights standard that you think the other party is likely to accept as fair; presumably, this standard will also benefit you.

- When you want to make it clear that if the dispute cannot be resolved, you will go to a third party for resolution and your argument will be based on a particular rights standard.

Power. Culture, emotion, and strategy are three reasons why disputants focus on power in negotiation. As we discussed earlier in this chapter, negotiators from hierarchical cultures spend proportionately more time discussing power when resolving disputes and when making deals than negotiators from egalitarian cultures. Regardless of culture, when one negotiator focuses on power, the other is very likely to reciprocate.[25] This may escalate the conflict to encompass task, procedural, and interpersonal issues and lead to an impasse or a very one-sided agreement.[26] Of course, many negotiators would be quite satisfied with a one-sided agreement, so long as it benefited them.

When people become emotional, as they often do when disputing, they are likely to lose perspective and be less receptive to other ideas and less cooperative.[27] When people feel threatened, anxiety reduces their capacity for rational thinking, and when people become angry, their focus may shift from the task to retaliation.[28]

There are also people who use power strategies and emotions strategically. Using emotional outbursts or tantrums strategically may be more common in individualist cultures than in collectivist cultures, where values for harmony and concerns for face limit the display of emotion in negotiations. Yet many of us know children and adults who throw strategic tantrums because they have learned that others will make concessions. Of course, the more frequently others make concessions to tantrums, the more tantrums become a learned negotiating strategy.

Despite helping you get what you want, tantrums may also have both emotional and strategic downsides. The emotional downside is that having strategic tantrums takes its own emotional toll. In following up some interest-based negotiation training we did in a labor management context, I was surprised to hear in the company focus group that "the relationship is much improved—Jeffrey [the union leader] doesn't throw tantrums anymore; he talks with us about interests." An hour later, Jeffrey told me he was "a new man." "In what way?" I asked. "You taught me how to negotiate using interests. You taught the others to listen and look for interests. I don't have to throw a tantrum to get them to the table, and I don't have to throw a tantrum to get them to engage in serious problem solving. You cannot imagine how my physical and mental health have improved!" I tell this story not to brag about our success in this instance but to point out that this negotiator was using tantrums strategically. He knew it, and the company people with whom he had to interact knew it. Moreover, doing so was taking a mental and physical toll on him—and probably on them too.

The strategic downside of using emotion at the bargaining table is that many people try to avoid negotiating with those who have a reputation for using emotion strategically. This is easier to do in deal making than in resolving disputes, where BATNAs are linked. In disputing, over time, people learn to deal with the other side's emotional outbursts by just saying no regardless of the merit of the claim. This escalates the costs of dispute resolution. Using emotion strategically is a risky use of power at the bargaining table.

There are some times when you will want to use power in dispute resolution negotiations. When you cannot get the other party to the table to talk, using power may convince him to come to the table. Examples of this strategic use of power come from international diplomacy. How many times in the past decade have the United States and its allies used massive air strikes to try to get a recalcitrant political leader to the table? Sooner or later the weaker party usually capitulates under the barrage. However, the cost of such a strategy to both sides is enormous. When you use power, you incur costs. In evaluating this strategy, it is important to consider realistically your costs and the costs to the other side.

You may also find it useful to resort to power when negotiations have broken down and all other attempts to restart them have failed. An example is Fusion's negative publicity campaign against Mitsubishi Electric when Mitsubishi rejected Fusion's claim that

Mitsubishi had violated Fusion's Japanese patents. Fusion's options at the time it instigated the negative publicity campaign were extremely limited. It could lump the claim, living with the risk that Mitsubishi Electric would take market share away from Fusion in Japan or demand royalty payments for Fusion's alleged violations of Mitsubishi Electric's patents. It could file its claim in the Japanese court system. Fusion's strategic decision was to choose the option that was most likely to encourage Mitsubishi Electric to come to the negotiating table. Clearly, when your BATNA is poor and you cannot get the other party to the table, using or threatening to use power may be strategically justifiable. Using power—or threatening to use it—communicates to the other party that the situation is no better than your BATNA and that you will be forced to go to your BATNA unless negotiations can be restarted.

A word on making threats. Threats are if-then statements about what you will do if the other party continues to do what he is doing. In the dispute over the rattling bicycles, one could imagine the U.S. buyer threatening the Chinese seller, "If you do not fix the rattle before shipping the bikes, then I will not release payment." Threats are very strong, very clear statements and so should be used strategically and only when the person making the threats is willing to act on them. People who make threats they do not intend to carry out lose credibility. Their threats are not believed and are unlikely to generate the desired outcome of restarting the negotiation.

There is an interesting question of whether disputants can talk about power in a purely informative way without one party inferring that the other is making threats. The U.S. bicycle buyer could say to the Chinese manufacturer, "You know, I still owe you money," without defining the conditions under which the money would be withheld. People do make these statements about power in dispute resolution negotiations. We see it throughout the transcripts of the Japanese disputants in the Summer Interns negotiation.[29] We also see it at the beginning and particularly right after the midpoint of the transcripts of U.S. disputants resolving a different dispute.[30]

The timing in the U.S. transcripts suggests that U.S. disputants talk about power early to try to gain dominance in the negotiation and again later when the structure of an agreement has appeared and they are trying to claim distributive gains.

The real question is not so much disputants' intent but how the information about power is received. My experience suggests that in the U.S. culture, information about power is either discounted as a negotiation ploy or taken as a serious threat. Even when the information is new to the other party, it is likely to be put in one category or the other. When we were studying union organizing campaigns in the United States, we would ask employees what the company spokesman had said in a meeting. We had transcripts of those meetings because the National Labor Relations Board in the United States regulates what can and cannot be said in such meetings, and companies and unions want to protect themselves.[31] The law prohibits direct threats—for example, to move the production facility to Mexico if the union wins the election. Companies are careful not to make them. Instead companies say things like, "Remember the employer who used to be down the street? When his plant voted union, he shut his doors and moved production to Mexico." When we asked employees what was said in the meeting, they would tell us, "He said that if we vote union, he's going to move production to Mexico." It seems that it may be difficult to talk about power in a purely informational way in cultures like the United States where there is less emphasis on power than interests and rights as dispute resolution strategies. Discussion of power in cultures like Japan, where we have seen that such discussion is normative, may not be as easily discounted or quickly taken as a threat.

Facts. Disputes are often about facts. The U.S. manager in making his claim for data might have said, "You said that the data I needed would be in the report this month." The Chinese manager might have replied, "I never promised you the data." If the disputants could agree on who said what, then presumably one would have the weight of a promise backing up the claimed position. Disputants complain about the other party—"If she would just admit what really went on, there would be no dispute." But of course, the other party's view of what really went on is different. Who is right and who is wrong? Will focusing on facts help resolve the dispute? Probably not, even if a neutral third party had overheard the U.S. and Chinese managers' conversation about the data and came forward to say, "I did not hear a promise," the U.S. manager's perception that a promise was made would still be valid to him. Sometimes it is helpful to share differing interpretations of the facts to delineate the areas of dispute. But trying to determine whose version of the facts is the truth is not likely to generate a resolution.

Interests. In general, if you want to find an integrative resolution to a dispute, one that preserves the resources, values, face of the disputants and others not at the table, and relationships as well, focusing on interests is the most reasonable approach. When you do not care about any of these issues but the bargaining range is very small or even not overlapping, focusing on interests is the only hope of resolving the dispute in negotiations.

There are the same risks in revealing interests in disputing as discussed in deal making. Your interests make you vulnerable. When information about interests is asymmetric, one party can take advantage of the other. It may also be more difficult to build trust in a disputing situation than in a deal-making one. Deal makers build trust by sharing information and using it to create a deal that works for both sides. The claim and its rejection, even when not emotional, interferes with the development of trust in disputing.

In sum, disputants need to be strategic about focusing on interests, rights, power, or facts. Each focus takes the negotiation toward a different type of outcome. Rights and power and facts focus on claiming and lead to distributive outcomes. Interests focus on creating value and integrative agreements. Interests, rights, and power are present in all dispute resolution negotiations. It is up to the disputants themselves to determine the strategic focus.

How to Change the Focus from Rights or Power to Interests. It is relatively easy to shift the focus from interests or facts to rights or power because deal-making and dispute-resolving negotiators reciprocate rights and power communications. What about shifting from power or rights to interests? Some of our recent research with U.S. negotiators suggests several ways that negotiations can be refocused from rights or power to interests.[32]

- *Do not reciprocate.* Disputants who refuse to echo or reciprocate the other party's rights or power communications significantly increase the likelihood that the other party will be deterred from continuing with this strategy. With some insensitive disputants, it may be necessary to redirect negotiations from rights or power several times before the point is made.

- *Declare the process ineffective.* Disputants who recognize that they are engaged in a rights or power contest or are spiraling over the true interpretation of the facts can label the process as counterproductive. For example, when disputing over what was promised, one party might suggest, "Let's agree to disagree and move on; this isn't getting us anywhere."

- *Combine reciprocity with a change of focus.* Some negotiators may fear that not reciprocating rights or power signals weakness. They may feel compelled to reciprocate to maintain their power position in the negotiations. Interestingly, among U.S. negotiators, combining a counterthreat with a change of focus to interests or a proposal for settlement is almost as effective as the "do not reciprocate" strategy in refocusing negotiations away from rights or power.

Dealing with Emotion. Disputes engage people's emotions. Sometimes disputants get so angry, hurt, or frustrated that they fail to control their emotions. It is useful to distinguish disputants who lose control over their emotions in negotiations as a strategy, like the union leader we worked with, and those who just lose control.

It is unwise to make concessions to either in response to an emotional outburst. There are a few other responses to those who just lose control:

- *Don't reciprocate with an emotional outburst.* Failing to confront anger with anger does not make you appear weak. The effect is just the opposite. Reciprocating the other disputant's emotional outburst draws you into her strategy and away from your own. It makes you appear unable to sustain your own strategic approach.

- *Don't take an emotional outburst personally.* Attributing an emotional outburst to something you did will only make you defensive and emotional and distract you from your preferred strategic approach. Attributing rejections to situational factors, such as understaffing, or to stable characteristics of the person ("She never says yes to anyone the first time") depersonalizes the rejection and should reduce emotions.

- *Deescalate and refocus on interests.* Use any of the techniques just discussed to shift the focus to interests.

- *Consider putting the party's behavior on the table.* Tell the other party directly that her emotional behavior is interfering with dispute resolution. Ask if there is something you can do to help reduce the emotional tension.

- *Try apologizing for the other party's emotional state.* "I'm very sorry you are so upset" goes a long way toward diffusing a hot emotional standoff.

- *Call for a cooling-off period.* Suggest taking a break from negotiations. You may need it as much as the other party.

- *Suggest involving a third party.* Third parties can often act to buffer disputants who seem to bring out the worst in each other.

Choosing How to Communicate. The major communication choices are face-to-face negotiations, electronic negotiations, and negotiating through agents. The major distinction among the three is social presence. In face-to-face negotiations, disputants are in each other's physical presence. They express and interpret verbal and non-verbal behavior. Electronic communications limit the expression of nonverbal behavior to pauses and silences but preserve communication of verbal behavior. Agents convey nothing of disputants' verbal or nonverbal behavior. The strategic question is when to use which type of communication.

Negotiating Electronically or Face to Face. The lack of social presence in electronically mediated communications has two effects on negotiations. First, it is more difficult to build trust and interpersonal relationships electronically than it is face to face.[33] When people communicate electronically, they are less inhibited by social norms. An angry disputant who would not slam a door in a claimant's face due to social inhibition may be more likely to bang the telephone receiver down or "flame" in an e-mail message. At least in the U.S. culture, it seems to be socially easier to say no via e-mail than on the telephone, and easier on the telephone than face to face. In terms of getting a hearing for a claim, at least in cultures that support direct confrontation, face to face seems to be the best venue. A second effect of electronic communications is that it may be more difficult to understand interests because the nonverbal nuances are lost.[34] Of course, when people are angry, they do not attend very well to informational nuances anyway. E-mail has the nice property that the claimant may lay out his claim or support it in great detail. He may go back and edit his statement and remove incendiary remarks. Just the process of thoroughly stating his claim may go a long way toward cooling the claimant's emotions. But beyond the general effects of electronic communications, we know very little about negotiating the resolution of disputes via electronic media, much less whether culture interacts with the media to affect the success of dispute resolution.[35]

Negotiating Through Agents. There are good reasons to use agents to resolve disputes and good reasons not to use them. Again the choice is a strategic one. Agents provide social distance. Social distance can increase the likelihood of resolving a dispute if disputants are extremely emotional. Social distance can also mean that disputants' interests do not quite get conveyed accurately and agreements reached by agents do not quite meet the disputants' interests. Agents may also have substantive expertise or technical knowledge that they can use to come up with creative solutions that disputants would not have thought of. Technical experts may also lose track of their charge in their enthusiasm to create something new. In short, agents need to be used for particular reasons and also need to be monitored. Their incentives must align their interests with the interests of their principals.[36]

Indirect Confrontation Without Third Parties

Most discussions of indirect confrontation focus on the role of third parties that are not agents of the disputants. There are a few other indirect ways to confront that do not involve third parties. In some situations, a claimant denied permission to act may act anyway. The Chinese bicycle manufacturer could have gone ahead and shipped the rattling bicycles to Germany, figuring that he would have more leverage with the shipment delivered on time. Though this seems like a pretty direct act, in fact it is an indirect way of using power to reduce the options of the U.S. middleman, who has to find out that the bicycles were shipped and find out that they rattled. A claimant may use nonverbal behavior to express dismay at a claim's being rejected. Slamming doors and pounding fists are nonverbal behavior; so are hanging up the telephone, refusing to respond to e-mail, and walking out of the area where negotiations are taking place. When negotiations between the Chinese government and the United States over most-favored-nation trade status seemed to be going nowhere, U.S. trade representative Charlene Barshefsky, the chief negotiator, had her team pack up and head for the airport. Chinese negotiators reopened negotiations.[37]

Another form of indirect confrontation is amassing information that you arrange to have delivered to the other party. The U.S.

manager, denied the data he wanted, might send the Chinese boss copies of reports from within his own company showing how the requested data were used to improve quality or reduce costs. Even more indirect, but perhaps more effective, he might arrange a trip for the Chinese boss, making sure that one stop would illustrate the data in use.

All these indirect confrontation methods put the claim back in front of the person or persons who rejected it. None of these methods is guaranteed to resolve the dispute; the most they can do is give the dispute a second hearing.

Indirect Confrontation and Third-Party Procedures for Dispute Resolution

Third parties are used in many cultures to facilitate the resolution of disputes. Disputants do not always have the option of choosing whether to involve third parties. Because their BATNAs are linked, one disputant can force the other into a third-party procedure. Whether you choose to involve a third party or the third party is forced on you, it is useful to have a systematic way of thinking about the implications of various third-party roles. One issue is whether the third party's focus will be interests, rights, or power. As we have seen, a dominant rights or power focus will result in a distributive outcome; an interests focus may result in an integrative agreement. Culture may play some role in how much the third party focuses on interests, rights, or power, although the role itself may also dictate a focus. Culture appears to influence how early in the dispute's history third parties become involved. It may also play a role in three other distinguishing characteristics of third-party roles. The first is whether the third party has authority to impose an outcome on disputants or can only try to help the disputants reach an agreement. The second is whether the third party is neutral or has interests that are aligned with one side. The third is the way the third party plays the role. Regardless of whether third parties get involved early or late, have authority or are neutral, they are viewed as effective when they facilitate an environment of respect, and this seems to generalize across cultures.[38]

Third-Party Focus on Interests, Rights, and Power: Role and Culture.

Some third-party roles limit the focus of the procedure. For example, judges and *arbitrators* (private judges) are required to make rights-based decisions. But other third-party roles allow the focus to shift among interests, rights, and power, much as the focus can shift in negotiations. The Chinese boss in the data dispute used his power to impose a resolution but gave a rights-based justification. Cultural norms may have prohibited him from considering interests. One could imagine a U.S. boss in the same position also using authority to impose a settlement, also using a rights-based justification, but also inquiring about the interests on both sides of the dispute. One of our studies of U.S. managers playing third-party roles indicates that the greater a manager's supervisory experience, the more likely the manager is to focus on the disputants' interests and facilitate rather than impose a settlement.[39] Mediators—third parties who are not authorized to impose settlements on disputants—will shift the focus from interests to rights to power and back while trying to encourage a settlement. Altogether there are three elements operating together—the third party's role, the third party's culture, and the third party's focus on interests, rights, or power—that affect whether the outcome of third-party intervention is or has the chance to be integrative, versus distributive or no agreement.

Timing of Third-Party Involvement and Culture.

Sometimes third parties, like the Chinese boss in the joint-venture example, get involved very early in disputes, often at the behest of one party. Other third parties, for example, mediators who try to help parties reach agreement or arbitrators who are hired by the parties to make a binding decision, enter a dispute only after the disputants or their agents have failed to negotiate an agreement. There seems to be a tendency toward early third-party involvement in disputes in hierarchical cultures, in cultures with strong values for harmony, and in cultures that prefer indirect confrontation. Involving a third party is normative in these settings because it is seen as a face-saving, harmony-preserving way to resolve the dispute. The Chinese boss told both the U.S. and the Chinese managers that the report would not be amended to provide the requested data. The boss's decision took saying no out of the lower-level Chinese manager's hands, allowing her to save face, and the U.S. manager did not have to experience rejection by a peer. In Chinese culture, being told no by a superior is more acceptable than being told no by a peer. But of course, the incident did not occur just within the Chinese culture. The U.S. manager evaluating the procedure through the lens of his own culture judged neither the process nor the outcome as face-saving, harmony-preserving, or just. From his cultural perspective, the boss should not have been involved at all, and there was greater loss of face being told no by the boss than by a peer. From his egalitarian, direct cultural background, you only involve the boss after negotiations have failed. From his perspective, negotiations never started.

The decision to involve third parties early in the dispute may also be motivated by a desire to develop political power. Third parties do not always have to have authority; they can be peers. Enlisting their involvement early in the dispute risks losing control over the process and outcome, but it may also generate support for your position. Many of the Hong Kong Chinese managers in the Summer Interns dispute decided to involve peers and higher-level managers in resolving how the program would be run in the future. They may have been motivated not only by collectivist interests but also by the desire to generate political support for their positions.

The major concern about the timing of third-party involvement is that because of the linked BATNAs, one disputant can involve third parties before the other is ready. As soon as a third party is involved, disputants give up more or less control over the procedure and the outcome. How much control depends on the third party's role.

Third-Party Roles and Authority. A major factor distinguishing third-party dispute resolution procedures is whether the third party has the authority to impose a settlement on the disputants. Bosses typically do, as do judges and arbitrators. Peers, like the other managers whom the Hong Kong Chinese involved in the Summer Interns dispute, and mediators can only influence outcomes via advice, framing, managing the process, or contributing their stature or expertise to one settlement proposal or another. If you have a choice of third party, one issue is whether to choose a third party with or without authority.

Procedures with Authority to Resolve Disputes That Cross National Cultural Boundaries. Litigation, arbitration, and hierarchy are three procedures that give third parties authority to resolve disputes. Litigation is a judicial procedure in which disputants or their agents argue their claim and a third party or occasionally a jury makes a final and binding decision. Disputants often prefer not to litigate disputes. When Mitsubishi Electric rejected Fusion's claim that Mitsubishi had violated Fusion's Japanese patent rights, Fusion had the option of litigating the claim in the Japanese court system. It chose not to. Litigation in the other party's legal system is seldom a very appealing choice for a number of reasons, including concerns about bias, the time and cost to litigate in another country, and the effect of litigation on future relationships.

Arbitration is a private, rights-based, adjudicative procedure. The arbitrator has authority to impose an outcome on the disputants, and legal systems generally enforce arbitrators' decisions within their own jurisdiction. Of course, disputants from different national cultures do not share legal systems. In the global arena, arbitrators' decisions are not so much enforced by judicial follow-up as by the norms of the marketplace. Parties who are not willing to abide by an arbitrator's decision may find their international options for doing business limited. When parties agree to arbitrate disputes, they name the commercial code under which arbitration will occur. This gets around the problem that commercial codes in many developing countries are rudimentary. They may also specify a source of neutral arbitrators and a process for picking one. This alleviates the problem that judges in some countries are not experienced in handling complex civil litigation. Parties can pick an experienced arbitrator, a retired judge, or a lawyer from a third country. Exhibit 3.12 lists some international sources of arbitrators. An important characteristic of arbitration is that arbitrators' decisions are private. Disputants who lose do not have to be concerned about losing face publicly. Exhibit 3.13 provides a brief description of the arbitration process.

Procedures Without Authority to Resolve Disputes. Why bother with a third-party procedure if the third party does not have the authority to resolve the dispute? In short, because third parties without authority are nevertheless frequently able to help disputants find acceptable settlements. They do so by controlling emotional outbursts and keeping the disputants focused on resolution instead of retribution. They do so by having better negotiation skills than the disputants have. They know how to look for and integrate interests. They know to construct proposals that link a future relationship to the resolution of the past dispute. They know to try to expand the scope of the dispute and get to the underlying issue or contract the scope and construct a non-precedent-setting agreement. They do so by engaging in reality testing with disputants, by making them focus hard and rationally on their BATNAs. Exhibit 3.14 describes the mediation process. The dispute resolution service providers in Exhibit 3.12 may also be good sources of mediators. Exhibit 3.15 explains what to look for when selecting a neutral mediator or arbitrator.

In the U.S. commercial context, mediation practiced by the four major U.S. mediation companies resulted in a 78 percent settlement rate.[40] Whether the case went to mediation voluntarily or because of a contract clause or a judge's action did not affect the settlement rate. Mediation was equally successful in settling personal injury disputes, contract disputes, and construction disputes. Cases

EXHIBIT 3.12. International Sources for Arbitrators and Mediators.

American Arbitration
  Association
140 West Fifty-First Street
New York, NY 10020
United States of America
Phone: (212) 484-4000
Internet: http://www.adr.org

Centre for Dispute Resolution
  (CEDR)
Princess House
95 Gresham Street, Third Floor
London EC2V 7NA
England
Phone: (011-44-171) 600-0500
Fax: (011-44-171) 600-0501
E-mail: mediate@cedr.co.uk
Internet: http://www.cedr.co.uk

China International Economic
  and Trade Arbitration
  Commission (CIETAC)
1 Fu Xing Men Wai Street
Beijing 100860
People's Republic of China
Fax: (86-10) 6851-1369
Internet:
  http://web.singnet.com.sg/~arbi
  ter/cietac.html

International Chamber of
  Commerce
ICC/UN Liaison Office
1212 Avenue of the Americas
New York, NY 10036
United States of America
E-mail: webmaster@iccwbo.org
Internet: http://www.iccwbo.org

UNCITRAL
Vienna International Centre
P.O. Box 500
A-1400 Vienna
Austria
Phone: (43-1) 21345-4060 or
  4061
Fax: (43-1) 21345-5813 or
  232156
E-mail: uncitral@unov.un.or.at
Internet:
  http://www.un.or.at/uncitral

World Intellectual Property
  Organization and Mediation
  Center
34, chemin des Colombettes
P.O. Box 18
CH-1211 Geneva 20
Switzerland
Phone: (41-22) 338-9111
Fax: (41-22) 740-3700
E-mail: arbiter.mail@wipo.int
Internet:
  http://www.wipo.int/eng/arbit

EXHIBIT 3.13. How Arbitration Works.

Arbitration has been an alternative to litigation for hundreds of years. It was used as early as the thirteenth century by English merchants who preferred to have their disputes resolved according to their own customs (the law merchant) rather than by public law. Commercial arbitration in the United States antedated the American Revolution in New York and several other colonies and is widely used today. Labor arbitration became widespread during the 1940s, and now more than 95 percent of all collective bargaining contracts contain a provision for final and binding arbitration. Additionally, arbitration is used to resolve disputes in the construction industry, disputes between consumers and manufacturers, family disputes, medical malpractice claims, securities disputes, attorney's fee disputes, and civil rights disputes. It is even used to resolve disputes about salaries to be paid to major league baseball players. . . .

Because arbitration is a private dispute resolution procedure, designed by the parties to serve their particular needs, it cannot be defined or described in a manner that will encompass all arbitration systems. Still, arbitration typically contains the essential elements of court adjudication, however, in that unless the parties agree otherwise, the only pretrial discovery will be that mandated by the arbitrator.

Additionally, the hearing is usually more informal than a court hearing, and the rules of evidence are not strictly applied. Finally, commercial arbitration awards typically contain only the arbitrator's award; commercial arbitrators do not provide reasons for their decisions. This practice is not followed in the labor context or in international commercial arbitration, where arbitrators, like judges, issue reasoned decisions. Most private arbitration systems provide the following:

- Joint selection and payment of the arbitrator
- Objective standards on which the arbitrator's decision is to be based (typically the terms of agreement between parties, the customs of the trade in which they conduct business, the applicable law, or some combination of these)
- Procedural rules to be applied by the arbitrator

Source: S. B. Goldberg, F.E.A. Sander, and N. H. Rogers, *Dispute Resolution: Negotiation, Mediation, and Other Processes,* 3rd ed. (Gaithersburg, Md.: Aspen, 1999), pp. 233–234. Reprinted with permission.

EXHIBIT 3.14. How Mediation Works.

Mediation is negotiation carried out with the assistance of a third party. The mediator, in contrast to the arbitrator or judge, has no power to impose an outcome on disputing parties.

Despite the lack of "teeth" in the mediation process, the involvement of a mediator alters the dynamics of negotiations. Depending on what seems to be impeding agreement . . . the mediator may attempt to:

- Encourage exchanges of information
- Provide new information
- Help the parties understand each other's views
- Let them know that their concerns are understood
- Promote a productive level of emotional expression
- Deal with differences in perceptions and interests between negotiators and constituents (including lawyer and client)
- Help negotiators realistically assess alternatives to settlement
- Encourage flexibility
- Shift the focus from past to future
- Stimulate the parties to suggest creative settlements
- Learn (often in separate sessions with each party) about those interests the parties are reluctant to disclose to each other
- Invent solutions that meet the fundamental interests of all parties

Mediators' strategies vary widely. Some mediators attempt to focus the negotiations on satisfying the vital interests of each party; others focus on legal rights, sometimes providing a neutral assessment of the outcome in court or arbitration. Some encourage the active participation of both lawyers and clients; others exclude either clients or lawyers from the sessions. Some mediators endeavor to maintain neutrality; others deliberately become advocates of a particular outcome or protectors of non-parties' interests.

Source: S. B. Goldberg, F.E.A. Sander, and N. H. Rogers, *Dispute Resolution: Negotiation, Mediation, and Other Processes,* 3rd ed. (Gaithersburg, Md.: Aspen, 1999), pp. 123–124. Reprinted with permission.

EXHIBIT 3.15. What to Look For When
Selecting a Neutral Third Party.

Ask for the résumés of several neutral parties who might serve on your panel or help with your individual case. Ask for a list of cases in which the individual has served as a neutral party and the names and addresses of parties and lawyers representing both sides of the dispute. Interview these parties about the neutral party.

For Mediators, Ask:

- Was the mediator a good listener?
- Did the mediator treat your side fairly?
- Did the mediator treat the other side fairly?
- Did the mediator come to understand your side's interests?
- Did the mediator help you to better understand the other side's interests?
- Did the mediator involve both sides in generating options for agreement?
- Did the mediator provide an interpretation of the law or contract relevant to the case? Was that interpretation requested by the parties? Did it help the resolution of the case?
- Was the mediator able to put the appropriate amount of pressure on the disputants to settle?
- Did the case settle?
- Would you use the same mediator again? Why or why not?

For Arbitrators, Ask:

- Was the arbitrator a good listener?
- Did the arbitrator treat your side fairly?
- Did the arbitrator treat the other side fairly?
- Was the arbitrator knowledgeable in the [relevant] area of law?
- Was the decision handed down in a timely fashion?

EXHIBIT 3.15. What to Look For When
Selecting a Neutral Third Party, *continued.*

- Was the decision written in language that the claimant could understand? (especially important for employee disputes)

- Did your side win or lose?

- Would you use the same arbitrator again? Why or why not?

You will receive more information that is directly relevant to your decision if you ask specific questions, rather than just ask the last question. If you can find a neutral party who receives praise from people on both sides of the dispute, chances are that person will be a good choice for you.

Source: J. M. Brett, S. B. Goldberg, and W. L. Ury, "Managing Conflict: The Strategy of Dispute Systems Design," *Business Week Executive Briefing Service,* 1994, 6, 22, tab. 9.

that did not settle were likely to be characterized by lawyers as "a party in search of a jackpot" or as "a situation in which it was not in the financial interest of one party to settle." These judgments were made after the fact and may be biased by the natural desire to attribute cause for failure to settle. However, if this bias were very strong, it would seem likely that many different characteristics would define the cases that did not settle. We questioned lawyers about twenty-one different characteristics. These were the only two that had a significant impact on the likelihood that a case would settle at mediation.[41] There are no comparable data for intercultural disputes. Intercultural mediation settlement rates might be somewhat lower if mediators have difficulty understanding one or the other parties' interests, due to cultural or communication biases. A solution is to have co-mediators, one from each of the cultures involved in the dispute.

Prosando, the Argentine company that claimed that High Tech, a U.S. company, had wrongfully terminated its contract, had to choose among litigation, arbitration, and mediation when negotiations with High Tech broke down. Litigation meant filing a lawsuit in the state of California, where High Tech was a major employer and the civil court system was eighteen months in arrears. Prosando could have chosen arbitration, but that would mean the end of its relationship with High Tech. Instead it chose to mediate, and High Tech agreed. Mediation in the U.S. commercial context typically takes less time than arbitration and is less expensive,[42] matters of concern to both parties. During confidential sessions with each party, the mediator learned that terminating the relationship might not be in the best interests of both parties. High Tech was still trying to break into the South American market, and Prosando had been making progress setting up a distributor network in Argentina and Chile but not elsewhere. The ultimate agreement did require High Tech to pay Prosando damages for termination, but it also set up a new and more restrictive agreement to work together in Argentina and Chile—clearly an outcome that would not have been possible had the dispute been arbitrated or litigated.[43]

A truly neutral mediator would not have a particular interest in preserving the relationship between the two parties. The mediator's interest was in getting a settlement. And he saw a way of getting the settlement by extending the relationship into the future, an option the High Tech and Prosando lawyers had not considered in previous dispute resolution negotiations.

Third-Party Interests and Neutrality. Third parties bring their own interests to dispute resolution settings. In some roles, like that of independent mediator in the Prosando–High Tech dispute, third parties are interested only in resolving the dispute and not in the nature of the agreement or its impact on a broader community of interests. Other third parties, like judges, are interested only in resolving the dispute within the guidelines of contract or law. But bosses, community officials, and government agents acting as third parties are usually interested in the substance of the resolution and its impact on the community. Third parties who bring their own substantive or community interests to the table are not neutral and are not perceived as neutral by disputants. They may promote their own interests, and in defense, disputants may be extremely strategic in the interests that they reveal.

But just as third parties with and without authority can be effective when they structure the situation so that disputants feel respect and control, third parties who are not neutral can be effective if they are able to facilitate an environment of respect and control. In addition to the structural features of the third-party role, the way the third party acts has an effect on dispute resolution.

Playing the Third-Party Role: Fairness, Respect, and Dignity. How third parties act affects whether the disputants think the third party is fair. Third parties who treat disputants in a neutral and unbiased fashion, who convince disputants that they are trustworthy, and who respect disputants' positions and interests receive the highest evaluations for fairness.[44] These three criteria are not totally due to the structure of the third-party role. Even third parties like bosses, who have authority to impose settlements have interests of their own and therefore lack neutrality, can promote an environment of fairness by paying attention to issues of neutral behavior, trust, and dignity.[45]

Disputants are concerned about the way third parties enact their roles because third parties' involvement in disputes comes at the expense of the disputants' control over the outcome and the process. There may be cultural differences in willingness to turn control over the outcome to a third party.[46] Disputants from collectivist and hierarchical cultures may be more accepting of third-party authority. They may presume that third parties will keep the interests of the collective in mind and will protect the weak from exploitation by the powerful. Disputants from individualist and egalitarian cultures probably neither make nor want to make such assumptions. They are concerned with furthering their self-interests and preserving their right to pursue those interests. Disputants from individualist and egalitarian cultures may be less accepting of third-party dispute resolution and then only when their best efforts at negotiating for themselves have failed.

There do not seem to be cultural differences in preferences for control over process. Studies in many cultures indicate that when third parties have the authority to impose outcomes, disputants prefer *adversarial procedures* to *inquisitorial procedures*.[47] When procedures are adversarial, disputants or their agents investigate the facts and present their own arguments to the judge. In inquisitorial procedures, an agent of the court investigates the facts and presents an opinion to the judge. The U.S. court system is an example of an adversarial system. The French court system, with its heavy reliance on experts, is an example of an inquisitorial system. The preference for the adversarial system appears to be due to the relationship that tends to develop between the disputants and the third party in the two different systems. Disputants who participate actively in resolving their dispute feel they are respected.[48] Their involvement may also lead to a sense of control over the outcome.[49] Adversarial procedures seem to involve disputants more than inquisitorial procedures. It is the difference between "It's my word against his" and "It's my word against his word against the expert's word." There is substantial evidence that mediation is preferred to arbitration for much the same reason.[50] Disputants generally rate mediation as more open and involving than arbitration, which is usually governed by judicial rules of evidence and turn taking. Also, in mediation, disputants retain control over the outcome, which they give up in arbitration.

Relational (respect) and instrumental (control) issues are concerns of people involved in disputes throughout the world.[51] Third-party procedures vary in the degree to which the procedure itself fosters respect and control. Third parties can also influence disputants' perceptions of respect and control by the way they play their roles. Why care about disputants' perceptions of respect and control? In short because perceptions of third-party fairness can affect whether the dispute gets resolved and whether the settlement gets implemented without further disputing.

Dispute Resolution Systems

Disputes are inevitable in cross-cultural relationships, and the costs may be significant. When there is hierarchy in a relationship, there is a system for resolving disputes, although not necessarily one that will encourage integrative agreements. When there is no hierarchy in a relationship, there is no system beyond negotiations for resolving disputes. When negotiations break down, parties may be too engaged in disputing to be able to think clearly about a system for resolving the dispute.

Dispute resolution systems have become widespread in egalitarian societies like the United States to direct disputes to low-cost procedures that also preserve the possibility of integrative outcomes.[52] A dispute resolution system can be as simple as an agreement to take disputes to a certain person or to a particular position in the organization or to negotiate first before doing so. It can be a contract specifying steps and procedures to be used to resolve disputes. It can be as elaborate a facility as the one IBM and Fujitsu set up to manage the transfer of computer technology after years of disputing over patent rights and royalty payments.[53] The North American Free Trade Agreement came with an elaborate dispute resolution system under which Canada, Mexico, and the United States have ceded the right to review domestic courts' decisions involving trade.

A key aspect of having a dispute resolution system is that it is in place before disputes occur. Once disputes have broken out, parties are often too emotionally involved to choose dispute resolution procedures wisely. Yet negotiating a system to resolve disputes at the same time as negotiating the deal may be difficult. It is rather like telling your fiancé right before the wedding that you want a prenuptial agreement to govern the dispensation of assets in the event of a divorce! Negotiators from collectivist cultures that value harmony, interpersonal relationships, and trust are not likely to be very open to negotiating a system for resolving disputes before any business has been transacted. Such a proposal is also very direct. Yet the effort may be worthwhile. A dispute resolution system sets up norms unique to your relationship about how you plan to deal with each other if disputes do occur. Such a system might have kept the dispute over data between the U.S. and Chinese managers from expanding from task conflict to procedural and interpersonal conflict. The U.S. manager would have known the appropriate way to make a claim, and the Chinese manager would have known the appropriate way to reject the claim according to the norms of the joint venture's dispute resolution system.

Exhibit 3.16 provides contract language for a three-tiered dispute resolution system: negotiation, mediation, and arbitration that can be easily adapted to relationships that involve parties from different cultures. Whether face-to-face negotiation is part of the system may depend on the parties' preferences for direct versus indirect confrontation. Mediation in some form should probably be part of the system so that there is a procedure beyond negotiation that preserves the possibility of an integrative agreement.

Excellent Dispute Resolvers

The inevitability of disputes within and between organizations and the misunderstandings, miscommunications, and misattributions that cultural differences add to the disputing environment mean that cross-cultural managers must be prepared to resolve disputes. Preparation requires understanding cultural differences in why and how claims are made and rejected and how disputes are resolved across cultures. It requires respecting preferences for direct versus indirect confrontation and facility with both direct negotiations and indirect third-party procedures. Disputants negotiating in a global environment need to understand how interests, rights, and power are construed in different cultures. They need to know when to focus on interests, rights, or power and how to change the focus and to deal with emotion. Disputants need to understand the effect on negotiations of different types of communication—face to face, through agents, or via electronic media. They need to be aware when indirect confrontation is occurring and how to deal with it. They need to recognize the different third-party procedures and the similarities and differences in third-party intervention in various cultures. They need to understand the importance of fairness, respect, and dignity when disputes must be resolved. Finally, they need to be prepared to set up dispute resolution systems when they negotiate deals so that they and their cross-cultural partners have their own norms for dispute resolution.

EXHIBIT 3.16. A Three-Tiered Dispute Resolution System.

CPR Institute for Dispute Resolution Model Contract Clauses

Negotiation
The parties shall attempt in good faith to resolve any dispute arising out of or relating to this Agreement promptly by negotiation between executives who have authority to settle the controversy and who are at a higher level of management than the persons with direct responsibility for administration of this contract. . . . All reasonable requests for information made by one party to the other will be honored.

All negotiations pursuant to this clause are confidential and shall be treated as compromise and settlement negotiations for the purposes of applicable rules of evidence.

Mediation
If the dispute has not been resolved by negotiation within [45] days of the disputing party's notice, . . . the parties shall endeavor to settle the dispute by mediation under the [then current] CPR Mediation Procedure [in effect on the date of this agreement]. Unless otherwise agreed, the parties will select a mediator from the CPR Panels of Distinguished Neutrals.

Arbitration
Any dispute arising out of or relating to this contract, including the breach, termination or validity thereof [which has not been resolved by a non-binding procedure as provided herein within [90] days of the initiation of such procedure,] shall be finally resolved by arbitration in accordance with the [then current] CPR Rules of Non-Administered Arbitration [in effect on the date of this agreement,] by [a sole arbitrator][three independent and impartial arbitrators, of whom each party shall designate one . . .] [three independent and impartial arbitrators, none of whom shall be appointed by either party]. . . . The arbitration shall be governed by the Federal Arbitration Act, 9 U.S.C. § 1–16, and judgment upon the award rendered by the arbitrator(s) may be entered by any court having jurisdiction thereof. The place of arbitration shall be _____. The arbitrator(s) [are] [are not] empowered to award damages in excess of compensatory damages [and each party hereby irrevocably waives any right to recover such damages with respect to any dispute resolved by arbitration].

Source: Copyright © 2000, CPR Institute for Dispute Resolution, 366 Madison Avenue, New York, NY 10017-3122; (212) 949-6490. Reprinted with permission. The CPR Institute is a nonprofit initiative of 500 general counsel of major corporations, leading law firms, and prominent legal academics whose mission is to install alternative dispute resolution (ADR) into the mainstream of legal practice.

4

Making Decisions and Managing Conflict in Multicultural Teams

Multicultural teams—groups of three or more people with diverse cultural backgrounds who must make decisions—are everywhere. These teams run the European Union (EU). They coordinate the global airline alliances, like One World and Star. They manage merged and acquired organizations. For example, Nissan, after selling a 37 percent stake to Renault, a French company, retains its Japanese chairman of the board but has a Brazilian-born CEO from Renault. They also direct global organizations. For example, in 1999, four of Ford Motor Company's six group vice presidents grew up outside the United States, including the chief executive and president. Multicultural teams manage international peacekeeping, relief, and development efforts.

The proliferation of multicultural teams is not the result of the latest fad in management but of the complexity and the challenges of living and working together in an increasingly interdependent world. Individuals simply do not have the breadth of knowledge and skills to accomplish multifaceted tasks, the time to complete big tasks, or the relationships to ensure that such tasks get done.

Teams bring essential resources to big complex tasks, but assigning a complex task to a team does not ensure successful task performance. Advances in European unity were at a standstill in June 2000, according to press commentary, because of vastly differing views of the future. Germany advocated a pooling of sovereignty by shifting power from national legislatures to a bicameral European parliament. France viewed pooling sovereignty as surrendering sovereignty. The result was virtually no debate about the destiny of Europe at the June 2000 meeting of EU leaders and much attention paid to small-scale disputes.[1]

There are three reasons why multicultural teams have difficulty achieving their goals. The first is because they must negotiate agreements in the context of difficult tasks (task conflict). The second is because they must resolve disputes about how to do the task (procedural conflict). The third is because task and procedural conflict often morph into interpersonal conflict (emotional outbursts, attributions of bad intentions, withdrawal).

Yet teams that experience substantial conflict can also produce creative ideas, meet deadlines with quality products, and make decisions over time that generate growth and prosperity. Research shows that when team minorities dissent, majorities are more likely to generate original and novel solutions to problems.[2] Organizations grow faster when top management teams engage in constructive debate.[3] Companies with top-management teams that engage in debate have a higher return on investment.[4] Headquarters teams doing nonroutine tasks perform better when they engage in task-related conflict accompanied by norms for openness than when they do not.[5] Cross-functional new-product teams are more innovative when they have a lot of disagreement about task design, if they have a norm for open expression of doubts, or if they engage in collaborative problem solving.[6]

Researchers think that when a team is engaged in a routine or repetitive task, all kinds of conflict are detrimental to performance. It is only when the task is nonroutine, for example, making decisions under conditions of uncertainty, that conflict appears to enhance team performance. A close look at the examples of successful teams suggests that at least three conditions have to be met if conflict is going to enhance rather than diminish team performance. First, the team needs systems for resolving task and procedural conflicts. These systems include information-sharing and information integration procedures that apply the knowledge, skills, and interests of team members to the complexities of the team's problem. Second, the team needs systems for preventing gratuitous and unnecessary conflict. These include procedures for clarifying tasks and for building trust and tolerance. Third, the team needs systems for channeling conflict and for dealing with dysfunctional conflict. These include norms for interaction and techniques for confrontation.

This chapter is about making decisions and managing conflict in multicultural teams. It begins with an overview of task, procedural, and interpersonal conflict, three reasons why multicultural teams have difficulty achieving their goals. It then turns to advice on how to organize multicultural teams to maximize their decision-making capabilities.

Sources of Conflict in Multicultural Teams

Task, procedural, and interpersonal conflict can interfere with the performance of multicultural teams. Culture can affect all three types of conflict.

Task Conflict

Multi-issue tasks seemingly pit team members against each other on one issue after another. Yet multicultural teams can reach high-quality decisions in this task environment if team members prioritize their interests across issues and trade off concessions on low-priority issues for either immediate or future concessions from other team members on high-priority issues.

Task conflict occurs in multicultural teams when team members deal with the task as though a single issue were at stake and seek a distributive outcome. A European pharmaceutical company expanding globally experienced this problem.[7] The company wanted to capitalize on efficiencies in getting the same drugs approved in the European Union, the United States, and Japan. It formed a multicultural team to identify duplicated efforts and to transfer learning from one national approval team to another. The first snag occurred because the team framed its task as whose standards would be used. Studies run to EU standards did not, according to the American team members, meet the standards of the Food and Drug Administration (FDA) in the United States. Trying to use European studies in the U.S. approval process generated frustration and irritation between U.S. and EU team members. At first, not fully understanding the differences in standards, the U.S. team members concluded that the Europeans were unable to do good research. The Europeans, also not understanding the differences in standards, were suspicious of why the U.S. members' standards were so strict.

Task conflict in the drug approval team was legitimate and cultural. Team members' different perspectives were grounded in the different regulatory environments they faced. In putting the team together, top management knew of these differences but charged the team with creating synergies out of them. Synergies could be efficiencies realized by sharing resources or by transferring knowledge from one effort to the other. Think about the natural conflict of interests in this situation that needs to be overcome to find synergies. The European team members describe their system; the U.S. members react, "That would never be acceptable in the United States." The U.S. team members describe their system, and the Europeans see the approach as cumbersome and overburdened by minutiae. The solution, easier suggested than realized, is to transform the single-issue task into a multiple-issue task where decisions across issues can take both sides' interests into account.

Procedural Conflict

Culture confounds multicultural teams' decision making because team members from different cultures often have very different ideas about how the team should go about making decisions. French and U.S. employees of Bull, an international information technology consulting organization, made a video discussing their different approaches to problem solving and the conflict it generates in their multicultural teams.[8] A U.S. manager says of the French, "They use a sort of Cartesian logic when approaching problems. It is important to them that they analyze the problem correctly, that they get the right conception of the problem." A French manager comments, "The Americans are much less concerned with having the proper intellectual approach to a problem or developing a clear logical structure. Their priority is getting quickly to the action even to the point of being partly wrong." One U.S. manager describes the French approach to decision making as "analysis paralysis." She says that so much analysis and attention to detail slows the process down. A French manager describes the U.S. approach as start, realize after three months it's not working, stop, change approach, and start over.

These cultural differences in problem solving described by Bull employees are the result of differences in the way managers and technicians were trained in school and were expected to perform at work before the merger that brought together the U.S. Zenith Data Systems and French Groupe Bull. Both French and U.S. employees describe the French approach as focusing on the negative—what is wrong with the suggested approach—and the U.S. approach as focusing on the positive—what is right. In yet another example of procedural conflict, a French woman describes an interchange with her U.S. manager. "He asked me to do a project. After he explained what he wanted, I asked a few clarifying questions and then asked when he wanted it. He said, 'Tomorrow.' I said, 'Tomorrow? That's not possible unless I compromise quality.' His response was, 'Why?'" It is clear from her reaction that it is not the French way to do something fast and yet with high quality.

These differences in approach to problem solving are neither trivial nor easy to bridge. Now that Bull is a global company with employees around the world, it needs to integrate the best of the French and American systems. But even if Bull develops its own corporate culture of problem solving, the differences in orientation between French and U.S. employees are going to continue. Bull is not going to change either the U.S. or the French school systems, and it is going to continue to hire employees from both. Bull not only needs a corporate approach to problem solving but also needs a system for resolving conflict when slower French and faster U.S. cultural approaches collide.

Interpersonal Conflict

Interpersonal conflict occurs when team members react to being denied an opportunity to express their ideas or to having their ideas rejected by feeling insulted or affronted. Psychologists point out that people feel affronted when their social identity is threatened.[9] *Social identity* is our sense of our own reputation, the impression we think we have made on others. People generally want to maintain a positive social identity, to be accepted and respected members of social groups to which they wish to belong or in which they must work.

Multicultural teams provide many opportunities for public confirmation and disconfirmation of social identity. Team members who look like us, talk like us, and agree with our views about the task or procedures reinforce our sense of who we are and what we know. They confirm our social identity. The Chinese call this social process *giving face*. But multicultural teams are by definition heterogeneous. Team members who look different, talk differently, or disagree with our views cause us to *lose face* and therefore threaten our social identity.

You will recall from Chapter One the Asian team member who withdrew from participating when her ideas were ignored. Her action was not an emotional outburst, but it was emotional nonetheless. Whereas before the incident she had been slowly increasing her participation, afterward she stopped participating altogether. She had lost face in the interchange and been shown that she was not a powerful player in the group.

People tend to hold others personally responsible for affronts to social identity. They may strike back immediately, pushing the team into open conflict, or hold back, waiting for an opportunity to extract revenge. Whether the response is immediate or delayed, when team members engage in leveling the social identity playing field by taking revenge, the team is not engaged in its task.

A retreat into *ethnocentrism* is another common response to threats to social identity in multicultural teams. When team members engage in ethnocentric thinking, they focus on the superiority of their in-group (people on the team with whom they share characteristics or interests) and the inferiority of the out-group (people on the team with whom they do not share characteristics or interests). When French and U.S. managers at Bull realized how differently they approached problem solving, each group engaged in ethnocentric thinking. French managers argued, "Our way is best because we do it right and we get the right answer." The U.S. managers argued, "Our way is best because there is no single right answer and we don't waste time looking for it."

French and U.S. employees of Bull were differentiating themselves in order to maintain a positive social identity.[10] Unfortunately, this only increases social distance and competition between the two warring groups. Increasing social distance is the same psychological phenomenon that occurs when two countries go to war. Each country's press emphasizes the *rights* of that country's values and the *wrongs* of the other country's values, resulting in in-group cohesion and a strong competitive orientation toward the out-group. Protecting social identity in multicultural teams by engaging in ethnocentric thinking only exacerbates social distance and hinders the integration of different cultural perspectives.

Yet another way to save face and maintain a positive social identity is to decrease social distance between in-groups and out-groups by exerting pressure for social conformity. European and U.S. managers on the drug certification team took this approach. Each cultural group tried to convince the other to adopt its protocols, arguing that its way was the right way. Of course, both groups were right: their way was right for their environment. It was the team's task to identify synergies that emerge from both cultures' environments.

Neither ethnocentric thinking nor social conformity pressure is a solution to the problem of creating synergies from differences among multicultural team members. Ethnocentric thinking can bring the team to a halt; if neither cultural group will accept the other's approach, no decisions get made, no problems get solved, no synergies get discovered. Social conformity pressure can also bring the team to a halt if neither side gives in to the pressure. If one side capitulates and the other side imposes its approach, the differences out of which synergies could be constructed are lost to the group. This loss is important because task conflict and procedural conflict are the resources from which teams construct innovative solutions to complex problems. There has to be a better way.

Making High-Quality Decisions and Managing Conflict in Multicultural Teams

Groups naturally jump into their tasks.[11] Members rely on norms imported from other group experiences for procedures[12] and use stereotypes and *categorization* (who looks like me, talks like me) to make judgments about likely friends and foes. This approach may work reasonably well even for complex, multi-issue tasks when there is little or no conflict over procedural norms and when cultural and individual differences are few. Unfortunately, multicultural teams must anticipate complex tasks, for which different team members will have different interests (task conflict), different approaches (procedural conflict), and *prejudices* and stereotypes about each other's culture.

Multicultural teams set themselves up for failure unless they start out by creating systems to resolve task and procedural conflict, to prevent gratuitous conflict, and to deal with dysfunctional interpersonal conflict when it inevitably arises.

Systems to Resolve Task and Procedural Conflict: Making Decisions in Multicultural Teams

Systems for resolving task and procedural conflict in multi-issue tasks include information-sharing and information integration procedures that apply team members' knowledge and skills to the team's task and help team members integrate their interests.

Information Sharing. Multicultural teams can reach high-quality decisions if they can apply their knowledge and integrate their interests. This requires sharing information. All the information search strategies discussed in Chapter Two apply to the multiparty situation:

- Give a little information.
- Ask for information.
- Build trust and treat others with respect.
- Do not make assumptions, and check out assumptions.
- Get reactions to multi-issue proposals.
- Suggest equivalent proposals.

Team members may be a little less reluctant to share information about priorities and interests than deal makers or dispute resolvers because the team's task provides a common goal. Common goals encourage cooperation. Cooperation encourages information sharing. Making group goals salient encourages information sharing.

Still team members may be reluctant to share information, fearing that by doing so they will make themselves vulnerable to exploitation and reduce their chances of achieving their goals. Setting a norm for *meaningful participation* is another way to encourage information sharing.[13] Meaningful participation focuses attention on two obligations of information sharing:

- Group members have an obligation to enter the group's discussion as their knowledge, expertise, or contacts become relevant to defining or acting on the group's task.

- Group members have an obligation to enter the group's discussion when they harbor doubts about the direction the group is taking or the feasibility of the group's plan.

Language, cultural, structural, and psychological barriers to meaningful participation need to be addressed because they interfere with information sharing.

Language Barriers   Language can be a powerful tool to exclude or include certain group members and therefore a barrier to meaningful participation. Examples of such language-based power practices include making personal remarks in a language some members do not understand or refusing to attend a meeting that will be conducted in another language. German members of various EU commissions threatened to boycott meetings at one point in 1999 when it was announced that only French and English translations would be provided.

Language can also be a source of misunderstanding. English was the working language of the pharmaceutical team, but not all team members were equally fluent. A French team member addressing a U.S. team member saying "I demand . . ." was perceived as rude until both members realized that the French member was using a direct but erroneous translation of *je demande,* a perfectly polite way of saying "I am asking . . ."

Language also can be a source of frustration and anger. French and U.S. employees of Bull discussed the frustration of trying to work in a second language. One manager said, "You feel like you've lost half of your body, you feel intellectually hampered, you get frustrated, and your emotion blocks your facility with the language; you get angry."

Teams need to confront their language problems. Failing to get information from group members because they are not fluent in the team's lingua franca threatens the viability of the team's project. Here are some things that might help:

- Discourage jargon; make available glossaries with translations of key terms.

- Use visual aids when collecting information from group members. Expand the positions and interests chart (Exhibit 3.1 in Chapter Three) by adding a column for every group member, and fill the chart in as the team discusses issues and interests. When presenting information to the team, use simple slides (lots of white space, main points, minimum of text), and make copies for all group members. When trying to reach agreement, write multi-issue proposals on a chalkboard or flipchart.

- Arrange for frequent breaks where team members can discuss what was going on in the meeting in their own language. Follow breaks with a question-and-answer session.

- Consider using an electronically networked meeting room with one or two central screens and a conference table with a small screen and keyboard at each place. These electronically supported meeting rooms are especially helpful when teams are brainstorming, working on documents, or coming up with multi-issue proposals for agreement.

- Adopt a team-endorsed way to stop a meeting and ask for clarification. For example, some teams give members flags to wave when they do not understand.

Regarding this last point, one European manager on the drug certification team described an incident in which humor eased misunderstanding and led to a clarification norm:

I was in a meeting with both French- and English-speaking colleagues, and we listened to a presentation by an American colleague. She's a very bright woman, and when she got into her story, she started talking very fast. My other colleagues and I were starting to have difficulty in following her when suddenly she started to regularly use "LOE." Now I was completely lost. I raised my hand, "What does that mean, 'LOE'?" "Oh," she said, "lack of efficiency." A few minutes later, I was lost again. I raised my hand again, saying, "LOU." "LOU?" she asked. "Yes," I said, "lack of understanding." We started to laugh. From then on, LOU became "ell-o-you," "hello you," our way of expressing ourselves when we don't understand anymore.[14]

If this European manager had not intervened and asked for an explanation, the team would have de facto developed a norm that tolerated misunderstanding. Instead this manager promoted a norm of understanding. His first polite intervention communicated "I respect you, but I need to understand you." His second humorous intervention communicated "We need a way to alert each other when we don't understand." "Ell-o-you" or "hello you" became the group's norm.

Cultural Barriers. Cultural values may also be a barrier to meaningful participation. Collectivism's emphasis on harmony and hierarchy's emphasis on deference to status do not encourage people with dissenting opinions to contribute their ideas. Team members from cultures where these values are strong may have difficulty participating in face-to-face open discussion, especially if their contribution is to dissent. Their culture's normative approach would not be to confront directly where face might be lost. Both high- and low-context communication norms can also be barriers. Direct communication may be offensive to group members from high-context cultures. Group members from low-context cultures may not understand indirect communication.

The multicultural team needs to develop its own culture of meaningful participation, but realistically, some group members will be more reluctant to share information than others for cultural reasons. Here are some ideas that may help:

- Charge someone in the group with monitoring meaningful participation. The team leader can do this, but the team leader is also trying to get the team to move ahead with its task. Someone else might be better, both because the team leader will be occupied with other matters and because the team leader may need to be reminded. The monitor can remind the group as a whole of its norms or take individuals aside and encourage them to participate.

- Have the whole team not only brainstorm the positive implications of an idea or approach but also separately brainstorm the negative implications. This makes dissenting opinions the responsibility of the whole group, not just a few members.

- Use e-mail for information gathering. E-mail has some important limitations that are discussed in the next section, but it also has some benefits. Power differences are minimized in an e-mail environment. People are less inhibited by social norms when communicating by e-mail.[15] Although this can be a problem, it can also encourage unrestrained participation of team members from cultures where harmony is highly valued and concerns for face is preeminent.[16] In cultures where saying no face to face is difficult, e-mail may actually facilitate communication about interests.

Another barrier that culture imposes on information sharing is misunderstanding and misattribution. People process meaning through the lens of their own culture. Direct eye contact implies honesty in the U.S. culture but is viewed as impolite in the Japanese culture. U.S. team members may distrust Japanese team members whose eyes are averted during conversation. Japanese team members may interpret the U.S. members' directness as rude and offensive. Either way, not only is meaning lost, but feelings are engaged and trust is challenged. French and U.S. members of a Bull team were exasperated with one another when the French, in keeping with their cultural norms, focused on the negative and the Americans focused on the positive. Here is some advice that may help deal with cultural misunderstanding:

- Find out if the annoying behavior is truly cultural, meaning that it is a group rather than an individual characteristic. Then find out what it means in the other culture.

For example, observing that many of my students in India seemed to be shaking their heads "no," I jumped to the cultural conclusion that they hated my class. Thinking I would do what I could to improve the next day's class, I asked my Indian host, "Do your students shake their heads back and forth like this when you are lecturing?" When he answered in the affirmative, I asked, "What does it mean?" "It means that they are listening intently," he told me.

Structural Barriers. Distance and time differences are the primary structural barriers to meaningful participation in multicultural teams. The team will need to experiment with alternative electronic communication media, learning when and how to use e-mail, computer conferencing, and teleconferencing effectively and when to insist on face-to-face interaction. A case in point: the members of the top-management team of a high-tech company hated their weekly meetings and loved e-mail, so they decided to make most of their decisions via e-mail, meeting face to face only to confront tough problems.[17] The result was that face-to-face meetings became like hand-to-hand combat. E-mail had eliminated the easy issues as well as the social manners that had made face-to-face meetings tolerable, if not enjoyable.

The major problem with electronic communication is that it increases social alienation. People working electronically do not identify with their groups as strongly as people working face to face.[18] When we had students from Canada, Mexico, and the United States working by e-mail on a joint North American Free Trade Agreement (NAFTA) project, instructors in all three cultures received frequent complaints that team members from the other cultures were not motivated, were holding up the project, and were therefore responsible for poor quality.[19] When we do not get regular communications from remote team members, we tend to assume that they are not working. When our e-mail is not answered promptly, we conclude that they just don't care enough about the project or, even worse, that people from their culture are lazy. We tend to attribute inactivity to willful negligence, not to environmental factors, such as time zone differences or access to e-mail, that are beyond the others' immediate control.

Attributions made to willful activity versus environmental factors exacerbate interpersonal animosity. The teams that produced the best NAFTA projects were the ones that developed norms relating to electronic communication. They recognized the potential pitfalls of e-mail and developed proactive strategies for dealing with coordination and logistical problems. Successful teams not only alerted each other about deadlines but also consistently confirmed receipt of material, keeping everyone up to date.

Here is some advice for overcoming the barriers to information exchange due to electronic communication:

- Set norms for use of e-mail. For example, decide if receipt of correspondence needs to be acknowledged, even when no substantive answer is necessary. Decide if all correspondence should go though the team leader or whether team members are expected to copy the whole team. Decide within what time frame e-mail should be acknowledged. Set up means for alerting others when a team member is unavailable.

- Minimize having the same team members participate in conference calls in the middle of their night. One multicultural team rotates its monthly conference by time zone, not by how many people on the team are in a time zone.

Psychological Barriers. One psychological barrier to efficient information sharing is that team members, especially those who are friends, tend to discuss common rather than dispersed knowledge.[20] Yet it is the dispersed knowledge that team members hold uniquely that gives the team leverage to do its task well. Meaningful participation does not imply that all group members participate equally at all times.[21] Focusing team members with relevant knowledge on the task while others are listening or doing something else is an efficient use of team resources.[22] It is also challenging to do. Here is some advice:

- The team leader and at least some team members need to have *transactive memory*. Transactive memory is knowledge of who on the team knows what.[23] For example, the member of the drug approval team who knows the most about EU standards may not be the same person who knows the most about setting up clinical trials in EU countries. When one or more team members have transactive memory, they can encourage the participation of the expert at the right time. When no one knows who is the expert, and the expert for whatever reason is unwilling to speak up, expertise is lost.

Another psychological barrier to information sharing is the tendency to focus on achieving group consensus or groupthink rather than on reaching a solution that integrates information. The Kennedy cabinet's management of the Bay of Pigs military operation to invade Cuba in 1961 is a widely cited example of groupthink. Members of the Kennedy cabinet had serious doubts about the wisdom of this invasion and the planning that went into it. Yet concerns about being accepted by other more hawkish members of the cabinet led them to keep their doubts to themselves. The invasion was a fiasco.

Teams that are overly concerned with the political repercussions of their decision can end up in this psychological trap. Groupthink leads to poor-quality decisions because groups tend to focus on a single objective when other objectives are also important. They fail to generate a full array of alternatives, fail to reassess alternatives in the light of new information, fail to examine the pros and cons of preferred alternatives, and fail to create contingency plans.[24]

The advice for avoiding cultural barriers to information sharing should also be helpful in avoiding groupthink. In addition, team members need to be assured of confidentiality and even protection:

- Have a norm of confidentiality. Some team members may be worried that their opinions will be broadcast beyond the group and therefore not express them, fearing harmful repercussions from outside the team.

- Protect team members from social ostracism. Some members may be worried that they will be shunned for expressing dissenting opinions. Team members should be assured that team membership is protected.

Information Integration for Mutual Gains. Multicultural teams that have shared diverse information and interests need a way to integrate that information and those interests if they are to reach high-quality decisions. Relying on imported norms is unwise, since team members from different cultural backgrounds are likely to have conflicting decision-making norms. For example, team members from a hierarchical culture may expect the team member with superior status to make the decision. Team members from an egalitarian culture may expect the majority to rule. Both *one party decides* and *majority rule* decision rules will almost certainly generate distributive outcomes. The people who have the power to make the decision will win and the others will lose. The decision will incorporate the interests of the winners but not the losers. Furthermore, the losers may be in a position to interfere with the implementation of the decision. There are situations when one party decides and majority rule are appropriate, but the only way to seek an integrative agreement, as opposed to falling into one by chance, is to use a *mutual-gains strategy*. A mutual-gains strategy focuses decision makers on integration where parties' interests are mingled in one or another of the types of agreement discussed in Chapter Three and summarized in Exhibit 3.2. When interests are integrated, the decision sweeps up all the potential value from team members' diverse information and interests. Also, because their interests have been addressed, team members should be motivated to work together to implement the decision.

Getting parties to reach integrative agreements is difficult in any circumstances. In deal making it is difficult because parties assume that the resource pie is fixed and that sharing information will be detrimental to their interests. In dispute resolving it is difficult because parties are usually emotional and distrust not only each other's motives but also the information provided. In teams it is difficult because of the multiplicity of issues and interests. However, there are some ways to structure team decision making to encourage integrative decisions. The first is to make sure that the group is set up to engage in meaningful participation. The second is to pursue a mutual-gains decision strategy.

Structuring the Issues for Integration. When multiple issues and options exist and team members' preferences are diffuse, reaching an integrative decision is usually possible. When issues and options are few or team members' preferences are focused on just a few options, reaching an integrative decision may not be possible, even if the team fully shares information about preferences and priorities. If an integrative decision does not seem feasible because of the structure of the task and the distribution of interests, there are several options to consider before giving up entirely on integration:

- Add issues or subdivide issues. Do whatever it takes to get more elements of the task on the table to work with simultaneously.

- Get commitment to long-term reciprocity. Long-term reciprocity takes advantage not only of the fact that team members have different preferences but also that some preferences are stronger than others. Teams whose members are cooperative, that is, concerned for both own and others' interests, operate with the implicit understanding that members whose interests are least affected by a decision should compromise when they can. In return for their cooperation on a less important decision, team members can expect support on a subsequent more important decision.[25]

Proposals. Proposals not only help get information about team members preferences and interests on the table but also integrate and distribute that information. The obvious way to integrate is to agree to a set of complex trade-offs that take into account all team members' interests. However, trading off among issues currently on the table is not the only way to realize mutual gains. Long-term reciprocity is an option. So are the other types of agreements to resolve disputes summarized in Exhibit 3.2: Decisions to experiment for a limited period and then evaluate give those team members who have reservations about a decision an important role in monitoring its progress. Non-precedent-setting decisions preserve future flexibility and let teams take into account unique circumstances. Decisions to minimize costs to members who are going to suffer losses build widespread commitment even among team members who will bear the costs.

Decision Rules. Fundamental to a mutual-gains strategy is a decision rule that requires a large proportion of the team's members to agree to the decision, either a two-thirds majority, *consensus*, or *unanimity*. These decision rules encourage information sharing and integration.

Majority rule implies that a decision can be reached with one person more than half of the group's members agreeing. Sometimes large factions or coalitions exist before the start of the information-sharing phase of group decision making. These *a priori majorities* place a damper on the sharing of information, especially the expression of minority views. Attention to minority views causes majority views to diversify.[26] Teams that let the majority rule are less likely to integrate than teams that must reach a unanimous agreement.[27]

Achieving a two-thirds majority usually requires that an a priori majority must gain members to control the group's decision. This often forces majority members to pay attention to the views of minority members. Consensus is a form of majority rule when there are no longer team members actively opposing a decision. Team members with doubts about the merits of a decision agree that the team should make the decision despite those doubts. Unanimity requires pleasing every single member of the group—an objective that may be impossible for multicultural teams to meet.

Voting has its own pitfalls.[28] When the decision rule requires a simple majority, the order in which alternatives are voted can affect the outcome. This is why it is preferable to rank alternatives rather than vote on them according to some sequence. Ranking, of course, has problems too. Team members may engage in strategic manipulation to make sure some undesirable option will lose.

Other decision rules reduce the likelihood of integration. When one party has the authority to make a decision, that member is usually expected to act in a self-interested way. As a result, other team members may hide information. The same is true when a coalition or *faction* has the authority to impose a decision. Factions are not motivated to learn about others' interests because integrating the interests of non–faction members is likely to dilute the gains available to distribute among faction members.

BATNAs. Teams have BATNAs in the same way that deal makers and dispute resolvers do. When a team is first formed, its BATNA is whatever will happen if the team cannot reach agreement. This BATNA, like deal makers' BATNAs, may have vastly different implications for different team members, or like dispute resolvers, team members may be able to impose their BATNAs on each other. The members whose interests will be hurt the most by no agreement will be the most motivated to reach agreement and likely the most cooperative and flexible. The team members whose interests will be hurt the least by no agreement are likely to be the least cooperative and make the most demands on the group. This means that any decision must be better than no agreement for the team as a whole and for each individual member. Trying to satisfy everyone motivates the search for mutual gains.

Little attention is paid to what exactly teams' BATNAs are, and this is an oversight when the goal is mutual gains. Consider the pharmaceutical team. If team members assume that their BATNA is the status quo—separate drug approval projects in Europe, the United States, and Japan—they are unlikely to be motivated to seek synergies and an integrative agreement. Yet the status quo may not be the BATNA. The pharmaceutical team would be more motivated to search for an integrative agreement if members knew that if they failed to reach agreement, an integrated drug approval program would be imposed on them. Attention paid to teams' BATNAs can motivate the search for integrative agreements.

Multiple Alternatives and Second Agreements. There are two different ways of searching for an agreement that maximizes mutual gains: brainstorm multiple alternatives and rank them, or seek a minimum agreement and try to improve it. After the team has shared information, it can use brainstorming to come up with multiple options and then rank the options. Brainstorming rules should apply: create as many ideas as possible; the more unusual the idea, the better; aim for quantity of ideas without worrying about quality; do not criticize options during brainstorming; and feel free to elaborate and extend others' ideas.[29] Review the types of integrative agreements in Exhibit 3.2. During brainstorming, options should be displayed visually so as to minimize misunderstanding. Ranking should be used rather than voting because it preserves options and forces the team to make its judgments in the context of realistic alternatives. The French employees at Bull might like this approach because it results in a single "best" decision. The Americans should like that many options are generated, not just one, and that this approach identifies a fallback option if something goes wrong with the first choice. Of course, this procedure takes time, and there is no guarantee that it will generate an integrative decision.

The second agreement requires reaching a first agreement and then trying to improve on it. After completing a positions and interests chart like that in Exhibit 3.1, teams might fill in another chart based on the least each member would agree to. Assuming that there is a least common denominator, the group then tries to improve on it. This procedure does not unleash as much in the way of creativity, but it does force team members to deal with issues simultaneously and so encourages integration. Of course, there are integrative agreements that generate a great deal of mutual gain and others that generate less. This procedure is unlikely to maximize mutual gain, for two reasons. First, team members may not be very motivated to engage in the hard work that may be required to improve the first decision. And second, the structure of the first decision may constrain creative thinking about alternatives.

Preventing Gratuitous and Unnecessary Conflict

Some conflict, particularly interpersonal conflict, can and should be avoided. A team with clear norms for sharing and integrating information will still have task conflict that can spill over into interpersonal conflict but should have relatively little procedural conflict. The first step, then, in avoiding unnecessary conflict is to have systems for decision making. There are a few other things that can be done as well. Task clarity goes a long way toward preventing unnecessary conflict. So do respect and tolerance for social and cultural differences, task-based trust, and norms for interpersonal interaction. Teambuilding, as it is typically practiced, does not necessarily build respect, tolerance, and trust that carry over to the task when interests are in conflict.

Task Clarity. When team members know what is expected of them and their expectations are consistent, conflict over the team's mission is less likely. It is management's responsibility to define the team's task, if possible. However, global management, to whom the team ultimately reports, and local management, to whom individual team members report, may have different perspectives on just what the team's task is. Part of a multicultural team's ongoing responsibility is to manage its relationships with global and local management. Consistent communications are essential to keep global and local management and the team itself focused on the same task.

Often multicultural teams have ill-defined tasks, not because management has foresworn its responsibility, but because there would be no need for a team if the task were clear. The first task of a multicultural team given no mission statement is to define its mission and sell it to global and local management. To develop and sell a mission, which implies acquiring the resources to carry out that mission, the team needs systems for making decisions.

Respect and Tolerance for Individual and Cultural Differences. There is a fine balance between tolerating differences and confronting them. Used selectively and freely, toleration can be a very effective way to reduce conflict.[30] Healthy marriages are probably the best example of how partners who have conflicting interests manage a shifting balance between confronting differences and tolerating them. Once I understood that my Indian students' head shaking was an expression of interest and not of rejection, it ceased to bother me. My toleration was stretched to its limits with my French students, who seemed to spend as much time talking to each other as listening to what was going on in the class. My host professors assured me that this was common in their classes too. But the background noise was interfering with my ability to understand the students with whom I was trying to have a dialogue, so I confronted and asked for silence. It lasted for the rest of that class but not the next. The students were quite surprised I had confronted them.

Several spoke to me after class, saying they had meant no disrespect. One even said to me, "You know, Professor, we were not talking about where we would go for coffee after class; we were talking about what you were talking about." I've been a professor too long to believe that explanation, however.

Trust. Trust reduces conflict in several ways. People who trust expect others to honor commitments, even commitments that are hard to define or hard to monitor.[31] With social pressure to honor commitments, people are more likely to do so, and fewer missed commitments mean fewer recriminations over fault and less conflict. Trust also reduces conflict in a more subtle way. When we trust someone, we expect benevolent behavior and tend to interpret what we see through the lens of our expectations. That same behavior exhibited by someone we distrust is easily attributed to malicious intent. So trust reduces conflict because it increases tolerance.

Norms for Interaction. Teams' norms for interpersonal interaction develop quickly as members start working together. Although team members import interpersonal interaction norms from prior experience just as they import decision-making norms, a lot of modeling also goes on. The way team members treat each other is very visible behavior; so are team members' reactions. Either disrespectful or respectful treatment of others can be rather quickly established as the group norm.

Stakeholder theory provides some guidelines for developing norms for interaction in teams. A *stakeholder* is a person with an interest. Stakeholder theory suggests that groups follow three principles:[32]

1. Accept that all stakeholders have legitimate interests.
2. Recognize that independent of further investigation, no one claim is superior to any other.
3. Treat other stakeholders with dignity and respect.

Note that these principles promote a team environment that is similar to the environment fostered by well-regarded third parties in dispute resolution. Norms of interaction based on stakeholders' principles reduce gratuitous and unnecessary conflict because they recognize the inevitability of differences and encourage toleration. They also provide a basis for trust that is depersonalized or group-based rather than individually based. Finally, norms based on stakeholders principles channel conflict toward an interest-based resolution.

The drug certification team developed the following set of interaction norms:

Don't

- *Don't* assume that the best ideas come from your own country or organization.
- *Don't* reject ideas that come from another place in the organization.
- *Don't* treat people from other parts of the company as second-class citizens.

Do

- *Willingly* listen to others' ideas.
- *Willingly* share your own ideas.
- *Willingly* change opinions.
- *Willingly* consider alternatives.
- *Willingly* admit there may be more than one right way.
- *Willingly* admit uncertainty.
- *Willingly* work together to reduce uncertainty.
- *Willingly* compromise (split the difference).
- *Willingly* reciprocate (your way this time, my way a future time).
- *Willingly* confront and talk through differences.

I would encourage them to add:

- *Willingly* make trade-offs.

Teambuilding. Teambuilding is supposed to transform a disparate set of individuals into a cohesive, coordinated team by breaking down social and cultural barriers and building trust. Teambuilding can be physically challenging, as teams trek through wilderness, build rope bridges, or sail tall ships under the distant but attentive supervision of experts who are being paid to ensure the safety of all parties. It can be fun and constructive when teams renovate community centers or parks. Pride in team accomplishment can also generate team identity—"we did this together."

What teambuilding typically does not do is replace cultural stereotypes with transactive memory that is relevant to the task. The team member who is awfully good at tying knots for the rope bridge may not be very good at solving the knotty problems associated with the team's task. The television programs *Big Brother* and *Survivor* represent the conflicting individual and group interests of multicultural, multi-issue task teams even better than teambuilding simulations in one important respect: in teambuilding simulations, team members' interests are aligned, whereas in real multicultural teams, members have individual and group interests that may conflict.

Building Trust and Tolerance in Multicultural Teams. Trust and tolerance acquired in the context of doing the task should help multicultural teams avoid unnecessary task and procedural conflict. It cannot hurt to get to know other team members as individuals in a fun setting. But there are also risks. Distrust generated in a physically challenging teambuilding setting may carry over into the intellectually challenging task setting, even though the two settings require very different skill sets. Multicultural teams need more than teambuilding as it is typically practiced to learn to work together effectively without gratuitous conflict. Talking through systems for decision making and then using and monitoring them should help teams build trust and tolerance. Systems generate expectations, use confirms expectations, and monitoring and adjustment builds trust.

Constructive Ways to Confront Dysfunctional Conflict

Dysfunctional conflict is not just shouting matches. Conflict is also dysfunctional when team members withdraw from meaningful participation and decisions are made without some team members' input.

What to do when dysfunctional conflict erupts? There are many options. The member charged with monitoring meaningful participation could intervene in private with the withdrawn member or with the group as a whole in the case of an outburst. The monitor also might be authorized to mediate between group members or between the disgruntled member and the group. The group might have a norm that members are expected to talk to each other when their tolerance is stretched to the limit and an emotional outburst or withdrawal is imminent.

It is possible to intervene in groups experiencing dysfunctional conflict and get them working together effectively,[33] but it is not easy. It is better to have conflict confrontation norms in place before conflict erupts. If the team I was observing had a conflict monitor, the woman who withdrew would have had a legitimate channel for expressing her feelings. She might have talked to the monitor instead of withdrawing. Or the monitor, sensing the woman's urge to withdraw, might have called a recess, taken the woman aside, confronted the situation, and possibly even engaged the group in a discussion of the underlying problem that this episode uncovered.

Conflict, even when associated with strong negative emotion, is not always bad for groups. Conflict lays bare important differences of opinion, and emotion conveys feelings. Emotional conflict can also be extremely dysfunctional for a group. Talking about emotions can be a powerful conflict management technique. Apology, especially when it is directed toward emotions ("I'm sorry you are upset"), is a good example. Sometimes an apology is sufficient to resolve the interpersonal conflict. At other times an apology reduces the tension between parties so that they can return to their task. Apology plays a central role in the resolution of disputes in Japan.[34] It is less used in dispute resolution in the United States because of rules of evidence that treat an apology as an admission of fault.[35] Used in the team setting, an apology focused on feelings need have no legal connotations and may be very effective in reducing interpersonal tension. The interest-based negotiation and third-party dispute resolution procedures discussed in Chapter Three can all be used in the team setting.

Effective Multicultural Teams

Sometimes all that multicultural teams need to be effective are systems that encourage information sharing and information integration and lead to integrative decisions. Yet just having the systems is often not enough. Team members need the skills and the motivation to use the systems. It is also very difficult for teams to use systems that lead to integrative decisions when the environment in which the team is embedded is focused on distributive outcomes.

Skills

The skills that team members need to use in decision-making and conflict management systems are the deal-making skills discussed in Chapter Two and the dispute resolution skills discussed in Chapter Three. Team training in those skills helps team members acquire them. Team training avoids singling out particular team members who for cultural or other reasons may not come to the group with much facility in focusing on interests. Team training also helps build interaction norms that can carry over into the workplace.

Motivation

Acquiring skills is one hurdle; using them is another. Team members have to be motivated to use their skills to participate meaningfully and seek high-quality integrative decisions. Culture complicates motivation because what is motivating in one culture may not be in another. Consider the following two incidents that occurred in two executive programs on different continents in the space of a week. A U.S. manager asked me for some advice. He said that his team was using his ideas but he was not getting any recognition. He was tired of "doing all the work and not getting any of the credit." He described a team that typically generated multiple alternatives, considered their pros and cons, and then selected the alternative that had the most team support. "By the time the team members reach a decision, they all own my alternative," he complained. That the group appeared to be using a pretty good process was not what this man wanted to hear. He wanted me to tell him how to get the team to recognize his contribution. I suggested that he start recognizing others' contributions, assuring him that the team would soon begin to model his behavior by giving him credit when credit was due. The point is not what advice I gave but rather the contrast with this next story. I sent materials for a four-day course in decision making to China two months in advance so that they could be translated. The young woman who was assigned to assist me had done a great job by any standard in organizing all the materials. Yet when I praised her in front of other staff members, I could tell that she felt very uncomfortable. "I'm just doing my job, Professor," she said. The public recognition that was so embarrassing to my Chinese assistant was exactly what the male manager required to maintain his meaningful participation in his team.

Structuring financial incentives for multicultural teams is at least as challenging as determining how to use nonfinancial incentives. Advice about team performance evaluation and pay structures suggests basic principles—establish target performance levels, quantify the criteria used to determine pay out, balance individual and team-based pay, determine timing of evaluation, and so on.[36] When teams are multicultural, this advice may be too pat. Performance and financial incentives need to be sensitive to cultural differences. Some team members, for example, may come from affiliates or organizations where pay is performance-based and others from affiliates where it is not. An incentive system that is normative and motivating to team members from some cultural backgrounds may be foreign and even offensive to others. Even the advice to involve the team members in devising their own incentive system[37] may be anathema to team members from hierarchical cultures where such decisions would normally be a responsibility of upper management. It is impossible to give specific advice about motivating team members beyond two generalizations: pay attention to motivation, and pay attention to cultural differences in what is motivating.

Environments for Effective Multicultural Teams

Multicultural teams are embedded in organizations or, in the case of joint ventures and alliances, in interorganizational relationships. Resources cross into the team at this boundary, and decisions pass out of the team. Most discussions of teams and their organizational contexts focus on resources, such as members' time, team space, and capital and assets. There is no question that these are important resources if a team is to be successful.

A more subtle resource is organizational support for the team's mission and systems. Organizations tend to use and reinforce the use of particular decision-making systems. One of the reasons multicultural teams may experience procedural conflict is that members from different parts of the organization or different organizations in the alliance have learned and are importing different decision-making procedures. A multicultural team trying to use a mutual-gains decision-making system may find it difficult to sustain its approach when embedded in an organization or alliance that relies heavily on decisions made by a single person or a small faction.

Multicultural teams need to be buffered from inhospitable environments by powerful organizational actors. Ideally, these are managers whose subordinates are team members and whose areas of responsibility are likely to be affected by team decisions. These managers need to be kept apprised of the team's progress, both its successes and its failures. The purpose of keeping powerful actors in the information loop is not to prepare them to intervene if the team has difficulties but rather to build their trust in and support for team activities. The rule of no surprises works well for multicultural teams managing their multifaceted interface with their environments.

Conclusion

Multicultural teams cannot be left alone to deal with task and procedural conflict as best they can. These teams need systems for making decisions and managing conflict that gather information and interests and integrate them into high-quality decisions. They need systems for preventing gratuitous and unnecessary conflict and systems for dealing with dysfunctional conflict when it occurs. Team members need the skills and motivation to use the systems. Teams need resources and protection from the organizations, joint ventures, and alliances in which they are embedded. Managing teams is extremely challenging; culture increases the challenge because culture affects team members' interests, the decision-making and conflict management procedures that they know and feel comfortable using, and their motivation.

5

Social Dilemmas

In the spring of 2000, the price of a barrel of crude oil skyrocketed because the Organization of Petroleum Exporting Countries (OPEC) once again agreed to production quotas. OPEC's saga of trying to agree to and then maintain oil production quotas is an example of a special type of multiparty decision making called a *social dilemma*.[1] The dilemma is whether to act in your own self-interest or in the interest of the collective. Acting to maximize self-interest—in this case, pumping oil—is always better for the individual OPEC country because that country gains revenue from higher volume. However, the rational pursuit of self-interest produces collective disaster.[2] When all OPEC countries increase their supply, the price of oil drops, and all oil-producing countries lose, though of course the oil-consuming countries win, a point taken up a little later.

Types of Social Dilemmas

There are several types of social dilemmas, including resource dilemmas, free-rider dilemmas, and competitive dilemmas. Although each type of dilemma has some unique characteristics, all have in common the tension between self-interests and collective interests.

Resource Dilemmas

Resource dilemmas are social dilemmas about the use of replaceable natural resources. Industries that extract or use replaceable natural resources—fishing, forestry, and agriculture—have to make decisions in the context of a social dilemma. If they extract too much, the resource will be depleted, but while they are depleting the resource, they are profiting greatly. Consider the fate of the "sweetheart" dining fish of the 1990s, the Patagonian toothfish.[3] Since this fish, also called the Chilean sea bass, was first introduced on the menus of American restaurants in about 1995, stocks have been depleted by 50 percent. Given the fish's increasing popularity, its slow rate of reproduction in the cold waters of the Antarctic, and its remote natural habitat, making the way it is caught and sold almost impossible to regulate, you should order this fish now. That way, when the fish becomes extinct (you of course helped make it so), you can boast that you tasted it once!

Resource dilemmas pose particular problems because surveillance of extraction and harvesting is often difficult, due to the remote locations of the resource. Resource consumers are also often spread across the globe and have no social identity as a group.

Free-Rider Dilemmas

A *free rider* is a person who does not personally contribute but benefits from the contributions of others. Free-rider dilemmas are social dilemmas about the decision to contribute to a public good. Tax evaders, despite paying no taxes, benefit from public services: they are free riders. Public radio and television in the United States are beset by the free-rider problem: a great many people listen or watch but do not make financial contributions during membership drives. The same can be said of teams. Free-rider team members who do not contribute nevertheless share in the team's rewards along with team members who do contribute. If the team is unsuccessful, the free rider, unlike other members of the team who contributed, will not feel exploited.

The first challenge in managing free riders is identifying who they are. The second challenge is instilling in them a sense of responsibility to contribute to the public good.

Competitive Dilemmas

Competitive dilemmas are multiparty *prisoner's dilemmas*, situations in which it is in one's self-interest to compete but in the collective interest to cooperate. OPEC is really just a small group of competitors trying to determine production quotas so that they can control the price of their product. Of course, in some cultures, collusive price setting is illegal, but OPEC is a global organization and not restricted by national laws. When explicit collusion is illegal, decision makers faced with a social dilemma can signal their competitors by the choices they make and publicize. Airfares and frequent flyer awards are good examples of this. Airlines do not collude in direct decision making like the OPEC countries. They do something more indirect. They announce a new fare increase a few days ahead of the date the fare will be implemented and wait to see what their competitors do. If the competitors match the fare, all share the market with higher margins. If the competitors do not match the fare, the initiator can roll back the fare increase and continue competing for market share at lower margins.

Competitive dilemmas are pervasive and complex because there are two sets of collective interests: the collective interests of the competitors and the collective interests of the consumers of the competitors' products. When OPEC nations make decisions about production quotas, there is no representative of the oil-consuming countries at the table. OPEC has to judge how much it can restrict production and increase prices before oil-consuming countries and consumers react, for example, by buying low-fuel-consumption cars or by releasing oil reserves. Consumers are not without power vis-à-vis a competitive cartel, but they have to coordinate their actions, and that may be difficult and take time. Meanwhile, if the cartel holds, it is reaping windfall profits.

The Ubiquity of Social Dilemmas

Social dilemmas are all around us. They may be local, involving the use of water in an area beset by drought, free-riding on a grade school history fair project, or competition between gas stations or fast-food restaurants on facing street corners. They may also be global, involving emissions that deplete the ozone level, free-riding as a member of a global airline alliance team, or competing for international market share of laundry detergent. Regardless of whether the dilemma is local or global, managing it requires balancing self-interests and collective interests.

Managing Social Dilemmas

Chapter Three introduced three ways to resolve disputes: interest-based approaches, rights-based approaches, and power-based approaches. When social dilemmas are out of balance, parties' behaviors are motivated by power. Each party's behavior is a function of its own self-interest and ability. Parties can continue to compete with one another until one or more exits or the resource is totally depleted. However, parties to a social dilemma can take a rights- or interest-based approach to managing the dilemma. Some approaches may be more acceptable to parties from some cultures than others.

Rights-Based Approaches

Rights-based approaches to managing social dilemmas involve either evoking a social norm—for example, equality, equity, need—or imposing a legal regulation. There are two problems with rights-based solutions.

One problem is that parties have difficulty agreeing what is a fair normative or legal standard. This is especially so when parties are receiving differential benefits. For example, one social dilemma that we have been studying involves representatives of four groups that are fishing for shark.[4] The rate at which sharks are taken for food and recreational purposes is greater than the rate of reproduction. Of course, the individuals involved in shark fishing for recreation are taking less than those who are fishing coastal waters in medium-sized boats, and they are taking less than the large commercial fishers. What is a fair standard for reducing fishing to a level where sharks are self-sustaining? Is it fair to ask each party to cut its take in half? Wouldn't that put an unfair burden on the small recreational fishing groups, especially when the large commercial fishing groups could rather easily switch to another fish? Should all take a cut proportional to their current harvest? Wouldn't that place an unfair burden on the large commercial fishing group? You get the point: in order to sustain the resource, self-interests must be sublimated to the collective interest of sustaining the population of sharks, but there is no uniformly fair way to do so in a social dilemma where benefits have been asymmetric. Furthermore, standards that are perceived to unfairly benefit one party over others are not self-regulating.

The second problem with rights-based approaches to resolving social dilemmas is that even when a normative standard is available or a legal standard is imposed, the incentives to defect in a social dilemma are sufficiently strong that surveillance and sanctions are usually necessary. When the standard is a norm and surveillance is easy, social sanctions may be sufficient to sustain cooperative behavior supporting the collective interest. For example, a team may minimize free riding by socially ostracizing members who fail to contribute their share or by besmirching their reputations. When the standard is a regulation, an agency may need to be created to carry out surveillance and sanctions. When the dilemma operates at a global level, international agencies may have authority for surveillance, but sanctions have to be imposed at the national level.

For example, there is no common legal enforcement mechanism for the international accord, signed by twenty-three nations, to protect various species of marine life, including the Patagonian toothfish. Even if there were an international endangered species marine police, consider the difficulty of enforcing toothfish fishing in the remote Antarctic Ocean. International regulations for managing social dilemmas have to be enforced by the separate signatories. Enforcement is expensive, and free riding occurs.

Our studies suggest that legal regulation may be more acceptable to parties from some cultures than from others. German managers focused more on rights and Japanese managers on power. However, U.S. managers were the most oriented to setting up rules and standards for future interaction.[5]

Interest-Based Approaches

An interest-based approach to managing a social dilemma involves realigning individual self-interests so that they are consistent with collective interests. This requires a shift in social identity from the self to the group coping with the social dilemma. The way to do this is to make group membership salient.[6] When group membership is salient, people's identity starts to shift toward the social identity of the group. Consider OPEC again. OPEC member nations have national self-identities. When OPEC nations are ignoring OPEC quotas, their self-identity is as a nation, not as a member of OPEC, whose standard they are ignoring. When OPEC nations are maintaining the group's quotas, their self-identity is aligned with the group—how else can they explain their compliance? Certainly not by self-interest.

Three techniques for making social identity salient are collective goals, contact, and recategorization. A *collective goal* may help parties recognize that they have a common interest in cooperating to satisfy self-interests. A major factor motivating OPEC members to renegotiate quotas and stick to them in 2000 was their common economic problems caused by low oil prices. OPEC members' collective goal of improving their individual economic situations was aligned with their self-interests. *Contact* places dispersed parties to a social dilemma in touch with one another. Contact works if it generates respect for differing interests and leads to trust that concessions will be reciprocated and commitments to quotas will be kept. One way to build trust is for all parties to take small cooperative steps that are easily monitored. Once there is an initial basis for trust, larger steps may be possible. *Recategorization* involves encouraging parties to a social dilemma to see themselves not as separate entities but as a single group confronting a common problem. This often involves invoking a superordinate category. For example, in dealing with oil-consuming nations, Saudi Arabia might represent itself as Saudi Arabia, the largest oil-producing country in the world, or as OPEC member Saudi Arabia. The distinction is subtle but important because the difference signals the priority of collective interests over self-interests.

These three techniques for making group identity salient may work somewhat differently for people from collectivist and individualist cultures. In collectivist cultures, the unit of social perception is the group, the self is viewed as interdependent with social identity groups, in-group goals have primacy over personal goals, and in-group harmony is valued. In contrast, the unit of social perception in individualist cultures is the individual, the self is viewed as an independent rather than a socially interdependent entity, personal goals are primary, in-group goals are secondary, and in-group confrontation is acceptable.[7]

The implication of these differences between collectivist and individualist cultures is that members of collective cultures should find it easier to align personal and collective interests than members of individualist cultures. Our studies comparing U.S., Japanese, and Chinese managers participating in the SHARC social dilemma confirm this prediction. Exhibit 5.1 shows that U.S. managers confronted with a decision to reduce harvesting from the current rate of 5,000 metric tons of fish to the sustainable 2,500 metric tons did not reduce their harvesting successfully when simply confronted

EXHIBIT 5.1. Harvesting in an Asymmetric Social Dilemma.

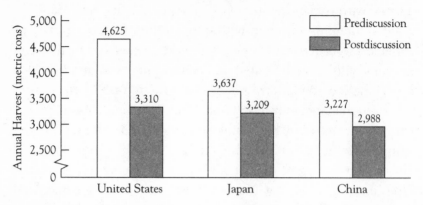

Note: Current annual harvest is 5,000 metric tons. A harvest that will sustain the resource is 2,500 metric tons.

with the problem. Only after we gave them an opportunity to discuss the harvesting problem were they able to reduce their harvesting significantly. Discussion also helped the Japanese and Chinese managers reduce their harvesting, but managers in both of these cultures were able to reduce harvesting significantly without discussion. In-depth analyses show that Japanese managers demonstrate as much self-serving or *egocentric bias* in their judgments of how much they deserve as U.S. managers. However, when making a harvesting decision prior to discussion, they harvested less, expected others in the group to harvest less, were more accurate in predicting the behavior of others, and took a more egalitarian approach to harvesting than U.S. managers did.[8] The Japanese managers' behavior suggests not only that they viewed each other as an in-group but also that their collectivist cultural norms gave them a basis for acting cooperatively in the social dilemma. They expected others to cooperate and did so themselves, confirming previous research on behavior in social dilemmas that shows strong relationships between expectations of others' cooperation and their own cooperation.[9]

How then to manage a social dilemma when parties are from individualist cultures? Exhibit 5.1 shows that communication helps managers from all three cultures, but especially managers from the United States. In the study contrasting U.S. and Japanese managers and in a previous study with just U.S. managers, communication helped the individualistic U.S. managers reduce their harvesting and be more accurate in predicting the harvesting behavior of others. The researchers speculate that hearing others articulate the logic for harvesting patterns that are different from one's own self-serving interests may lead parties to reassess their judgments of fairness. However, communication may have the same effect even if what group members discuss is not relevant, because it enhances group identity,[10] leading to recategorization. Communication may also develop commitment to a distribution norm that maximizes a collective goal, or it may assure others of each member's intention to cooperate.[11]

The risk in using recategorization to increase group salience is that the most effective way to encourage recategorization is to increase in-group salience by creating a contrast with an out-group. Group members making decisions in social dilemmas are twice as likely to cooperate when they are in an intergroup situation than when they are not.[12] This is the very familiar situation that causes the formation of alliances among nations with seemingly disparate interests against other nations or alliances. Strategists frequently use out-groups to increase cooperation among in-group members.

In weighing alternative strategies for making group identity salient and encouraging cooperation in social dilemmas, several culture-related cautions should be heeded. First, whom parties from a collectivist culture define as the out-group and whom they define as the in-group may not be the same as whom members of individualist cultures select.[13] Second, members of collectivist cultures tend to make sharper distinctions between in-groups and out-groups than members of individualist cultures do.[14] Third, members of collectivist cultures tend to cooperate more with members of their in-groups and compete more strenuously with members of out-groups than members of individualist cultures.[15]

The final question concerns what predictions can be made and advice extended for making social identity salient in the multicultural situation when parties to a social dilemma have different cultural backgrounds. Behavior in such a context may be affected both by the party's own cultural values and by expectations of others' behavior. If others are viewed as out-group members, competitive choices are likely, especially if the party is from a collectivist culture. Thus interventions to shift social identity may be necessary before the group can reach agreement on normative or regulatory standards.

Conclusion

The first step in becoming more effective in managing social dilemmas is to recognize that all dilemmas are a balance between self-interests and collective interests. The requirement to balance those interests will not disappear no matter how effectively the dilemma is managed. The challenge is to manage the balance. Regulation may be the obvious approach, but there are more subtle and more psychological approaches, including collective goals, contact, and recategorization, that may limit the need for regulation and work effectively where regulation and enforcement are not practical.

6

Government At and Around the Table

"Mickey and Minnie Go to Hong Kong" read the headlines in November 1999 as the Disney company and the Hong Kong government announced a deal after thirteen months of protracted negotiations. The agreement called for a $316 million direct investment by Disney for a 43 percent stake and $419 million from the Hong Kong government for a 57 percent stake. Hong Kong will also extend a $787 million loan and arrange $296 million in commercial loans. Total cost: $1.8 billion, with $1.5 billion coming from Hong Kong.[1]

Why did Disney choose Hong Kong instead of a China location where there would be no travel restrictions for Chinese citizens? Why partner with Hong Kong instead of an investor-developer as Disney did in Tokyo? Analyzing the motives of Disney, a global entertainment company, and Hong Kong, a relatively small government, helps illustrate how factors that are in the background in same-culture negotiations often move to the foreground in negotiations that cross cultures. Given the economic realities of doing business in China, a government partner was probably the only alternative. Why, then, Hong Kong instead of, say, Shanghai? Disney no doubt considered the economic and political stability of the former British colony. Disney may also have been betting on the power of the British-trained Hong Kong bureaucracy and the vestiges of British influence in the way Hong Kong is run. Disney is a family entertainment company with a squeaky-clean reputation. It may also have had concerns with corruption had Disney chosen an alternative site in China.

These issues: the interests of governments, political and economic stability, the power of the bureaucracy, dealing with corruption, and the legal context for dispute resolution that Disney either considered or should have considered in deciding to build its Asian theme park in Hong Kong are the focus of this chapter.

If government is not actually at the table in negotiations that cross political boundaries, it is around the table. Government provides the political and legal context for negotiations. In same-culture negotiations, this context is a fixed backdrop, and unless challenged, for example, in a dispute over the application of a law, it affects both parties similarly. When negotiations cross cultural boundaries, they occur in a context of ideological, political, and legal pluralism. Pluralism makes cross-cultural negotiations much more complex than same-culture negotiations.

The Interests of Government in Cross-Cultural Negotiations

Governments play an important role in international business. Even when cross-cultural negotiations occur between two private enterprises, ideological, political, and legal differences provide both a challenge and an opportunity. Recall the example in Chapter Three of the dispute resolution negotiations that occurred between Fusion Systems and Mitsubishi Electric. Fusion claimed and Mitsubishi counterclaimed patent infringement. Contributing to the dispute were differences in the two countries' patent laws. The U.S. system is designed to reward creativity by protecting individual inventors' rights from being infringed on by developments that do not constitute substantial innovation. The Japanese patent system, in contrast, is designed to encourage the rapid diffusion of new technological advances. After several rounds of frustrating negotiations, Fusion, as one of its negotiating strategies, lobbied successfully to involve the Office of the U.S. Trade Representative and the U.S. Congress in the dispute.[2]

In the Hong Kong–Disney negotiations, the Hong Kong government was at the table as a party, not in the background. Even with the expansion of capitalism after the fall of the Soviet Union, governments in many parts of the world participate in all sorts of business: controlling imports and exports, banking and insurance, and even some manufacturing and agriculture. Deals that in some parts of the world would be negotiated between private parties are made in other parts of the world with government ministries and state-owned corporations.

Having the government at the table raises a number of special issues for the cross-cultural negotiator. Governments' principal goals may not be cost or profitability but surely will be social, economic, and political. Governments serve at the behest of their populace and sometimes the military. In general, officials in power prefer to remain in power. It is not unreasonable to assume that political survival is an underlying interest. Governments, especially in developing countries, may also be less concerned about costs than politics because the costs of projects are often borne by international agencies, such as the U.S. Import-Export Bank or the World Bank. Although loans must be paid sometime in the future, politicians and bureaucrats, not unlike others whose incentives focus them on short-term gains, are frequently willing to sacrifice the future for immediate gains.

As in all negotiations, parties' interests make them vulnerable, and governments are no exception. Just as governments' interests are not necessarily the same as those of a private company, neither are governments' vulnerabilities. Where private companies are vulnerable to the opinions of financial markets that normally value change, governments are vulnerable to the opinions of their political supporters, religious organizations, labor unions, and the military, all groups that frequently prefer the status quo and strenuously resist change.

In 1996, Daewoo Electronics offered to buy Thomson Multimedia, a French state-owned electronics company. As part of its offer, Daewoo pledged to provide three thousand jobs and invest $1 billion in Thomson by 2000. Unemployment in France in 1996 was 12.6 percent.[3] "In an abrupt about-face and under domestic political pressure, France canceled the sale after its privatization commission objected to the provision that would cede control of the consumer-appliance maker to the South Korean company. The vice president of Daewoo Electronics said, 'There was no reason to worry about any change in working conditions and welfare' and that he hoped that the French unions, prime opponents of the deal, would realize that it was 'in their best interests and the best way to secure growth.'"[4] Although the French government's decision may seem vindicated in light of Daewoo's financial problems associated with the Asian economic crisis, the decision in 1996 was political, not prescient.

When negotiating with a government agency, there are two things you must do:

- Identify the government's interests by anticipating the reactions of various stakeholders to your initiative.

- Seek the support of those stakeholders to avoid their resistance and the risk of an aborted deal.

Ideology: Private Investment, Profits, and Individual Rights

Understanding a government's ideology should also help a cross-cultural negotiator understand its interests and vulnerabilities. Ideology refers to the theory underlying a government's social, economic, and political programs. Ideology is one aspect of culture that is likely to affect the issues that negotiators think need to be resolved, their positions on those issues, and their interests or the reasons for taking particular positions. Three elements of ideology that invariably complicate cross-cultural negotiations, at least when one party is from the United States, are private investment, profit, and individual rights.[5] Cultures differ fundamentally with respect to their positions on each of these three aspects of ideology.

U.S. negotiators generally view private investment as good. Economic incentives associated with private ownership generate efficiencies and profits to be reinvested and hence economic growth that in turn brings jobs and increases the standard of living. Negotiators from other cultures may not look so positively on private investment, especially when that private investment is foreign investment, as in France's refusing to sell Thomson to Daewoo. Exhibit 6.1 shows the 1999 World Economic Forum's rankings of fifty-nine nations in terms of economic competitiveness. The top five nations were Singapore, the United States, Hong Kong, Taiwan, and Canada. The bottom five were Russia, Ukraine, Zimbabwe, Bulgaria, and Bolivia. The index used for the rankings is based on eight criteria: openness to trade and investment, the role of the state, finance, infrastructure, technology, management, labor, and institutions.[6]

Another ideological reservation about private investment is that it can be viewed as generating wealth for a small group of investors by exploiting workers and/or the environment. Governments seek to maximize the benefits and minimize the costs of private foreign investment through regulation. However, so long as resources and low-cost labor are not equally distributed throughout the world and regulation limits but does not prohibit exploitation of workers or resources, private investors will seek profits from investments in developing countries.

Governments may not be as concerned with profits as with social or political ends. Some governments would be satisfied if foreign investments just broke even after taxes (although of course governments realize that the prospect of breaking even would not be likely to motivate foreign investment in the first place). Negotiators representing private enterprise, by contrast, generally view profit as good. Profit is a just reward for risks taken and efforts applied by the individual company. Without the incentive of profit, companies would not be motivated to take risks or apply effort. The private-enterprise view of profit is that because it can be reinvested, it will induce economic expansion, which is a benefit to all of society. This view of

EXHIBIT 6.1. Global Competitiveness Rankings for Fifty-Nine Nations, 1999.

1999 Rank (1996 Rank)	Country	Index[a]
1 (1)	Singapore	2.12
2 (4)	United States	1.58
3 (2)	Hong Kong	1.41
4 (9)	Taiwan	1.38
5 (8)	Canada	1.33
6 (6)	Switzerland	1.27
7 (5)	Luxembourg	1.25
8 (15)	United Kingdom	1.17
9 (17)	Netherlands	1.13
10 (26)	Ireland	1.11
11 (16)	Finland	1.11
12 (12)	Australia	1.04
13 (3)	New Zealand	1.01
14 (13)	Japan	1.00
15 (7)	Norway	0.92
16 (10)	Malaysia	0.86
17 (11)	Denmark	0.85
18 (27)	Iceland	0.59
19 (21)	Sweden	0.58
20 (19)	Austria	0.58
21 (18)	Chile	0.57
22 (20)	Korea	0.46
23 (23)	France	0.44
24 (25)	Belgium	0.39
25 (22)	Germany	0.39
26 (32)	Spain	0.37
27 (34)	Portugal	0.16
28 (24)	Israel	0.15
29 (–)	Mauritius	–0.09
30 (14)	Thailand	–0.10
31 (33)	Mexico	–0.20
32 (36)	China	–0.27
33 (31)	Philippines	–0.31

1999 Rank (1996 Rank)	Country	Index[a]
34 (28)	Costa Rica	–0.33
35 (41)	Italy	–0.36
36 (38)	Peru	–0.37
37 (30)	Indonesia	–0.39
38 (46)	Hungary	–0.39
39 (35)	Czech Republic	–0.40
40 (28)	Jordan	–0.51
41 (39)	Greece	–0.60
42 (37)	Argentina	–0.65
43 (44)	Poland	–0.67
44 (42)	Turkey	–0.70
45 (–)	Slovak Republic	–0.72
46 (–)	El Salvador	–0.72
47 (43)	South Africa	–0.74
48 (–)	Vietnam	–0.85
49 (29)	Egypt	–0.86
50 (47)	Venezuela	–1.09
51 (48)	Brazil	–1.20
52 (–)	India	–1.30
53 (–)	Ecuador	–1.34
54 (40)	Colombia	–1.48
55 (–)	Bolivia	–1.50
56 (–)	Bulgaria	–1.50
57 (–)	Zimbabwe	–1.65
58 (–)	Ukraine	–1.94
59 (49)	Russia	–2.02

Source: World Economic Forum.

[a]The index is based on eight criteria: openness to trade and investment, the role of the state, finance, infrastructure, technology, management, labor, and institutions.

profit is a "variable pie" mentality—the generation of resources be-
gets resources, but the "fixed pie" mentality is also widespread—
profits gained by investors are viewed as resources claimed from
others. How, then, does a negotiator representing a private company negotiate the repatriation of profits from investment in a
country whose government does not wholly embrace the ideology
of the free market?

Advice for Dealing with Government Interests, Particularly Human Rights Issues

There are some approaches that are not likely to be successful.
Although all members of a society may not ascribe to its ideologies,
it is unlikely that a negotiator, especially one representing the government, will flout ideological premises by negotiating an agreement
that contradicts a dominant ideology. It is also unlikely that a negotiator representing a private company will succeed in persuading the
government negotiator to abandon one ideology in favor of another.
Ideologies are firmly held convictions that are reinforced by social-
ization and by interaction with social institutions. They will not be
easily changed by persuasion. In addition, the integrative negotiator's fundamental strategy for resolving differences by making trade-
offs may not be successful when the differences are ideological.
Making ideological trade-offs implies that the ideology is not a social
cornerstone and portends the toppling of those social institutions
that have the ideology as a foundation. This is simply not within the
purview of commercial transactions or dispute resolution.

In short, when acting alone, negotiators must find agreements
that do not challenge conflicting ideologies. To do so takes discipline and creativity. Discipline is required to restrain the tendency
to be ethnocentric about your culture's ideologies. Getting into an
ideological struggle will not increase the likelihood of a negotiated
agreement. Creativity is required to find agreements in the spaces
between ideologies. Understanding the other party's ideology is the
first step toward negotiating an agreement. Collect economic devel-

opment plans, and meet with government officials to find out the government's priorities and the interests underlying them. Often an agreement can be structured to be consistent with an investor's interests and with a government's development policy. A widely cited example of creativity that overcame ideological differences about the repatriation of profits is the agreement in the 1970s and 1980s between the government of the Soviet Union and the Pepsi-Cola Company. Pepsi agreed to buy and export vodka in lieu of re-patriating profits from selling soft drinks in the Soviet Union.

When acting in consort with other companies, negotiators may be able to confront ideology more aggressively and find nonnegoti-ated paths of ideological resistance. General Motors and other com-panies following the Sullivan Principles in South Africa during apartheid are an example. Leon Sullivan was a GM director at the time when its board was debating whether or not to withdraw its business from South Africa because of the government's policies toward nonwhites. Sullivan designed a policy of passive disobedi-ence of the law that required treating white and nonwhite employ-ees differently. GM convinced other multinational corporations to join in flouting the law and treating all employees equally regard-less of race. The South African government, not wanting to lose the foreign investment represented by this group of multinationals, did not prosecute. It also did not capitulate. After ten years, Sul-livan concluded that the principles had not succeeded, and GM withdrew from South Africa until the end of apartheid.

Protection of the rights of the individual is a social and politi-cal tenet, not an economic one, but as the South African example illustrates, private companies become ensnared in conflict over this ideology. Protection of the rights of individuals is a fundamental tenet of Western philosophy; sublimation of the interests of the individual to the interests of the community is a fundamental tenet of Eastern philosophy. Governments that are not satisfied with other governments' positions on human rights use trade opportu-nities as leverage to bring about social and political change. Exam-ples abound: trade embargoes on South Africa during apartheid, the refusal of the European Union and the United States to aid Serbia after the war to end ethnic cleansing in Kosovo, protracted negotiations between the United States and China over its entry into the World Trade Organization. These conflicting political agendas limit companies' movement into new markets. They also raise ethical questions about whether a company should operate in a country whose government condones human rights violations.

There are both ethical and economic issues to be considered when deciding to operate in a country where rights violations (at least from a Western perspective) are rampant.[7] The ethical issue is the morality of contributing to the economy and thereby supporting a government that condones human rights violations. The economic problems need not occur in the country where the violations occur; they may occur at home, where rights-monitoring interest groups can organize public opinion in the press, at shareholders' meetings, and on an ongoing basis by visiting individual members of the corporate board and the executive committee. The World Trade Organization meetings in Seattle in 1999 and Washington, D.C., in 2000 drew thousands of activists whose demonstrations disrupted negotiations for the Millennium Round of multilateral trade agreements.

Political and Economic Stability

Where there is economic opportunity there is also risk. There is risk that the economic conditions that made the deal like BP's acquisition of Sidanko favorable will change. Sidanko's economic problems were certainly due in part to the drop in world oil prices between 1997 and 1999. There is risk like that experienced by Enron in India: Enron reached an agreement with the Congress Party to build a power plant at Dabhol, in the Indian state of Maharashtra, in February 1995. One month later, the Congress Party lost its majority in the state's government to a coalition of two other parties, Shiv Sena and BJP, that had been brought to power using the slogan "Drive Enron into the Sea." The new state government set up a committee to investigate the agreement with Enron, and six months later, even though construction had begun, the state minister canceled the project.[8] Cross-cultural negotiators need to hedge their deals as much as possible against such risks. They also need to be willing to renegotiate.

Hedging Political Risks

One strategy for hedging against political change is to frame the deal in the general interest of the citizens. Political parties find it easier to embrace arrangements with foreign investors that contribute to the general interest than arrangements that cater to the interests of a special group. Enron's power plant agreement had this characteristic. The state of Maharashtra was in dire need of additional electrical power. Enron's plant was critical to other aspects of the state's development plan. After a period in which the power plant project was placed on hold, new negotiations between Enron and the Shiv Sena–BJP coalition were successful in reframing the agreement along lines acceptable to the new government's interests. The second agreement included reducing Enron's profit margins (from 27 to 29 percent to 20 to 22 percent), adding a 30 percent Maharashtra state partner, and building a hospital, school, and training center near the plant.[9]

Another strategy, at least in democratic states, is to maintain cordial relations with members of minority parties as well as with members of the majority party. After Enron's first contract was canceled, its divisional CEO, Rebecca Mark, set up a semipermanent base for herself in India.[10] She was joined there by Kenneth Lay, the company's chairman. Together these two top-ranking executives met repeatedly with government officials at the state and national levels and with local party officials from BJP and Shiv Sena. The ongoing presence of the two high-ranking company officers signaled Enron's willingness to seek a second negotiated agreement, even though its lawyers in London were moving ahead with arbitration (Enron's BATNA). Enron's team in India held one-on-one meetings with as many Shiv Sena and BJP party leaders and politicians as possible, as well as with journalists and other opinion leaders. Enron was no novice in negotiating with national governments. What Enron learned in India was how much attention needs to be paid to local government.

Relationships are important in all cultures and overwhelmingly important for successful negotiations in some. Maintaining relationships across the political spectrum and at national and local levels, prior to, during, and after the negotiation, is a wise investment for the cross-cultural negotiator. Enron may not have been able to develop relationships across the political spectrum in advance of the change in government, but once the government did change, Enron maintained daily contact with officials between April and August, when the contract nevertheless was canceled. The new government, given its campaign slogan, was probably not in a position to reopen negotiations with Enron without first following through on its political threats. The contacts between April and August and Mark and Lay's personal presence after the contract was canceled kept the focus on relationships and a new agreement rather than on Enron's very unappealing BATNA to arbitrate its losses.

Hedging Economic Risks

There are two related types of economic risks associated with cross-cultural negotiations. The first is the economic stability of the country in which the negotiated deal is to be enacted. The second, a closely related issue, is the stability of its currency. When a country becomes economically unstable, its currency will collapse. However, even without economic instability, currency may lose value. For example, the euro consistently lost ground against the dollar and the yen during its first year (1999), despite economic stability in Europe.

Economic stability means controlled growth, controlled inflation, and controlled unemployment. The benchmark, at least throughout the 1990s, seemed to be single digits on all three indicators. Rampant growth, as was characteristic of the Asian economies in the mid-1990s, is alluring to foreign investors. Although many multinational corporations experienced significant losses when the Asian economic bubble burst, beginning with the Thai baht's dramatic downfall during the summer of 1997, most were hedged by the diversity of their markets and the continuing strength of the U.S. economy. Hedging against the economic stability of a country means having investments in more and in less risky markets.

Hedging against currency fluctuations depends on whether the money is movable or immovable.[11] Movable money is currency that is easily convertible—dollars, yen, euros; immovable money is currency that is not freely convertible and for which governments "regulate the entry to, possession in, and exit from their territories of both foreign and local currencies."[12]

Hedging against movable money currency fluctuations can be managed in the futures market or in the negotiated deal. Hedging in the futures market essentially shifts the risk to a third party.[13] Our focus here is negotiations.

One way to negotiate a hedge against currency fluctuations is to limit the term of a contract or to include a renegotiation clause that specifies the conditions under which the contract will be reopened. Both types of contracts prevent parties from being locked into prices that make no sense for either of them given changes in currency valuation. Consider the fate of a Thai company producing athletic shoes for a U.S. company. The agreement, negotiated in 1996, provided that the Thai company be paid entirely in baht at a rate that at the time provided it with profits over its costs, all of which were paid in baht. This was a reasonable deal for both companies when it was negotiated. However, when the baht lost its value in the summer of 1997, the U.S. company began making extraordinary excess profits. It was able to buy many more baht for the same amount of dollars. This made the shoes cost the U.S. company less, but it was still selling the shoes for the same price in dollars as before the baht decreased in value. Because of inflation that accompanied the drop in the baht, the Thai company was no longer making money on the shoe contract.

Why would negotiators, especially ones from countries whose currencies are stable, enter into a contract that essentially rules out excess profits due to currency fluctuations? The question itself is cultural, for negotiators from hierarchical cultures might not even consider this a question. It is the negotiator from the egalitarian-individualist culture (such as the United States), where all parties look out for their own interests, who may find it difficult to contemplate a renegotiation clause. For example, in the 1990's Rubbermaid was the leading brand-name maker of common kitchenware and household items like laundry baskets. But when the price for the main component in its products, resin, more than tripled between 1994 and 1996, Wal-Mart [Rubbermaid's biggest customer] balked at paying increased prices. When Rubbermaid insisted, Wal-Mart relegated the manufacturer's items to undesirable shelf space and used its market power to promote a Rubbermaid rival.[14] According to Carl Steidmann, an economist with Pricewaterhouse-Coopers, Wal-Mart is the "epitome of capitalism."[15]

The negotiator from the hierarchical-collectivist culture is more likely to presume that risk must be shared and accept that unforeseen circumstances are legitimate reasons for reopening negotiations. When cultures value relationships, negotiators are more likely to think that windfall profits due to currency fluctuations are to be made in the currency markets, not at the cost of the viability of your business partner.

When money is immovable, it is more difficult to repatriate profits in a hard currency. After all, the reason the country has instituted currency controls is to reduce currency flight. In this situation, it is essential to negotiate arrangements for payment. Creativity and expert advice are key. Many options have been used more or less successfully. Negotiating a foreign currency allotment from the country's central bank is one approach. Beware, however: central bank regulations can change abruptly, and new regulations can be applied retroactively. Structuring the transaction so that profits are withdrawn in ways other than cash is acceptable in some countries with currency restrictions. Two examples are royalties on technology and inflated prices for raw materials. And there is always countertrade. Indeed, some countries require countertrade as part of any agreement. Be especially careful to find out prior to negotiating a price whether countertrade will be required because the transaction costs of countertrade will change the cost structure of the deal. There are various forms of countertrade with different transaction cost structures. Pepsi for vodka, the countertrade arrangement with the Soviet Union, is an example of pure barter. Other countertrade examples are more indirect—for example, in exchange for supplying shoe manufacturing equipment to a Thai company, taking payment in shoes manufactured by that company, or agreeing to buy for hard currency products produced in the host country or to reinvest profits in other host-country companies. Countertrade makes deals possible where otherwise there would be none. However, it is not without risks. The Soviets offered Pepsi vodka, Lada cars, or caviar. Pepsi wisely stuck close to its own business by limiting its countertrade to vodka. Coke took the much less attractive Lada deal, underestimating the cost of transporting these automobiles to the U.S. market and, even worse, U.S. consumers' aversion to buying them.

Power of the Bureaucracy

In December 1985, the French national government, in a dramatic change in policy regarding foreign investment, signed a letter of intent with Disney to construct and operate a theme park twenty miles outside of Paris in Marne-la-Vallée. Before a final agreement could be negotiated, however, a conservative government replaced the socialist government, and Disney was introduced to thirty-six new French negotiators. Joe Shapiro, Disney's lead negotiator, said: "It was like coming to the United States and trying to make a deal with the President of the United States, the Secretary of Defense, the Secretary of State, the Secretary of Transportation; and it also has to be approved by the House and the Senate. Then you have to make a deal with the governor of California, the county of Los Angeles, the city of Los Angeles, the Burbank Redevelopment Agency, and you have to go to the southern California rapid transit people."[16] A final agreement was not signed until March 1987. Jean-René Bernard, who eventually became the lead negotiator for the French side, did not have an easy time of it either. The vocal socialists in France argued strongly that the government's money should be spent on housing and other immediate economic needs rather than lending Disney $770 million, or about 40 percent of the cost of the entire project, and investing $150 million to build an extension of a commuter rail line. Local French farmers resisted the government's efforts to acquire their land.

Negotiating globally, it is wise to learn about the bureaucracy at all levels of the government. What you are seeking is information that will help you discover bureaucratic interests relevant to negotiating the deal and implementing it.

- What is the country's bureaucratic structure?
- Are policy decisions made or only implemented by the bureaucracy?
- What decisions are implemented at what level of the bureaucracy?
- How do bureaucrats get their jobs? Are they elected, appointed, hired on merit?
- What are the relationships between various agencies and between national and local levels?
- Is there a climate of corruption and extortion?

Some bureaucratic interests should be easy to anticipate. When the French branch of an international consulting firm signed a contract to audit the efficiency of several ministries of a North African nation, the consultants were stymied by lack of cooperation. In negotiating the contract, the consulting firm failed to understand two important facts. First, bureaucrats in the ministries being audited feared that the consultants' report would be damaging and that they would lose their jobs directly for lack of efficiencies or indirectly as a result of the implementation of the efficiencies suggested by the consultants. It is usually valid to assume that bureaucrats will resist change. Second, the consultants failed to understand that they were being used as pawns by the hiring ministry to gain prominence over the audited ministries. It is also usually valid to assume that there are competing factions within bureaucracies, either between ministries or between national and local agencies.

Other bureaucratic interests may be unique to the context of the negotiations, and therefore local advice is essential. The lack of warmth with which the Disney managers were initially received by local government officials in Marne-la-Vallée was no doubt due to many factors beyond the Americans' desire for the French bureaucracy to respond more quickly. Local government officials were not consulted about the negotiations that led to the choice of Marne-la-Vallée over sites in Spain. The French have a love-hate relationship with American culture, and there was widespread distaste for the culture represented by Disney theme parks and the types of jobs that such parks provide.

One pitfall in dealing with a bureaucracy is failing to understand the bureaucracy's interests. Another pitfall is underestimating its power. Bureaucracies are usually entrenched. Their BATNA is usually to keep operating as they have always done, outlasting the pressures of elected parties and foreign investors. To get a bureaucracy to change requires helping the bureaucracy understand that change will occur regardless of the bureaucracy's interests. Then smart bureaucrats, realizing they cannot stop change, will likely participate in order to protect their interests, and smart foreign investors will let them do just that.

Disney in France initially misjudged both the interests of the local Marne-la-Vallée bureaucracy and its power. The site Disney and the French government chose for what has become today Disneyland Paris was an agricultural community. Local governments were not involved in the negotiations leading to the site selection. Distressed by the threat a Disney park posed to their traditional lifestyles, the communities and their officials reacted. Some probably harbored the hope that Disney would choose another location. At one point, striking farmers blocked the entrance to the park itself.[17] In the end, the communities used their considerable moral power to force Disney and the French national government to pay attention to their needs. Disney, possibly misled by the enthusiasm of French tourists for Walt Disney World in Florida, had not anticipated the reaction of the French interests to foreign investment, commercial development, and America's Mickey Mouse culture.

Dealing with Corruption

Bureaucracies can also be rife with *corruption*—the unethical use of authority for the purpose of personal gain, including situations in which the rules of participation are unclear, changing, differentially applied, or tainted by nepotism, bribery, extortion, or embezzlement. Yet a practice that is unethical in one culture may be perfectly acceptable in another. Cronyism—handing out political appointments according to who knows whom rather than according to qualifications—has characterized business in Asia for centuries. These practices did not prevent the Asian miracle of the 1990s, and it is difficult to blame them for the 1997–1998 Asian financial crisis, given that the 1999 recovery was not accompanied by wide-scale reforms. Whether these practices are viewed as unethical or not and whether they characterize the bureaucracy or private relationships or both, government in some countries in 1999 (Russia and Indonesia are two examples) was incapable of enforcing anticorruption laws. Thus cross-cultural negotiators must be prepared to deal with corruption.

Negotiators' ethical standards affect their reservation prices. Ethical standards provide a criterion in addition to BATNA for determining at what point the negotiator should walk away from the table. Therefore, cross-cultural negotiators need to have a clear understanding of their own ethical standards. They also need to know what they can do about unethical behavior on the part of others.

The U.S. Foreign Corrupt Practices Act, passed in 1977, prohibits the use of bribery and extortion and provides an ethical guideline for U.S. negotiators. U.S. companies routinely brief their negotiators not to pay bribes, give in to extortion, or accept personal gifts. The twenty-nine member countries of the Organization for Economic Cooperation and Development (OECD) have signed the organization's Convention on Combating Bribery in International Business Transactions. The convention targets the offering side of the bribery transaction in an effort to eliminate the supply of bribes to foreign officials. Signatories take the responsibility for the activities of companies registered in their states. Signatories are passing and implementing tough legislation against transnational bribery with dissuasive sanctions. OECD has recommendations against the tax deductibility of bribes, for combating corruption in aid-funded procurement, and ending money laundering. Exhibit 6.2 lists the twenty-nine OECD members and the five nonmember nations that have signed the convention. The World Bank, with 181 member countries, has adopted guidelines that make companies found to have engaged in corrupt or fraudulent practices in competing for or in executing a bank-financed contract ineligible to bid on future bank-financed contracts.[18]

Despite the growing recognition that corruption has a corrosive impact on poor countries, corruption thrives when companies are willing to pay officials for contracts. Allegations filed on July 28, 1999, by the Lesotho government against Masupha Sole, former head of the Highlands Water Project in Lesotho, a southern African kingdom, charge that twelve international companies bidding

EXHIBIT 6.2. Signers of the OECD Convention on Combating Bribery of Foreign Public Officials in International Business Transactions.

Member Signatories

Australia	Hungary	Poland
Austria	Iceland	Portugal
Belgium	Italy	Spain
Canada	Japan	Sweden
Czech Republic	Korea	Switzerland
Denmark	Luxembourg	Turkey
Finland	Mexico	United Kingdom
France	Netherlands	United States
Germany	New Zealand	
Greece	Norway	

Nonmember Signatories

Argentina
Brazil
Bulgaria
Chile
Slovak Republic

Source: Organization for Economic Cooperation and Development.

on dam-building and engineering projects paid Sole $2 million for consideration.[19]

Advice for Making Ethical Decisions in Cross-Cultural Negotiations

Negotiators who lack a legal standard on which to base ethical judgments must determine their own ethical course, balancing profits and ethics to generate a companywide policy, or make ethical choices on a situation-by-situation basis. Anyone involved in making ethical decisions recognizes that there is much more to being an ethical negotiator than merely conforming to the standards of the Foreign Corrupt Practices Act or the OECD convention. Negotiation itself poses a dilemma of honesty. The more open you are about your preferences, the more vulnerable to exploitation you become. There are incentives in negotiation to misrepresent your preferred settlement or reservation price, to bluff by making false threats or promises, to falsify by introducing untrue information, to deceive by leading others to draw false conclusions, and to disclose information selectively. There are no professional, national, or international guidelines for managers that provide ethical standards for resolving the dilemma of honesty in negotiation. These standards are at the discretion of the negotiator.

How, then, does a cross-cultural negotiator, or any negotiator for that matter, construct standards for ethical conduct? Moral philosophy suggests two approaches.[20] *Utilitarianism* judges the morality of an act by the consequences it produces, and those consequences are evaluated against either a "greatest good" criterion or against a set of principles. The philosophy of *relativism* judges the morality of an act by its acceptability in the context.

Relativism justifies engaging in corruption in corrupt environments; yet even in the absence of an international anticorruption treaty, many companies on principle refuse to engage in or support corrupt practices. Why do they do so when in the short term, paying the bribe means getting the business and not paying means losing the bid to a company that will? They do so because they believe that an ethical basis for interaction is a fundamental structural imperative for a democratic society and a free economy. The decision whether to engage in or reject corrupt practices is ultimately a social dilemma. If all parties engage in corrupt practices, trust will be low, transaction costs will be high, and integrative potential will go unrealized. If all parties refuse to engage in corrupt practices, trust will be high, transaction costs will be low, and integrative potential will be realized. The interesting case is when some parties reject corrupt practices and others engage in them. Research and theory suggest that in large groups in which some parties are ethical and others unethical, over time the ethical parties will choose to interact with each other, ultimately generating an environment for which unethical parties are unfit.[21]

Cooperation is ultimately a long-term utilitarian response. In the short term, being ethical costs. "Just say no," the strategy suggested by a Mexican government official when questioned about corruption at a Latin American business conference at Kellogg, satisfies your own ethical standards. However, it does nothing to change the practice of corruption and may mean that you will lose the business opportunity. (Caving in to extortion, of course, reinforces the practice and may cause it to escalate.)

Negotiators willing to apply moral imagination can sometimes generate strategies that may actually stymie an unscrupulous opponent. Like the Wicked Witch of the West in *The Wizard of Oz* who could not stand water, corruption cannot sustain itself in the spotlight of publicity. Corruption thrives in environments in which information is controlled and withers in the light of public scrutiny. As part of its response to the Asian financial crisis, the International Monetary Fund (IMF) pressed countries to publish more financial information, which is now available on its Web site (http://www.imf.org). In Indonesia in 1999, the fact that government was unable or unwilling to prosecute corruption did not stop the Indonesian Bank Restructuring Agency from resorting to a strategy of shaming. It began publishing the names of the country's one hundred worst debtors in local newspapers.[22]

Choosing to expose corruption and holding people accountable for actions that have inflicted harm on others is a negotiation strategy itself. Confronted with corruption and being unwilling to acquiesce, the global negotiator must consider the costs and benefits of whistle-blowing. Exposing corruption takes moral courage. It is much easier to simply cut your losses and walk away from corruption than to face it down. For these reasons, when confronting corruption, a collective response is likely to be stronger and more effective than an individual response. Parties who would not confront corruption on their own may be willing to engage in joint action. Those who are willing to confront corruption will be more powerful. As the companies that subscribed to the Sullivan Principles and collectively disobeyed South African law learned, it is more difficult to be prosecuted when acting in concert.

How far can a cross-cultural negotiator go in confronting a corrupt opponent? Should negotiators acting on the part of their organizations give financial support to encourage the overthrow of a corrupt government? Traders and merchants have done so for centuries, and there is a vivid modern example in ITT's involvement with the CIA to destabilize the political situation in Chile and help usher in the Pinochet regime.[23] Current theorizing about business ethics draws the line at collaborating in the overthrow of governments. Besides, at the end of the twentieth century, the IMF seems to have taken on this role. Its outgoing head, Michel Camdessus, acknowledged that the IMF "created the conditions that obliged President Suharto to leave his job" as president of Indonesia and that President Boris Yeltsin of Russia was warned by the IMF that the same forces could end his control in Russia.[24]

Companies who find themselves facing corruption in global negotiations have at least the following options:

- Publicizing the corruption
- Uniting with other firms to resist the corruption

- Promoting local laws and institutions to contain the corruption

- Leaving or choosing not to invest at all

Legal Context for Dispute Resolution in Cross-Cultural Negotiations

There is a risk inherent in all negotiations that the goodwill and good intentions generated at the negotiation table will fade when parties must turn to implementation. In cross-cultural negotiations, so much can go wrong: the central bank refuses to authorize the repatriation of profits in hard currency, the goods you were to receive in barter have not been supplied, building permits are delayed, your technicians' visas have been revoked. Planning for dispute resolution during deal making is especially important when negotiating globally because cross-cultural deals are captives of legal pluralism: two or more tax systems, two or more legal systems, and two or more court systems. Rather than cope with legal plurality after disputes arise, it is wise to plan for dispute resolution at the time the deal is negotiated.

Negotiators who are reluctant to raise such issues before a deal is finalized, fearing that doing so will taint the trust developed during negotiation, should keep in mind that a sovereign state has the power to take property, cancel contracts, and halt business activity.[25] Any of those actions will cost you money. If you are not willing to cut your losses and leave, if you want to be compensated, who will make the decision? Without a dispute resolution clause that specifies judicial jurisdiction, the most you can hope for is hometown justice—decisions by local courts that may elevate national interests above those of foreign investors.

A dispute resolution clause should specify the jurisdiction to which the contract terms are subject. English common law dominates international business,[26] but any legal system that has a well-specified commercial code will do. The clause should state that in the event of a dispute, the parties should endeavor to negotiate a resolution. Specifying the form of that negotiation, for example, direct negotiation between disputing parties, may not be wise, as parties from some cultures may be uncomfortable negotiating the resolution of disputes in that manner and prefer to involve third parties. Regardless of the direct or indirect negotiation preferences of the cultures involved, the dispute resolution clause also should provide for neutral third-party assistance, in the form of mediation and arbitration, that is outside the influence of either of the disputing parties. In mediation, as described in Chapter Three, the third party tries to facilitate an agreement but does not have the authority to impose a settlement. When parties hope to continue their relationship, mediation is the preferred third-party procedure, as a mediator may be able to help the parties negotiate a settlement that preserves the relationship. When the relationship has ended and the claim is for damages, arbitration may be preferable because it is binding.

Conclusion

Government plays an important role in cross-cultural negotiations. Often in global negotiations, government is at the table as a party. In that case, government's interests, ideologies, and ethics need to be dealt with directly. When government is not a party, global negotiators must still deal with the ideological, political, and legal differences that are a subtext to their positions on the issues being negotiated.

Understanding the ideological, political, and legal environment of a global negotiation may make the difference between an agreement and an impasse. It may make the difference between a deal that is profitable for the private company and a deal that meets the government's social and political standards. It may make the difference between a dispute that can be resolved in private, where a relationship can be preserved, and a dispute that is argued in a public forum, where relationships are irrevocably broken. Such understanding does not come without effort and investment. It requires study and planning; it requires time, patience, and creativity; it requires weighing the advice of legal and cultural experts; and sometimes it requires moral courage.

7

Culture Matters

The premise of this book is that national culture matters when parties negotiate. Yet as technology makes our world smaller and smaller, some analysts argue that we are moving rapidly toward one global culture, especially in the context of business. As English has come to dominate global business transactions, won't Western negotiation strategies soon dominate global negotiations? Isn't it just a matter of time until the culture of negotiation is direct confrontation and direct information sharing, where self-interests motivate targets and BATNAs underlie reservation prices? The answer is probably not, and there are several reasons why not.

Cultural differences in negotiation strategy are not trivial. There is quite a bit of evidence that culture affects the way people negotiate. There are cultural differences in negotiators' goals (self-interests versus collective interests), their conception of power (status versus BATNA), their use of influence (sparingly versus strongly), and the way they share information (direct versus indirect). There are cultural differences in negotiators' preferences for direct and indirect confrontation when resolving disputes and in their willingness to participate meaningfully in multicultural teams and to cooperate when self- and collective interests are in conflict. There are cultural differences in the contexts in which negotiations occur, especially in the role of government.

There are good reasons for these cultural differences that make it unlikely that Western negotiation strategies will dominate global negotiations or that strategic adjustments made to smooth cross-cultural economic interactions will cause major cultural change in same-culture interactions. The model in Chapter One suggests that culture affects negotiators' interests and priorities and their strategies for getting what they want in a negotiation. Cultural differences in interests and priorities are linked to differences in cultural values and cultural ideologies. Homogenization of negotiators' interests and priorities would require a homogenization of cultural values and ideologies. This seems unlikely given that homogenization is antithetical to the nature of individualist cultures.

Cultural differences in negotiation strategy are tied to cultural norms for interaction in interpersonal situations that are not limited to economic activity. For example, cultural norms govern interpersonal relations in the family, in the community, in schools, and in social and political organizations. A shift in negotiating strategy to resolve a dispute cross-culturally is not likely to generalize to economic or noneconomic interactions at home and in the community. The Western manager in the U.S.-Chinese joint venture who learned to involve the Chinese boss in conflict within the venture is unlikely to involve his boss in conflicts when posted back to the United States, where such behavior is not normative.

If you want to be an effective negotiator in a global environment, reaching integrative agreements and claiming distributive value, you are going to have to recognize that culture does matter and be prepared for cultural differences at the negotiation table. It may be a little bit easier to deal with interests and priorities that are culturally based than with negotiation strategies.

Interests and Priorities

Be prepared for interests and priorities to have a cultural basis. If you are proposing to bring economic development to a region, find out how people in the region feel about economic development before you get to the negotiation table. Prepare for the negotiation by understanding the culture. See how the culture is classified according to the cultural values of individualism versus collectivism and egalitarianism versus hierarchy.[1] Do some background research so that you have a good understanding of the other negotiator's political, economic, and social environment. Make sure you have your own interpreter. Use your interpreter to help you understand the cultural factors influencing the other party's interests and priorities.

Once you understand the other party's interests and priorities, you can treat them as you would interests and priorities in a domestic negotiation. First, they should be respected and treated seriously. Interests that may seem irrational to you may be firmly grounded in cultural values and cultural tradition. Second, keep your own interests in mind. Third, propose trade-offs. Do not give up easily searching for an integrative agreement.

Negotiation Strategy

Dealing with cultural differences in negotiation strategy requires making decisions about whether to adjust your strategy to the other side's or to maintain your own. Sometimes there is no choice. At other times maintaining your preferred strategy may put you at a disadvantage in terms of claiming distributive value.

Confrontation

If you prefer direct confrontation, you may have to adjust your strategy when in conflict with someone who prefers indirect confrontation. You cannot negotiate with someone who will not talk with you! Remember that in a dispute, BATNAs are linked. If the other party does not want to negotiate directly but does want to involve a third party, his BATNA is your BATNA. What to do? The first step is preparation. If you think the other party is likely to prefer indirect confrontation, you have to decide whether to even try direct confrontation. You will want information about how this party normally manages conflict situations to help you make this decision. Before you choose a strategy, consider the other party's BATNA. If he refuses to talk directly, what will he do? What third party might he involve in the conflict? Think about what third party is likely to support his interests. Consider other third parties that you might involve preemptively who might be favorable to your interests.

When making decisions in multicultural teams, indirect confrontation may be more effective than direct confrontation when managing procedural and interpersonal conflict. However, if the task requires the knowledge, skills, and commitment of all the team members, task conflict needs to be confronted directly. Chapter Four discusses how to develop team identity and meaningful participation norms that can be used both to encourage and to control participation in team decision making. Chapter Four also describes the mutual-gains decision strategy that can generate integrative agreements rather than the distributive outcomes likely if one party decides or the majority rules.

Information Sharing

If you prefer direct information sharing, you may have to adjust your strategy when negotiating with someone who prefers indirect information sharing or else risk being taken advantage of. The advantage of direct information sharing is that when it works as it is supposed to work, what might be called quick trust develops. As the parties reveal their interests and those interests are treated with respect, the parties begin to develop a relationship based on mutual respect and reciprocity. If reciprocity does not develop, the negotiator who reveals the most information is likely to get the worst of a distributive outcome.

Using proposals does not generate quick trust because the process does not require that first vulnerable step of revealing information. (Proposals can be anchored to maximize your own gains.) But proposals can be extremely useful. They link integrative and distributive outcomes. They also act like a truth serum when negotiators are less than forthcoming about their interests. It is easy to reach integrative agreements when negotiators are willing to exchange information directly about preferences and priorities. The problem is that even within cultures that rely on direct information sharing, negotiators may be reluctant to share information. Regardless of whether most of your negotiations occur in a direct or an indirect culture, you will want to be proficient using proposals.

Influence

If you are from a hierarchical culture where negotiations are about influencing the other party and you are negotiating with someone from an egalitarian culture where influence attempts are kept to a minimum in negotiations, be aware that you may initiate a conflict spiral and an impasse. Conflict spirals are a risk in any culture when negotiators become focused on who is right and who is wrong or who has the most power, whether that power has to do with status or alternatives. In our studies, Japanese negotiators used influence freely both in deal making and dispute resolution.[2] Nevertheless, Japanese negotiators reached agreements that were almost as integrative on average as those of the top-performing Israelis (see Exhibit 2.6). This is evidence that a focus on influence in negotiation does not have to generate conflict spirals and impasses or skewed distributive agreements. However, consider what might happen in a cross-cultural negotiation between a Japanese negotiator used to relying heavily on influence strategies and a U.S. negotiator who is used to using influence sparingly but is prepared to reciprocate influence with influence. If the Japanese negotiator uses influence, the U.S. negotiator is likely to reciprocate, and a conflict spiral is likely to ensue. When we invited Japanese managers working for Japanese companies in the United States to negotiate with U.S. managers, the result was low joint gains (see Exhibit 2.6), but the reason was not as we expected, a conflict spiral. Japanese-U.S. cross-cultural negotiators used less influence than Japanese same-culture negotiators and less influence than U.S. same-culture negotiators.[3] Japanese negotiators adjusted their use of influence from what is normative in their culture.[4] They avoided a conflict spiral, but they did not create integrative value.

There is a place for influence strategies in negotiation. Chapter Three points out two situations in which to use influence: when a negotiator will not come to the table[5] and when negotiations have broken down and all other attempts to restart them have failed. However, our studies of Japanese negotiators suggest a different way to think about using influence in hierarchical cultures like theirs where using influence in negotiation is normative. Underlying the Japanese negotiators' influence attempts is a presumption that their side deserves more from the other. When both sides think they are entitled and deserve more, negotiators can either reach an impasse or get creative. The Japanese negotiators' motivation to integrate came from below, so to speak, from their confidence in their power. In contrast, the Israeli negotiators' motivation to integrate came from above, their high targets reflecting their self-interests.

Cooperative and Individualistic Motivation

If you are from a collective culture and tend to cooperate with in-group members and compete with out-group members, you may be disadvantaged when negotiating across cultures unless you make some strategic adjustments. Cooperative negotiators are capable of integrating, but they risk compromising and reaching a distributive outcome. High self-goals, a sense of entitlement, and good alternatives motivate negotiators to search for alternative settlements. That search may turn up an integrative agreement. When both negotiators are cooperative and there is a large area of agreement, there may not be enough tension in the negotiation to motivate negotiators to search beyond a satisfactory but suboptimal outcome. Searching for an integrative agreement does not have to be a power contest. The process of searching for an integrative agreement can be hard on the relationship, but it does not have to be. The direct information-sharing approach builds a relationship of trust during the process of sharing the information needed to construct an integrative agreement.

Excellent Global Negotiators

Excellent global negotiators know that to make deals, resolve disputes, and reach decisions across cultural boundaries, they must exercise strategic flexibility. Although culture will very likely affect negotiators' interests and priorities, negotiators need do nothing out of the ordinary to integrate those interests once they understand them. It is the process of understanding negotiators' interests that is likely to require strategic flexibility when negotiating across cultures. So long as strategy stays within ethical boundaries, excellent global negotiators are less concerned how their interests are met than that their interests are met.

Notes

Preface

1. Disney sources include M. Landler, "Mickey and Minnie Go to Hong Kong," *New York Times*, Nov. 3, 1999, pp. C1, C14; R. Grover, *The Disney Touch* (Homewood, Ill.: Business One/Irwin, 1991); S. Waxman, "The Key to the Magic Kingdom," *Washington Post*, Oct. 13, 1992, p. C1.

2. M. H. Bazerman and M. A. Neale, *Negotiating Rationally* (New York: Free Press, 1992); D. G. Pruitt, *Negotiation Behavior* (Orlando, Fla.: Academic Press, 1981); L. L. Thompson, *Making the Team* (Upper Saddle River, N.J.: Prentice Hall, 1999); L. L. Thompson, *The Mind and Heart of the Negotiator* (Upper Saddle River, N.J.: Prentice Hall, 1998); W. L. Ury, J. M. Brett, and S. B. Goldberg, *Getting Disputes Resolved: Designing a System to Cut the Costs of Conflict* (San Francisco: Jossey-Bass, 1988; Cambridge, Mass.: Harvard Program on Negotiation, 1993); L. R. Weingart, R. J. Bennett, and J. M. Brett, "The Impact of Consideration of Issues and Motivational Orientation on Group Negotiation Process and Outcome," *Journal of Applied Psychology*, 1993, 78, 504–517.

3. The negotiation exercises that I have used in data collection, as well as the exercises that I use in teaching culture and negotiation, are available on CD along with teaching notes from Dispute Resolution Research Center, Kellogg Graduate School of Management, Northwestern University, Evanston, IL 60208,

847-491-8068, *drrc@northwestern.edu*, http://www.kellogg.
nwu.edu/research/disp_res/index.htm.

Chapter One

1. N. Banerjee, "BP's Losses in Russia Seen as a Warning for
   Investors," *International Herald Tribune*, Aug. 13–14, 1999, pp. 9, 13.

2. Individuals are members of many different cultural groups in addition
   to their nation-state. Furthermore, cultural subgroups are embedded
   within nation-state cultural groups. This all gets rather confusing. So
   when doing cultural research, it is imperative to identify the type of
   group you are studying. In our studies, negotiators bring their individual differences to the table; they bring their employer's culture to the
   table, the culture of their ethnic group, and their national culture.
   We are interested only in the cultures of nation-states, and those cultures are relevant only if there are systematic differences between
   them. This requirement is a reasonably high hurdle for the research. If
   there are no differences between national cultural groups, then there
   is no basis for drawing cultural inferences.

3. A. L. Lytle, J. M. Brett, Z. I. Barsness, C. H. Tinsley, and
   M. Janssens, "A Paradigm for Confirmatory Cross-Cultural
   Research in Organizational Behavior," in L. L. Cummings and
   B. M. Staw (eds.), *Research in Organizational Behavior* (Greenwich,
   Conn.: JAI Press, 1995).

4. S. T. Fiske and S. E. Taylor, *Social Cognition* (New York: McGraw-
   Hill, 1991).

5. U.S. companies apparently do not learn well from each other's
   experiences. Mondavi Vineyards announced in May 2000 that it
   was planning to lease a forested hillside above Aniane, near Mont-
   pellier, to produce France's first foreign-owned *vin de terroir*.
   Mondavi expected Aniane's 2,120 inhabitants to be pleased that
   this fine American company would be pumping $8 million into the
   local economy over the next ten years. Instead, villagers protested
   the destruction of the communal forest where they hunt wild boar;
   V. Walt, "French Village Unwilling to Welcome Mondavi," *International Herald Tribune*, July 20, 2000, p. 11.

6. Ury, Brett, and Goldberg, *Getting Disputes Resolved.*

7. J. French and B. Raven, "The Bases of Social Power," in D. Cartwright (ed.), *Studies in Social Power* (Ann Arbor, Mich.: Institute for Social Research, 1959).

8. R. Fisher, W. Ury, B. Patton, *Getting to Yes* (New York: Penguin, 1991).

9. Office of the U.S. Trade Representative, "USTR Kantor Makes Preliminary Decision That EU Banana Regime Harms U.S. Interests" (press release), Jan, 9, 1999.

10. G. Hofstede, *Culture's Consequences: International Differences in Work-Related Values* (Thousand Oaks, Calif.: Sage, 1980); S. Schwartz, "Beyond Individualism/Collectivism: New Cultural Dimensions of Values," in H. C. Triandis, U. Kim, and G. Yoon (eds.), *Individualism and Collectivism* (London: Sage, 1994); H. C. Triandis, *Individualism and Collectivism* (Boulder, Colo.: Westview Press, 1995).

11. J. C. Turner, *Rediscovering the Social Group: A Self-Categorization Theory* (Cambridge: Blackwell, 1987).

12. Triandis, *Individualism and Collectivism.*

13. Hofstede, *Culture's Consequences;* Schwartz, "Beyond Individualism/Collectivism."

14. W. B. Gudykunst, G. Gao, K. L. Schmidt, T. Nishida, M. H. Bond, K. Leung, G. Wang, and R. A. Barraclough, "The Influence of Individualism-Collectivism, Self-Monitoring, and Predicted Outcome Value on Communication in Ingroup and Outgroup Relationships," *Journal of Cross-Cultural Psychology,* 1992, *23,* 196–213.

15. A more technical and psychologically insightful explanation for why negotiators from collectivist cultures are reluctant to use confrontation focuses on the importance of in-groups in these cultures. In-groups provide social identity to their members. In a collectivist culture, group-based social identity is very important because individual needs and values are subordinate to collective needs and values. People do not want to risk ostracism from in-groups that confer identity and social benefits. For this reason, cooperation and harmony with in-group members is emphasized. Confronting a member

214 NOTES

of an in-group signals a lack of respect for that person, and for yourself, since you are both members of the same social identity group; Turner, *Rediscovering the Social Group*; see also the discussion of direct and indirect confrontation in Chapter Three of this book.

16. As a member of a Western culture, I admit that I find it difficult to understand how being told no indirectly by the boss is going to preserve my relationship with my peer, whom I originally asked for something and who did not respond to that request. Some things about culture you just have to accept, and one of them seems to be that in some cultures, involving the boss (indirect confrontation) is seen as a way of preserving the peer relationship and in others it is not. Recognizing the difference does not mean that you have to accept it as your own way of interpreting the situation, just that there is another way to frame the same situation that is legitimate in other cultures.

17. Schwartz, "Beyond Individualism/Collectivism."

18. K. Leung, "Negotiation and Reward Allocations Across Cultures," in P. C. Earley, M. Erez, and Associates, *New Perspectives on International/Industrial Organizational Psychology* (San Francisco: Jossey-Bass, 1997).

19 Leung, "Negotiation and Reward Allocations Across Cultures."

20. J. M. Brett and T. Okumura, "Inter- and Intra-Cultural Negotiation: U.S. and Japanese Negotiators," *Academy of Management Journal*, 1998, *41*, 495–510.

21. E. T. Hall and M. R. Hall, *Understanding Cultural Differences* (Yarmouth, Maine: Intercultural Press, 1990). See also M. Rajan and J. Graham, "Nobody's Grandfather Was a Merchant: Understanding the Soviet Commercial Negotiation Process and Style," *California Management Review*, Spring 1991, pp. 40–57.

22. Leung, "Negotiation and Reward Allocations Across Cultures"; M. W. Morris, K. Leung, D. Ames, and B. Lickel, "Views from the Inside and Outside: Integrating Emic and Etic Insights About Culture and Justice Judgments," *Academy of Management Review*, 1999, *24*, 781–796.

23. J. M. Brett, D. L. Shapiro, and A. L. Lytle, "Breaking the Bonds of Reciprocity in Negotiations," *Academy of Management Journal*,

1998, *41*, 410–424; W. L. Adair, "Reciprocity in the Global Market," unpublished doctoral dissertation, Department of Management and Organizations, Northwestern University, 2000.

24. Adair, "Reciprocity in the Global Market."

Chapter Two

1. Bazerman and Neale, *Negotiating Rationally*.

2. A. E. Tenbrunsel and M. H. Bazerman, "Working Women," in J. M. Brett (ed.), *Teaching Materials for Negotiations and Decision Making* [compact disk] (Evanston, Ill.: Dispute Resolution Research Center, Northwestern University, 2000).

3. The difference in the two reservation prices is $10,000 per episode times 100 episodes, or $1 million.

4. This class from Hong Kong University of Science and Technology has a rich mix of cultures. We asked participants to identify their primary culture and included only those who identified Chinese culture as primary.

5. Max Bazerman, Tetsushi Okumura, and I disciplined ourselves to coordinate our introduction to Cartoon. Our discipline minimizes the chance of instructor effects. In addition, in reporting data, I have aggregated classes across instructors and years. Such aggregation serves to increase group size and generate better estimates of prototypical behavior. However, if a strong prototype does not emerge from aggregated data, between-group differences will not be significant.

6. Because some buyer-seller pairs integrate and therefore do better as a team than others, controlling for sellers' net gains helps us focus on the distributive aspect of the negotiation. It also lets us focus on cultural differences that are not contaminated by unique buyer-seller interactions.

7. E. A. Locke and G. P. Latham, *A Theory of Goal Setting and Task Performance* (Upper Saddle River, N.J.: Prentice Hall, 1990).

8. Bazerman and Neale, *Negotiating Rationally*.

9. V. L. Huber and M. A. Neale, "Effects of Self and Competitor Goals on Performance in an Interdependent Bargaining Task," *Journal of Applied Psychology*, 1987, *72*, 197–203; S. Siegel and L. Fouraker, *Bargaining and Group Decision Making: Experiments in Bilateral Monopoly* (New York: McGraw-Hill, 1960).

10. Bazerman and Neale, *Negotiating Rationally*.

11. D. M. Messick and C. McClintock, "Motivational Bases of Choice in Experimental Games," *Journal of Experimental Social Psychology*, 1968, *4*, 1–25.

12. The social motives theory does not have a category for people whose choices in interdependent situations are dominated by concerns for the collective. Theorizing about people from collectivist cultures suggests that their social motives may vary, depending on whether the social interdependence is with an in-group or an out-group member. People are generally cooperative with in-group members; Turner, *Rediscovering the Social Group*. Because people from collective cultures are supposed to make stronger in-group versus out-group distinctions than people from individualist cultures, their social motives when dealing with an out-group member are expected to be competitive; Leung, "Negotiation and Reward Allocations Across Cultures"; Triandis, *Individualism and Collectivism*.

13. That there were few competitive negotiators in our study may have little to do with the distribution of competitive negotiators in these cultures or others. Kellogg and its academic partners screen applicants to this executive M.B.A. program; it is quite possible that applicants with competitive social motives were not selected for the program.

14. W. L. Adair, J. M. Brett, A. Lempereur, T. Okumura, C. H. Tinsley, and A. L. Lytle, *Culture and Negotiation Strategy* (Evanston, Ill.: Dispute Resolution Research Center, Northwestern University, 1998).

15. K. Leung and M. H. Bond, "The Impact of Cultural Collectivism on Reward Allocation," *Journal of Personality and Social Psychology*, 1984, *47*, 793–804.

16. The data in Exhibit 2.10 are from transcripts of same-culture negotiations. Each statement made by each speaker was coded. The

analysis reported in Exhibit 2.10 is based on a two-way table of five columns and two rows. There is a column for each culture. One row is for the frequencies of use of direct influence attempts, and the other row is for the frequencies of use of all other substantive discussion. A cell (row-by-column intersection) indicates the frequency with which direct influence was used across groups in a particular culture. Multiplying a column total (number of phrases used in a culture) by a row total (number of direct influence attempts across cultures) and dividing by the total number of phrases in all cultures provides an expected value for each cell. The difference between the actual values and the expected value indicates which cultures were using direct influence more (positive) or less (negative) than would be expected, given the number of coded statements by negotiators from that culture and the number of direct influence statements across cultures. Standardizing the residuals just puts everything on the same scale with zero as the neutral point. A chi-square statistic is used to evaluate the significance of the result. All results in the exhibits in Chapter Two are statistically significant, with a probability of less than 1 percent.

17. Keep in mind that these data are not mean values. The results do not indicate that the Japanese made *more* direct influence attempts than the U.S. negotiators. Rather, the data indicate that *relative to what else was discussed* in the Japanese same-culture negotiations, there was a lot of discussion that was categorized as direct influence. Likewise, the results do not indicate that the Israelis made fewer direct influence attempts than the U.S. negotiators. Rather, they spent less time on this type of influence relative to what else they discussed.

18. M. Olekalns, personal communication, Aug. 19, 1999.

19. D. G. Pruitt and S. Lewis, "Development of Integrative Solutions in Bilateral Negotiation," *Journal of Personality and Social Psychology*, 1975, *31*, 621–633.

20. Brett, Shapiro, and Lytle, "Breaking the Bonds of Reciprocity in Negotiations."

21. Adair, "Reciprocity in the Global Market."

22. Brett and Okumura, "Inter- and Intra-Cultural Negotiation."

23. Adair, "Reciprocity in the Global Market."

24. J. Graham, D. K. Kim, C. Y. Lin, and M. Robinson, "Buyer-Seller Negotiations Around the Pacific Rim: Differences in Fundamental Exchange Processes," *Journal of Consumer Research*, 1988, *15*, 48–54.

25. M. A. Neale and M. H. Bazerman, "The Effects of Framing and Overconfidence on Bargainer Behavior," *Academy of Management Journal*, 1985, *28*, 34–49.

26. D. Dialdin, S. Kopelman, W. L. Adair, J. M. Brett, T. Okumura, and A. L. Lytle, *The Distributive Outcomes of Cross-Cultural Negotiations* (Evanston, Ill.: Dispute Resolution Research Center, Northwestern University, 1999); see also D. L. Hartnett and L. L. Cummings, *Bargaining Behavior: An International Study* (Houston, Tex.: Dame, 1980).

27. L. R. Weingart, L. L. Thompson, M. H. Bazerman, and J. S. Carroll, "Tactical Behavior and Negotiation Outcomes," *International Journal of Conflict Management*, 1990, *1*, 7–31.

28. Adair, "Reciprocity in the Global Market."

29. Previous research on negotiation has labeled this proposal and counterproposal process of negotiating "heuristic trial-and-error search"; Pruitt, *Negotiation Behavior*. The name implies a random process and integrative outcomes based on luck. Yet this is clearly not a random strategy in cultures where it is normative.

30. Weingart, Bennett, and Brett, "Impact of Consideration of Issues and Motivational Orientation."

31. Weingart, Bennett, and Brett, "Impact of Consideration of Issues and Motivational Orientation."

32. H. Raiffa, *The Art and Science of Negotiation* (Cambridge, Mass.: Belknap Press, 1982).

33. The sellers are generally pleased when they write up their results but less pleased when the instructor insists that they also post their results if the contingency is not activated.

34. W. L. Adair, T. Okumura, and J. M. Brett, "Culturally Bound Negotiation Scripts and Joint Gains in U.S. and Japanese Intra- and Intercultural Dyads," *Journal of Applied Psychology*, forthcoming.

35. A. L. Lytle, J. M. Brett, and D. L. Shapiro, "The Strategic Use of Interests, Rights, and Power to Resolve Disputes," *Negotiation Journal*, 1999, *15*, 31–52.

Chapter Three

1. P. J. Carnevale and D. G. Pruitt, "Negotiation and Mediation," *Annual Review of Psychology*, 1992, *43*, 531–582.

2. W.L.F. Felsteiner, R. L. Abel, and A. Sarat, "The Emergence and Transformation of Disputes: Naming, Blaming, and Claiming," *Law and Society Review*, 1980–1981, *15*, 631–654.

3. Ury, Brett, and Goldberg, *Getting Disputes Resolved*.

4. Triandis, *Individualism and Collectivism*.

5. C. H. Tinsley and J. M. Brett, "Managing Workplace Conflict in the U.S. and Hong Kong," *Organizational Behavior and Human Decision Process*, forthcoming.

6. A video of a mediation of the Prosando–High Tech dispute is available from CPR Institute for Dispute Resolution, 366 Madison Avenue, New York, NY 10017; http://www.cpradr.org.

7. K. Leung and M. W. Morris, "Justice Through the Lens of Culture and Ethnicity," in J. Sanders and V. L. Hamilton (eds.), *Handbook of Law and Social Science* (New York: Plenum, 1996).

8. C. H. Tinsley, "Culture's Influences on Conflict Management Behaviors in the Workplace," unpublished doctoral dissertation, Department of Organization Behavior, Northwestern University, 1997; C. H. Tinsley, "How We Get to Yes: Predicting the Constellation of Strategies Used Across Cultures to Negotiate Conflict," *Journal of Applied Psychology*, forthcoming.

9. Tinsley coded every subject-verb clause that was uttered: 4,456 in the German discussions, 5,814 in the U.S. discussions, and 2,891 in the Japanese discussions. (Japanese discussions were in Japanese and then translated.) She then entered the data in a code-by-culture table, using twenty-three codes across the three cultures. The cells in the table are the frequencies that disputants in a culture used a

code category. The row totals are the frequencies across cultures of the use of a code category. The column totals are the frequencies of all codes in a culture. If you multiply row total times column total and divide the result by the overall number of subject-verb sequences, you get an expected value. If you subtract the observed value from the expected value, the residual will be positive if the culture used the code category more than expected and negative if that culture used the code category less than expected. Standardized residuals are easier to interpret than raw residuals because if the culture is using the category of behavior as expected, the standardized residual will be zero. The statistical significance of the residuals can be evaluated with a chi-square statistic. Significant chi-squares are associated with Exhibits 3.4 through 3.10.

10. L. Pye, *Chinese Commercial Negotiating Style* (Cambridge, Mass.: Oelgeschlager, Gunn, & Hain, 1982); T. Fang, *Chinese Business Negotiating Style* (Thousand Oaks, Calif.: Sage, 1999).

11. R. Tung, "Strategic Management Thought in East Asia," *Organizational Dynamics*, 1994, *22*(4), 55–65.

12. R. M. Emerson, "Power Dependence Relations," *American Sociological Review*, 1962, *27*, 31–41.

13. J. J. Di Stefanno, *Canada-China Computer Crisis Case* (London, Canada: University of Western Ontario, 1994).

14. C. H. Tinsley, "Models of Conflict Resolution in Japanese, German, and American Cultures," *Journal of Applied Psychology*, 1998, *83*, 316–323; Tinsley, "Culture's Influences"; Tinsley, "How We Get to Yes."

15. Tinsley and Brett, *Managing Workplace Conflict*.

16. Tinsley, "Culture's Influences"; Tinsley, "How We Get to Yes."

17. E. T. Hall, *Beyond Culture* (New York: Anchor/Doubleday, 1976); S. Ting-Toomey, "Intercultural Conflict Styles: A Face Negotiation Theory," in Y. Kim and W. B. Gudykunst (eds.), *Theories in Intercultural Communication* (Thousand Oaks, Calif.: Sage, 1988).

18. E. Goffman, *The Presentation of Self in Everyday Life* (New York: Doubleday, 1959).

19. S. Tjosvold and C. Hui, *Showing Respect Among Chinese: A Study on Social Face in Conflict* (College Park, Md.: International Association for Conflict Management, 1998).

20. Tjosvold and Hui, *Showing Respect Among Chinese*.

21. T. R. Tyler, E. A. Lind, and Y. J. Huo, *Culture, Ethnicity, and Authority: Social Categorization and Social Orientation Effects on the Psychology of Legitimacy* (Berkeley: University of California Press, 1995).

22. D. Spero, "Patent Protection or Piracy: A CEO Views Japan," *Harvard Business Review*, 1990, 68(5), 58–67.

23. Ury, Brett, and Goldberg, *Getting Disputes Resolved*.

24. Lytle, Brett, and Shapiro, "Strategic Use of Interests, Rights, and Power."

25. W. L. Adair, "Exploring the Norm of Reciprocity in the Global Market: U.S. and Japanese Intra- and Intercultural Negotiations," *Academy of Management Proceedings*, 1999; Adair, "Reciprocity in the Global Market."

26. Brett, Shapiro, and Lytle, "Breaking the Bonds of Reciprocity in Negotiations."

27. K. A. Jehn, "Workplace Conflict," in B. M. Staw (ed.), *Research in Organizational Behavior* (Greenwich, Conn.: JAI Press, 1999).

28. L. H. Pelled, "Demographic Diversity, Conflict, and Work Group Outcomes: An Intervening Process Theory," *Organizational Science*, 1996, 7, 615–631.

29. Tinsley, "Culture's Influences"; Tinsley, "How We Get to Yes."

30. Lytle, Brett, and Shapiro, "Strategic Use of Interests, Rights, and Power."

31. J. G. Getman, S. B. Goldberg, and J. B. Herman, *Union Representation Elections: Law and Reality* (New York: Russell Sage Foundation, 1969).

32. Brett, Shapiro, and Lytle, "Breaking the Bonds of Reciprocity in Negotiations"; Lytle, Brett, and Shapiro, "Strategic Use of Interests, Rights, and Power."

33. S. S. Keisler and L. Sproull, "Group Decision Making and Communication Technology," *Organizational Behavior and Human Decision Processes*, 1992, *52*, 96–123.

34. Keisler and Sproull, "Group Decision Making and Communication Technology."

35. There seem to be more electronic dispute resolution sites on the Web every day. Enter "dispute resolution" in any of the major search engines, and a long list of dispute resolution service providers will appear. Some offer virtual service exclusively. Research on settlement rates in the different electronic formats is not yet available. One experiment done by posting an offer to mediate on eBay's customer service page generated about two hundred hits in two weeks. Of those, half had either settled on their own or were not eBay-connected disputes. Of the hundred that were mediated electronically, fifty settled; E. Katsh, J. Rifkin, and A. Gaitenby, "E-Commerce, E-Disputes, and E-Dispute Resolution: In the Shadow of 'eBay Law,'" *Ohio State Journal of Dispute Resolution*, 2000, *15*, 705–734.

36. J. Z. Rubin and F.E.A. Sander, "When Should We Use Agents? Direct vs. Representative Negotiation," in J. W. Breslin and J. Z. Rubin (eds.), *Negotiation Theory and Practice* (Cambridge, Mass.: Program on Negotiation, Harvard Law School, 1995).

37. C. Barshefsky, address at the J. L. Kellogg Graduate School of Management, Northwestern University, Mar. 14, 2000.

38. Leung and Morris, "Justice Through the Lens of Culture and Ethnicity."

39. R. Karambayya, J. M. Brett, and A. L. Lytle, "Managerial Third Parties: The Effects of Formal Authority and Experience on Third-Party Roles, Outcomes, and Perceptions of Fairness," *Academy of Management Journal*, 1992, *35*, 426–438; R. Karambayya and J. M. Brett, "Managers Handling Disputes," *Academy of Management Journal*, 1989, *32*, 687–704.

40. J. M. Brett, Z. I. Barsness, and S. B. Goldberg, "The Effectiveness of Mediation: An Independent Analysis of Cases Handled by Four Major Service Providers," *Negotiation Journal*, 1996, *12*, 259–270.

41. Brett, Barsness, and Goldberg, "The Effectiveness of Mediation."

42. Brett, Barsness, and Goldberg, "The Effectiveness of Mediation."

43. CPR Institute for Dispute Resolution, film available from http://www.cpradr.org.

44. T. R. Tyler and E. A. Lind, "A Relational Model of Authority in Groups," in M. Zanna (ed.), *Advances in Experimental Social Psychology* (Orlando, Fla.: Academic Press, 1992).

45. J. M. Brett, *Third Parties* (College Park, Md.: International Association of Conflict Management, 1998); Karambayya, Brett, and Lytle, "Managerial Third Parties"; Karambayya and Brett, "Managers Handling Disputes."

46. Tyler, Lind, and Huo, *Culture, Ethnicity, and Authority.*

47. United States: J. Thibaut and L. Walker, *Procedural Justice: A Psychological Analysis* (Mahwah, N.J.: Erlbaum, 1975). Britain, France, and Germany: E. A. Lind, B. E. Erickson, N. Friedland, and M. Dickenberger, "Reactions to Procedural Models for Adjudicative Conflict Resolution: A Cross-National Study," *Journal of Conflict Resolution*, 1978, 2, 18–341. Hong Kong: K. Leung, "Some Determinants of Reactions to Procedural Models for Conflict Resolution: A Cross-National Study," *Journal of Personality and Social Psychology*, 1987, 53, 898–908. Japan and Spain: K. Leung, Y. F. Au., J. M. Fernandez-Dols, and S. Iwawaki, "Preferences for Methods of Conflict Process in Two Collectivist Cultures," *International Journal of Psychology*, 1992, 27, 195–209.

48. Tyler and Lind, "A Relational Model of Authority in Groups."

49. D. L. Shapiro and J. M. Brett, "Comparing Three Processes Underlying Judgments of Procedural Justice: A Field Study of Mediation and Arbitration," *Journal of Personality and Social Psychology*, 1993, 65, 1167–1177.

50. Shapiro and Brett, "Comparing Three Processes."

51. Leung and Morris, "Justice Through the Lens of Culture and Ethnicity."

52. K. A. Slaiku and R. H. Hasson, *Controlling the Costs of Conflict: How to Design a System for Your Organization* (San Francisco:

Jossey-Bass, 1998); C. A. Costantino and C. S. Merchant, *Designing Conflict Management Systems: A Guide to Creating Productive and Healthy Organizations* (San Francisco: Jossey-Bass, 1995); Ury, Brett, and Goldberg, *Getting Disputes Resolved.*

53. American Arbitration Association, *International Business Machines Corporation v. Fujitsu Limited,* American Arbitration Tribunal, Sept. 15, 1987, case no. 13-I-117-0636-85.

Chapter Four

1. E. Drozdiak, "Facing Big Tasks, EU Dithers," *International Herald Tribune,* June 22, 2000, pp. 1, 4.

2. D. Gruenfeld, M. C. Thomas-Hunt, and P. Kim, "Cognitive Flexibility, Communication Strategy, and Integrative Complexity in Groups: Public Versus Private Reactions to Majority and Minority Status," *Journal of Experimental Social Psychology,* 1998, *34,* 202–226.

3. K. Eisenhardt and C. B. Schoonhaven, "Organizational Growth: Linking Founding Team Strategy, Environment, and Growth Among U.S. Semiconductor Ventures," *Administrative Science Quarterly,* 1990, *35,* 504–529.

4. T. L. Simons, L. H. Pelled, and K. A. Smith, "What Kinds of Difference Make a Difference? How Diversity Interacts with Debate in Top Management Teams," *Academy of Management Journal,* 1999, *42,* 662–673.

5. K. A. Jehn, "A Multimethod Examination of the Benefits and Detriments of Intragroup Conflict," *Administrative Science Quarterly,* 1995, *40,* 256–282.

6. K. Lovelace, D. L. Shapiro, and L. R. Weingart, "Maximizing Cross-Functional New Product Teams' Innovativeness and Constraint Adherence: A Conflict Communications Perspective," *Academy of Management Journal,* forthcoming.

7. This example was constructed from a project done with Maddy Janssens and Ludo Kuenen. The company is real and the incidents are real, though not all occurred on the same team, as is represented here for the purpose of simplicity.

8. Bull Worldwide Information Systems (http://www.bull.com, 2000), *Cultural Diversity at the Heart of Bull* (video) (Yarmouth, Maine: Intercultural Press, 1992). All quotations are from this video.

9. M. Hewstone and K. Greenland, "Intergroup Conflict," *International Journal of Psychology*, 2000, *35*, 136–146.

10. H. Tajfel and J. C. Turner, "An Integrative Theory of Intergroup Conflict," in W. G. Austin and S. Worchel (eds.), *The Social Psychology of Intergroup Relations* (Pacific Grove, Calif.: Brooks/Cole, 1979).

11. J. R. Hackman, K. R. Brousseau, and J. A. Weiss, "The Interaction of Task Design and Group Performance Strategies in Determining Group Effectiveness," *Organizational Behavior and Human Performance*, 1976, *16*, 350–365.

12. K. L. Bettenhausen and J. K. Murnighan, "The Emergence of Norms in Competitive Decision-Making Groups," *Administrative Science Quarterly*, 1985, *3*, 20–35.

13. M. Janssens and J. M. Brett, "Meaningful Participation in Transnational Teams," *European Journal of Work and Organizational Psychology*, 1997, *6*, 153–168.

14. M. Janssens, L. Kuenen, and J. M. Brett, "Valuing Cultural Diversity," unpublished report, 1998, p. 14.

15. Keisler and Sproull, "Group Decision Making and Communication Technology."

16. A. Rosette, J. M. Brett, A. L. Lytle, and Z. I. Barsness, *The Effect of Computer-Mediated Communications on Negotiated Outcome and Behavior in Chinese and American Culture* (Evanston, Ill.: Dispute Resolution Research Center, Northwestern University, 1999).

17. M. Schrage, *No More Teams! Mastering the Dynamics of Creative Collaboration* (New York: Doubleday, 1995).

18. Thompson, *Making the Team*.

19. Z. I. Barsness, J. M. Brett, and L. Eden, "Developing Real-World Skills: Managing Virtual Transnational Teams." Paper presented at the annual meeting of the Academy of International Business, Vienna, Oct. 7–10, 1998.

20. E. Peterson and L. L. Thompson, "Negotiation Teamwork: The Impact of Information Distribution and Accountability on Performance Depends on the Relationship Among Team Members," *Organizational Behavior and Human Decision Processes*, 1997, *72*, 364–383.

21. Janssens and Brett, "Meaningful Participation in Transnational Teams."

22. D. Wegner, "Transactive Memory: A Contemporary Analysis of the Group Mind," in B. Mullen and G. Goethals (eds.), *Theories of Group Behavior* (New York: Springer, 1986).

23. Wegner, "Transactive Memory."

24. Thompson, *Making the Team*.

25. Weingart, Bennett, and Brett, "Impact of Consideration of Issues and Motivational Orientation."

26. Gruenfeld, Thomas-Hunt, and Kim, "Cognitive Flexibility, Communication Strategy, and Integrative Complexity."

27. L. L. Thompson, B. Mannix, and M. H. Bazerman, "Group Negotiation: Effects of Decision Rule, Agenda, and Aspiration," *Journal of Personality and Social Psychology*, 1988, *54*, 86–95.

28. Thompson, *Making the Team*.

29. Thompson, *Making the Team*.

30. M. Roloff and D. Ifert, "Conflict Management Through Avoidance: Withholding Complaints, Suppressing Arguments, and Declaring Topics Taboo," in S. Petronio (ed.), *Balancing the Secrets of Private Disclosure* (Mahwah, N.J.: Erlbaum, 1999).

31. Thompson, *Making the Team*.

32. Janssens and Brett, "Meaningful Participation in Transnational Teams."

33. Ury, Brett, and Goldberg, *Getting Disputes Resolved*.

34. H. Wagatsuma and A. Rosette, "The Implications of Apology: Law and Culture in Japan and the United States," *Law and Society Review*, 1986, *20*, 461–498.

35. S. B. Goldberg, F.E.A. Sander, and N. Rogers, *Dispute Resolution: Negotiation, Mediation, and Other Processes*, 3rd ed. (Gaithersburg, Md.: Aspen, 1999).

36. Thompson, *Making the Team*; S. E. Gross, *Compensation for Teams: How to Design and Implement Team-Based Reward Programs* (New York: AMACOM, 1995).

37. Thompson, *Making the Team*.

Chapter Five

1. Social dilemmas are also called commons problems; G. Hardin, "The Tragedy of the Commons," *Science*, 1968, *162*, 1243–1248. Hardin explained that if one member of a group of farmers who shared a common grazing area added one more cow to his herd, he would benefit, but if all the farmers added an additional cow, the common grazing area would be exhausted, to the detriment of all.

2. Thompson, *Mind and Heart of the Negotiator*, pp. 226–227.

3. "Patagonian Toothfish," *New York Times Magazine*, Apr. 11, 1999, p. 23.

4. The original research using the SHARC exercise was done by K. A. Wade-Benzoni, A. E. Tenbrunsel, and M. H. Bazerman, "Egocentric Interpretations of Fairness in Asymmetric, Environmental Social Dilemmas: Explaining Harvesting Behavior and the Role of Communication," *Organizational Behavior and Human Decision Processes*, 1996, *76*, 111–126. The comparative cultural research is reported in K. A. Wade-Benzoni, T. Okumura, J. M. Brett, D. Moore, A. E. Tenbrunsel, and M. H. Bazerman, *Behavior and Expectation in Asymmetric Social Dilemmas: A Comparison of Two Cultures* (Evanston, Ill.: Dispute Resolution Research Center, Northwestern University, 1999).

5. See the Summer Interns study described in Chapter Three; see also Tinsley, "Culture's Influences"; Tinsley, "How We Get to Yes."

6. Hewstone and Greenland, "Intergroup Conflict."

7. Triandis, *Individualism and Collectivism*.

8. Wade-Benzoni, Okumura, Brett, Moore, Tenbrunsel, and Bazerman, *Behavior and Expectation in Asymmetric Social Dilemmas*.

9. Wade-Benzoni, Tenbrunsel, and Bazerman, "Egocentric Interpretations of Fairness."

10. P.A.M. Van Lange, W.B.G. Liebrand, D. M. Messick, and H.A.M. Wilke, "Social Dilemmas: The State of the Art: Introduction and Literature Review," in D. M. Messick, W.B.G. Liebrand, and H.A.M. Wilke (eds.), *Social Dilemmas: Theoretical Issues and Research Findings* (Oxford, England: Pergamon Press, 1992).

11. Van Lange, Liebrand, Messick, and Wilke, "Social Dilemmas"; R. M. Dawes, J. McTavish, and H. Shaklee, "Behavior, Communication, and Assumptions About Other People's Behavior in a Commons Dilemma Situation," *Journal of Personality and Social Psychology*, 1977, *35*, 1–11.

12. G. Bornstein and M. Ben-Yosef, "Cooperation in Intergroup and Single-Group Social Dilemmas," *Journal of Experimental Social Psychology*, 1994, *30*, 597–606.

13. T. M. Probst, P. J. Carnevale, and H. C. Triandis, "Cultural Values in Intergroup and Single-Group Social Dilemmas," *Organizational Behavior and Human Decision Processes*, 1999, *77*, 171–191.

14. Triandis, *Individualism and Collectivism*.

15. K. Leung, "Some Determinants of Conflict Avoidance," *Journal of Cross-Cultural Psychology*, 1998, *19*, 125–136.

Chapter Six

1. Landler, "Mickey and Minnie Go to Hong Kong."

2. Spero, "Patent Protection or Piracy."

3. U.S. Census Bureau, *Statistical Abstract of the United States*, Vol. 108 (Washington, D.C.: Government Printing Office, 1998), p. 842.

4. D. Kirk, "Korean Executives Lash Out at France over Thomson," *International Herald Tribune*, Dec. 12, 1996, pp. 1, 4.

5. G. Salacuse, *Making Global Deals* (New York: Times Books, 1991).

6. A. Friedman, "Singapore Is Ranked Most Competitive," *International Herald Tribune*, July 14, 1999, pp. 10, 12; see also the World Economic Forum Web site, http://www.weforum.org.

7. There are many sources of information about human rights practices. The U.S. State Department publishes *Human Rights Practices*

Reports. Organizations such as Amnesty International, PEN International Writers' Union, and Physicians for Human Rights publish their own specialized reports. The American Association for the Advancement of Science publishes a Web-based directory of human rights resources (http://shr.aaas.org/dhr.htm). Information on the PBS documentary on human rights and globalization can be found at http://www.pbs.org/globalization/.

8. "Enron Project Is Reconsidered in India," *New York Times*, Oct. 6, 1995, p. D4; A. Gottschalk, "Enron Project in India May Be Alive and Well: Firm Hears Deal Wasn't Canceled," *Journal of Commerce*, Aug. 17, 1995, p. 5B.

9. K. J. Cooper, "Wattage to India: U.S. Firm Set to Resume Work on Giant Power Project," *Washington Post*, Feb. 5, 1996, p. A12.

10. R. Mark, address at the J. L. Kellogg Graduate School of Management, Northwestern University, Apr. 17, 1996.

11. Salacuse, *Making Global Deals*.

12. Salacuse, *Making Global Deals*, p. 137.

13. Professor Torben Andersen, my colleague at the J. L. Kellogg Graduate School of Management, Northwestern University, comments that hedging against currency fluctuations is straightforward in simple situations but difficult and almost intangible in more complex settings. He suggests the following references: D. K. Eiteman, A. I. Stonehill, and M. H. Moffett, *Multinational Business Finance*, 8th ed. (Reading, Mass.: Addison-Wesley, 1998), esp. part 3 on the hedging decision; A. C. Shapiro, *Multinational Financial Management*, 6th ed. (Upper Saddle River, N.J.: Prentice Hall, 1999), esp. part 2 on managing exposure; P. Sercu and R. Uppal, *International Financial Markets and the Firm* (Cincinnati, Ohio: South-Western, 1995), esp. part 3 on risk management.

14. L. Kaufman, "As Biggest Business, Wal-Mart Propels Changes Elsewhere," *New York Times*, Oct. 22, 2000, Business/Financial Desk Archives.

15. Ibid.

16. Grover, *The Disney Touch*.

17. Waxman, "Key to the Magic Kingdom."

18. See Fiduciary Policies on the World Bank's website: http://www. worldbank.org.

19. P. Blustein, "Lesotho Bribery Charges Read Like 'Who's Who of Dam-Builders,'" *International Herald Tribune*, Aug. 14, 1999, pp. 9, 13.

20. R. J. Lewicki, J. A. Litterer, J. W. Minton, and D. M. Saunders, *Negotiation*, 2nd ed. (Burr Ridge, Ill.: Irwin, 1994).

21. D. L. Messick and W.B.G. Liebrand, "Individual Heuristics and the Dynamics of Cooperation in Large Groups," *Psychological Review*, 1995, *102*, 131–145.

22. W. Arnold, "Indonesia's Chief Repo Man Takes on the Elite," *International Herald Tribune*, July 29, 1999, p. 8.

23. N. David, *The Last Two Years of Salvador Allende* (Ithaca, N.Y.: Cornell University Press, 1985).

24. D. Sangler, "Longtime I.M.F. Director Resigns in Midterm," *New York Times*, Nov. 10, 1999, p. C1.

25. Salacuse, *Making Global Deals*.

26. T. Buerkle, "U.K. Firms Lead as Law Goes Global," *International Herald Tribune*, July 13, 1999, pp. 11, 12.

Chapter Seven

1. One caution: neither Hofstede nor Schwartz, whose research underlies Exhibits 1.4 and 1.6, surveyed managers. We have not studied nearly as many cultures as they did, but we have surveyed managers. Our surveys confirm Hofstede and Schwartz's categorization of egalitarian and hierarchical national cultures more frequently than the categorization of individualistic and collectivist national cultures. It may be that managers in any culture are more individualistic than the cultural average because of their engagement in economic activity; J. M. Brett, W. L. Adair, A. Lempereur, T. Okumura, P. Shikhirev, C. H. Tinsley, and A. L. Lytle, "Culture and Joint Gains in Negotiation," *Negotiation Journal*, 1998, *14*, 55–80. Note that the widely consulted work by T. Morrison, W. Conaway, and G. Borden, *Kiss, Bow, and Shake Hands* (Holbrook, Mass.: Adams Media, 1996), is largely based on Hofstede's and Hall's research.

2. W. L. Adair, T. Okumura, and J. M. Brett, "Negotiation Behavior When Cultures Collide: The U.S. and Japan," *Journal of Applied Psychology*, forthcoming; Tinsley, "Culture's Influences"; Tinsley, "How We Get to Yes."

3. Adair, Okumura, and Brett, "Negotiation Behavior When Cultures Collide."

4. Why they changed is a fascinating question with multiple answers. Japanese companies nominated these managers for the programs in which these data were collected because they spoke fluent English and were primarily responsible for representing their company to U.S. customers, suppliers, or clients. One explanation for why they did not use influence in negotiations is that they had learned while working in the United States that heavy use of influence in negotiations is not normative there. Another is that they perceived their status as a foreign company operating in the United States as low and their alternatives as poor. Given this situation, it is possible that they were using little influence in their business negotiations in the United States and that this carried over to their cross-cultural negotiations in the program.

5. Be careful to rule out the possibility that the reason the negotiator will not come to the table is that she is taking an indirect route.

Glossary

Adversarial procedure   Process in which disputants or their agents investigate the facts and present their own argument to the third party; compare *inquisitorial procedure*.

A priori majority   Large factions or coalitions that exist before the information-sharing phase of group decision making begins.

Arbitrator   In dispute resolution, a private third party who serves as a judge and makes a final and binding decision.

BATNA (best alternative to a negotiated agreement)   What each negotiator will do in a deal-making situation if no agreement is reached; what will happen to negotiators if they fail to resolve a dispute or reach an agreement.

Categorization   Sorting of people into types or categories based on superficial information about them, such as culture, language, race, or sex.

Claim   A demand for something due.

Collective goal   A goal that is shared by group members who also have goals that are based on self-interests.

Collective interests   The interests of an identifiable group of people who may not be participating directly in the negotiation but will be affected by the agreement.

Collectivism   A cultural value that promotes the interdependence of individuals with the social groups to which they belong and supports collective interests over self-interests as the predominant life value.

Compatible issues Issues on which negotiators on both sides want the same outcome.

Competitive social motive Concern for maximizing one's own outcome at the expense of the other party's outcome.

Concession An act of yielding.

Conflict The perception of opposing interests, involving scarce resources, goals, or procedures.

Confrontation A meeting between negotiators, either directly (face to face or electronically), or indirectly (via a third party or nonverbal behavior).

Consensus A form of majority rule when no team members publicly oppose a decision, though they may do so in private.

Contact Face-to-face interaction among diverse members of a group intended to help them build mutual respect and trust.

Contingent contract An agreement to change the negotiated outcome in a specific way based on the occurrence of a future event.

Corruption A situation in which the rules of participation are unclear, changing, or differentially applied or in which nepotism, bribery, extortion, or embezzlement is involved.

Culture The unique character of a social group, including the values and norms shared by members of the group and the group's social, economic, political, and other institutions.

Deal-making negotiations Negotiations to buy and sell.

Decision-making negotiations The process of arriving at an agreement when there are multiple potential and conflicting choices; the process by which multicultural teams reach agreement.

Direct influence strategies Strategies that urge compliance to avoid negative consequences for the party being influenced; they include persuasion, argument, substantiation, and threats.

Dispute resolution negotiations Negotiations to resolve the conflict resulting from a claim being made and rejected.

Dispute resolution system A hierarchical set of dispute resolution procedures that provide opportunities to reach integrative agreements at more than one stage and provide for final resolution of the dispute.

Distributive agreement   An agreement in negotiation that allocates a fixed set of resources.

Egalitarian culture   A culture that aspires to social equality, especially in political, social, and economic affairs.

Egocentric bias   The belief that you deserve substantially more than another person in exactly the same circumstances.

Ethnocentrism   The belief that your culture's way of doing something is the best way.

Face   Personal honor and socially based respect.

Faction   A group that accounts for less than a majority.

Fairness standards   Decision rules that presumably provide a just distribution.

Free rider   A group member who does not contribute to the group but benefits from the group's efforts.

Hierarchical culture   A culture that accepts social inequality in political, social, and economic affairs.

Ideology   A collection of principles and precepts that provide the basis for making choices about the structure of institutions.

Impasse   The outcome when negotiators cannot reach agreement and discontinue negotiating.

Indirect influence strategies   Strategies that urge compliance to avert negative consequences for the influencing party; appeals to sympathy are an example.

Individualism   A cultural value that promotes personal independence and gives self-interest a high priority among important life values.

Individualistic social motive   Concern for oneself irrespective of the consequences for the other party.

Influence   Trying to produce a desired effect in another person—in negotiation, usually an attempt to obtain a concession.

Information   Knowledge or intelligence that is communicated.

In-group   A group to which an individual belongs and from which that individual may derive social identity.

Inquisitorial procedure   Process in which an agent of the court investigates and presents an opinion and arguments to the judge; compare *adversarial procedure*.

Institution   A public organization that structures social interaction.

Integrative agreement   An agreement in negotiation that expands the resources to be allocated beyond those resources that would be available if one party took all or two parties compromised (split their differences) on all issues.

Integrative potential   The maximum possible value available to negotiators if they agree to all compatible issues and make all efficient trade-offs.

Interests   The reasons why negotiators take the positions they do; negotiators' needs, fears, and concerns.

Interpersonal conflict   Disputes over personal responsibility and blame.

Litigation   A judicial procedure in which disputants or their agents argue their claim and a third party makes a final and binding decision.

Lumping it   Deciding not to make a claim public or not to pursue a claim that has been rejected.

Majority rule   A decision rule whereby the alternative preferred by more than half of the members of a group becomes the alternative chosen by the group.

Meaningful participation   Group discussion engaged in according to the principle that group members have an obligation to speak up when their knowledge, expertise, or contacts become relevant as well as when they harbor doubts about the direction the group is taking or the feasibility of the group's plan.

Mediator   In dispute resolution, a private third party who tries to facilitate an agreement but does not have the authority to impose an outcome on the disputants.

Motivation   The factor or factors urging a person to act.

Multicultural teams   Groups of three or more people with diverse cultural backgrounds who must make decisions together.

Mutual-gains strategy   A group decision-making strategy that has a goal of reaching an integrative decision.

Negotiation The process of conferring among two or more inter-dependent parties to arrive at an agreement about some matter over which they are in conflict.

Net value In deal making, the anticipated return minus the costs, including the costs of negotiating.

Norm Any standard of appropriate behavior in social interactions.

One party decides A decision rule that permits one member to choose the alternative for the group.

Other interests The interests, concerns, and priorities of the other negotiators.

Out-group Any group in which an individual is not a member.

Power The ability to influence others to concede to your wishes.

Preferences Positions; the outcomes that negotiators want.

Prejudice An ungrounded positive or negative opinion.

Priorities The order of importance of a set of issues.

Prisoner's dilemma A two-party social dilemma; a situation in which self-interests lead one to compete but collective interests lead one to cooperate.

Procedural conflict A dispute over means, including the dispute resolution process itself.

Prosocial social motive Concern for both one's own outcome and the other party's outcome.

Prototype The cultural pattern or model, based on the average or modal characteristic of a culture.

Recategorization Building a new social identity based on group membership rather than on independent attributes of the self.

Relativism Judging the morality of an act by its appropriateness in the context.

Reservation price The most a negotiator is willing to offer or the least a negotiator is willing to take and still reach agreement.

Rights Standards of fairness or law that can be used to resolve disputes; similar to fairness standards in making deals.

Self-interests The negotiator's own interests, concerns, and priorities.

Social dilemma A multiparty decision-making situation in which, if everyone acts to maximize personal gain, everyone is worse off than if everyone acts to maximize collective gain; yet acting to maximize personal gain is always better for the individual.

Social identity   A sense of one's own reputation, the impression one thinks one has made on others.

Social motives   The types of choices that people make in situations like negotiation in which they are interdependent.

Stakeholder   A person with an interest.

Stereotype   A belief that everyone from a given culture will be like that culture's prototype.

Strategy   An integrated set of behaviors chosen because they are thought to be the means of accomplishing the goal of negotiating.

Synergy   A result that is greater than the sum of its parts.

Target   The components that would constitute an ideal settlement; goals in negotiation and standards against which to judge opening offers, concessions, and final offers.

Task conflict   A dispute over goals and resources.

Threat   An expression of an intention to do harm; an if-then statement about the other party's actions and the consequences if the party persists in them.

Trade-offs   Conceding on low-priority issues in order to gain on high-priority issues.

Transaction costs   The costs of negotiating.

Transactive memory   Knowledge of who on the team knows what.

Unanimity   Agreement among all team members.

Utilitarianism   Judging the morality of an act by its consequences.

Value   A judgment of what is important in social interactions and other aspects of life.

Value-claiming negotiation   Negotiation to reach a distributive agreement.

Value-creating negotiation   Negotiation to reach an integrative agreement.

Index

A

A priori majorities, 155

Adversarial procedures, 131

Advice: on avoiding psychological barriers to information sharing, 152; on confrontation and culture, 205–206; on cultural differences in negotiation strategy, 205–209; on electronic communication in multicultural teams, 150; on ethical decisions, 197–200; on government interests, 184–186; on influence, 58–60, 207–208; on information sharing, 63, 148, 152, 206–207; on interests and priorities, 88–89, 204–205; on opening offers in distributive negotiations, 44; on power, 58–60, 103; on proposals and equivalent proposals, 68–69; on rights-based dispute resolution, 96–97, 97–98; on setting BATNAs and reservation prices, 28; on setting targets in distributive negotiations, 44; on social motives, 47; on threats, 112

Agents, negotiation through, 117–118. *See also* Third parties

Apologies, 162–163

Arbitration, 122–123, 125

Arbitrators: limited focus of, 120; selecting, 127–128; sources for, 124

B

"Banana wars," 13

Barshefsky, C., 118

Bazerman, M., 215n5

Bernard, J.-R., 192

Best alternative to a negotiated agreement (BATNA), 13; in egalitarian cultures, 19; for information integration in multicultural teams, 155–156; linked in dispute resolution, 99–100, 205–206; reservation prices and, 25–26; setting, 26, 28; sharing information about, 70–72; as source of power, 48; unlinked in deal making, 98–99

Body language, cultural interpretation of, 148–149

BP, and Sidanko, 1, 25, 186

Brainstorming, 156

Bribery. *See* Corruption

Bull: cultural misunderstanding in, 149; interpersonal conflict in, 142; language difficulties in, 145; procedural conflict in, 139–141

Bureaucracies, government, 191–194

Buyers, caution on power and influence of, 59–60

C

Camdessus, M., 199

Canadian manager, in dispute with Chinese employee, 100–101

Cartoon simulation, 29–37; coding scheme for, 50–55; contingent contracts in, 72–74, 218n33; cultural differences in integrative agreements and distributive outcomes with,

Mark, R., 187, 188

Meaningful participation: cultural barriers to, 147–149; language barriers to, 145–147; psychological barriers to, 151–152; structural barriers to, 149–150; to encourage information sharing, 144–145

Mediation, 123, 128–129; description of, 126; to resolve interest-based dispute, 87–88

Mediators: focus of, 120; selecting, 127; sources for, 124

Mitsubishi Electric, dispute with Fusion Systems, 99, 105–106, 111–112, 122, 178–179

Mondavi Vineyards, 212n5

Motivation: culture as affecting, 12; in multicultural teams, 164–165; social motives in integrative negotiation as, 44–47, 208–209; targets in distributive negotiation as, 41–44

Multicultural teams, 136–166; barriers to goal achievement by, 137, 138–143; conflict enhancing performance by, 137–138; confronting dysfunctional conflict in, 162–163; defined, 136; environments for, 165–166; information integration in, 152–157; information sharing in, 144–152; meaningful participation in, 144–152; motivation in, 164–165; preventing conflict in, 157–162; proliferation of, 136; skills of, 163; types of conflict in, 138–143

Multiple alternatives, 156–157

Mutual-gains decision strategies, 152–157

N

National cultures: economic competitiveness rankings of, 181, 182–183; egalitarian vs. hierarchical, 18; as focus of book, xvii, 6, 212n2; individualist vs. collectivist, 16; low- vs. high-context, 21

Negotiation: cross-cultural, reasons for concern about, 24–25; cultural aspects affecting, 6–8; fundamentals of, 2–6; lying in, 67–68, 71–72; nonparticipation in, 141, 208, 231n5; types of, 2–3. *See also specific types of negotiation*

Negotiation strategies: complex link between culture and, 22–23; cultural features affecting, 15–21, 208–209;

culture as affecting, 8, 9–14, 205–209; dealing with cultural differences in, 205–209; defined, 6; persistence of cultural differences in, 203–204

Net value, 26, 28–29

Nissan, Renault buying stake in, 12

Nonparticipation by negotiator, 141, 208, 231n5

Norms: as affecting negotiation, 7, 9–10; as approach to managing social dilemmas, 170–171; for interaction in multicultural teams, 159–161

North American Free Trade Agreement (NAFTA): dispute resolution system, 132; e-mail use in project on, 150

O

Okumura, T., 215n5

One party decides, 152

Opening offers, 43–44

Organization for Economic Cooperation and Development (OECD), 195, 196

Organization of Petroleum Exporting Countries (OPEC), 167, 169–170, 172–173

Out-groups, 15, 175

P

Participation: meaningful, 144–152; negotiator's refusal to engage in, 141, 208, 231n5

Patagonian toothfish, 168, 172

Pepsi-Cola Company, agreement between Soviet Union government and, 185, 191

Pharmaceutical company: language difficulties in, 145, 146–147; task conflict in global expansion by, 138–139

Political risks, in dealing with governments, 186–188

Positions and interests chart, 85

Postsettlement settlements, 69–70, 157

Power: advice and cautions about, 58–60; defined, 13, 98; dispute resolution based on, 98–103, 110–113; in hierarchical vs. egalitarian cultures, 19–20; sources of, in deal-making negotiations, 47–48; used in deal-making negotiations, 48–60

Power distance, 17